Human Resource Management in the Philippine Setting

TOMAS D. ANDRES

New Day Publishers
Quezon City
1991

Published by
New Day Publishers
11 Lands St., VASRA
P.O. Box 167, 1100 Quezon City
Philippines
Tel.: 99-80-46

Cover Design by Toti Orias

ISBN 971-10-0348-1

PREFACE

HUMAN RESOURCE MANAGEMENT IN THE PHILIPPINE SETTING gives the reader a comprehensive understanding of the concepts, trends, principles, systems and researches involved in the science and art of managing people. This is the first book on Philippine personnel/human resource management that discusses the art and science of managing people, not from the time of hiring to firing, but from human resource planning to the time of human resource accounting.

This book is a modest effort to present the most complicated concepts, principles and systems on human resources management on a level which the average Filipino student of Management can grasp. We have also tried to situate these principles in a Philippine setting.

This book is intended for individual reading as well as for use as a text for training programs in Personnel Management, Human Resource Management, and Human Behavior.

Tomas Quintin Donato Andres

Ateneo de Manila University

ACKNOWLEDGMENTS

The author is indebted to those authorities in the field of personnel administration, human resource management, psychology, business management, and related disciplines who shared their insights with him as well as others who helped shape and complete this book. He therefore, wishes to give due recognition to the following:

Fellow personnel and human resource management practitioners in the Personnel Management Association of the Philippines, Philippine Society for Training and Development, Bankers Association for Personnel Management, and the Construction Industry Board Foundation; officials of the Ministry of Labor and Employment, National Manpower and Youth Council, University of Life, Development Academy of the Philippines, and other government agencies; his fellow-professors and former students in Far Eastern University, University of the East, Rizal Technological College, Eulogio "Amang" Rodriguez Institute of Science and Technology, De La Salle University, Polythechnic University of the Philippines, Marikina Institute of Science and Technology, Southeast Asian Interdisciplinary Institute; his former colleagues in personnel and human resource management in the organizations where he has worked; the human resource management consultants, experts and professors whose experiences and lectures he was privileged to hear in the State University of New York, in Labor Management College of New York in Buffalo, and in various universities and conferences in Europe, America, Japan, India and Canada.

Special thanks are due the following: Atty. Natty Roma of the Bureau of Labor Relations of MOLE; Robert D. Turner, Vice President of Employee Relations of Hanes Group; Lari Stanton, Freddie Jimenez, and Rolf Schoeder of Aris (Philippines) Inc., Victor Floresca, General Manager of Rohm and Haas Philippines, Inc.; and Rodolfo I. Garcia, President of Astra Pharmaceuticals (Philippines), Inc. as well as all those authorities whose names have eluded the writer's memory. As much as possible, the writer acknowledges all the sources used in the book; however, some authors or sources were not acknowledged explicitly due to inadvertence or lack of documentation on the part of the writer. To them, a sincere apology and gratitude are given.

Last but not least, his thanks and gratitude are due his loving wife, Pilar Corazon and his kids: Thomas Philamer, Pilar Philamer, Pierre-angelo Philamer, Lord Philamer, Patrician Philamer and Bernard Philamer.

This book is dedicated to all business, educational, government, professional, religious and civic organizations who have availed themselves of the author's services as Human Resource Management Consultant and Practitioner, particularly those who have adapted in their organizations the Philippine-based MANAGEMENT BY FILIPINO VALUES SYSTEM which the author has pioneered and established.

MARAMING SALAMAT PO SA PAGTANGKILIK NINYO SA SARILI NATING SISTEMA NG PANGANGASIWA NG MGA TAUHAN.

CONTENTS

PART THREE—HUMAN RESOURCE PLANNING AND PROCUREMENT

PART FOUR—HUMAN RESOURCE DEVELOPMENT AND MANPOWER TRAINING

PART FIVE—HUMAN RESOURCE MAINTENANCE AND CONSERVATION

PART SIX—HUMAN RESOURCE INFORMATION, ACCOUNTING, AND MEASUREMENT

A GUIDE TO THE TEACHER

Human Resource Management focuses on personnel administration as regards management: developing and administering policies and programs leading to effective organization, qualified employees, equitable treatment, advancement opportunities, and job security.

The purpose of a Human Resource Management course is to develop knowledge and understanding, attitudes and values, and skills, as follows:

1. Understanding, attitudes and skills needed to be gained in a general activity area of management:
   a. The nature of the activity area
   b. The functions into which the activity area is subdivided
   c. Contributions of the activity area to the success of the overall enterprise
   d. Problems involved in directing the activity area
   e. Relation of the personnel administration activity area to other activity areas of management

2. Understanding, attitudes and skills to be gained regarding the functions into which the activity area is subdivided:
   a. What each function is
   b. The purpose of each function
   c. Relation to other functions in the personnel administration activity area
   d. Other activity area functions to which the function may be related
   e. Conditions which make the function important

f. Conditions which make the function unimportant

3. Knowledge and understanding, attitudes and values, and skills in the most-used methods of carrying out each function and subfunction of the personnel administration activity area

4. Knowledge of how to proceed effectively.

It will be wise to examine other textbooks on human resource management and, perhaps, adopt one or two of them to supplement this textbook. Also, become familiar with the current literature provided by personnel management/industrial relations periodicals.

Conduct the course with assigned readings, discussions based on the reading assignments, lecturettes, live case discussions, written analyses of cases, research paper, project paper, group report, group activities and examinations. Reading assignments should be completed before the classes for which they are assigned. The readings will provide a common denominator upon which to base class discussions.

Discussion based on the readings will clarify concepts, enlarge perspectives, deepen insights, and develop the ability to apply concepts to real Philippine situations. Assigned chapters of the book will serve as the starting points for discussion.

Formal lecture presentation may be used at your discretion. Lectures will extend and supplement various topics and provide additional and different perspectives on them. In relation to the textbook readings, do not organize the lectures to duplicate the readings. Augment the text material with your lecture by presenting personnel management principles as practised in the Philippines.

PART ONE

THE ART AND SCIENCE OF HUMAN MANAGEMENT

---

1. **Contemporary Views and Concepts on Human Resource Management**

2. **Human Resource Management in the Philippines**

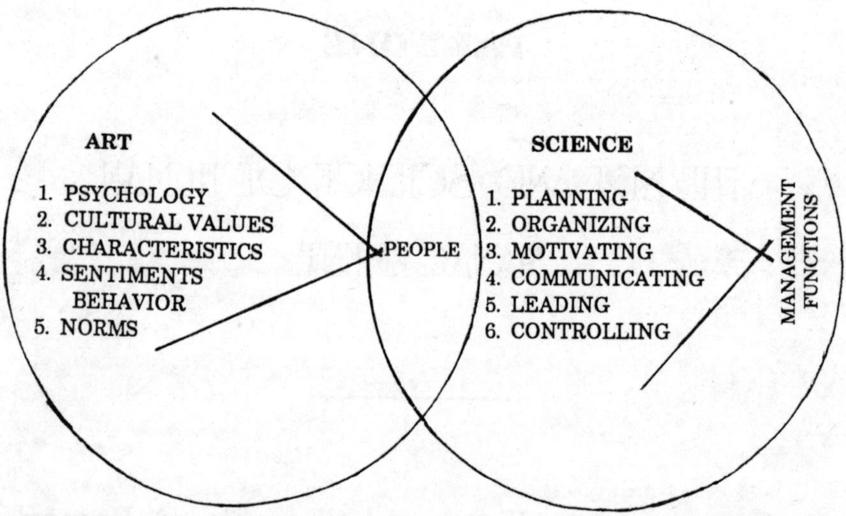

Human Resource Management as an Art and a Science

Is Human Resource Management an art or a science? There are two schools of thought regarding this matter. Those who say that it is a science affirm that Human Resource Management must follow strict and rigid scientific rules and principles in human resource programs. The other school of thought, that Human Resource Management is an art emphasizes differences among the workers regarding their cultural values systems which must be taken into consideration in the design and implementation of human resource programs.

1

CONTEMPORARY CONCEPTS ON HUMAN RESOURCE MANAGEMENT

MANAGEMENT is the art and science of directing human effort to control the forces and utilize the materials of nature for the benefit of man. Management is a science because it is a body of systematized knowledge based on general principles which are verifiable in business practices. It is also an art because the manager, after gaining knowledge from education, experience or observation uses imagination, originality, and foresight to apply such knowledge.

The functions of management may be grouped into planning, organizing, directing and controlling. No organization can be effective without human resource management. In business and industry the kind of human resource management applied can be the cause of success or failure. The primary objective of any organization is to utilize its human resources to the optimum extent feasible.

The Nature of Human Resource Management

Human Resource Management has been accepted as an integral part of management in business and industry. However, it is one of the most misunderstood phases of modern business management. Many firms still have no clear idea of what human resource management is, and much less of the role it plays in the organization. In fact many companies in the Philippines still refuse to set up a human resource department or division worthy of the name. Even the objectives which some otherwise forward-looking companies envision for their human resource departments vary greatly with the attitude of top management.

Companies in the Philippines may be classified into four groups on the basis of management's attitude toward a human resource department.

The *first group* consists of companies with a human resource department that assumes a negative, defensive attitude toward union activity. Some of these companies think of creating a human resource department only after they find themselves swamped with labor troubles such as when a union is being formed or a strike is shaping up. Then a human resource department is hurriedly knocked up as management's counter measure against labor union activities. Management will then call for a specialist to handle the human resource problems.

The *second group* consists of firms which set up a human resource department because other companies have done so. In these cases, the man assigned to head the department usually performs only clerical work such as keeping employee records and running errands for top management. Under such a set-up, the human resource manager is a mere clerk.

The *third group* of companies establish their human resource departments to accommodate someone who does not fit anywhere else in the organization and use this department as a dumping ground. The pet man of a top executive of the firm may be appointed human resource manager regardless of his fitness for the job.

The *fourth group* consists of companies which establish their human resource department so as to develop healthy employer-employee relations or to maintain and improve existing relationships, whether or not there are any existing unions. The human resource department enjoys the full backing of the top management and has a well-planned and efficiently administered program. Top management fully supports its policies and programs. The human resource manager is given the authority he needs.

Human resource includes the total knowledge, skills, creative abilities, talents, and aptitudes of an organization's work force, as well as the values, attitudes and beliefs of the individuals involved.[1] Human Resource Management comprises the performance of all functions involved in planning for, recruiting and selecting, developing, utilizing, and rewarding, the human resources of an organization. Human Resource Management, therefore, is that branch of business management concerned with securing and maintaining the right quantity and the right quality of people needed for the company to meet its objectives.

Human Resource Management seeks and develops ways of bringing out the best in people in any work organization so that they can contribute most towards the corporate goals and at the same time enhance their opportunities to achieve their own personal goals. Like all other resources, human resources must be effectively applied.

Human Resource Management Retrospect and Prospect

Human resource management at its primitive stage began during the Middle Ages with free employment relationships among contemporary personnel. The growth of towns and villages provided a new demand for goods and services as well as employment for those seeking to escape their positions as serfs within the fe udal system.[2] Skilled artisans banded together to form guilds which established controls and regulations pertaining to their respective trades, and most important, the right of individuals to enter and practice the trade.[3]

Then came the Industrial Revolution which stimulated the growth of factories resulting from the availability of capital, free labor, power-driven equipment, improved production techniques, and a growing demand for manufactured goods. This can be considered the beginning of modern human resource management wherein significant progress had been made in organizing, coordinating, motivating, and controlling the activities of large numbers of personnel who were working in a particular area. Although people were employed in great numbers then, the factory owner maintained sole direction and control of labor. Thus further research and improvement were needed to provide for the health, safety, and morale of the workers.

By the beginning of the nineteenth century, scientific management was necessitated by rising labor and overhead costs which forced management to devote more effort to improvement of work methods and the development of standards by which employee efficiency could be judged. Frederick W. Taylor (1856-1915), the "Father of Scientific Management" emphasized work standards, methods improvements, and financial incentive systems, opening the eyes of human resource managers to the fact that employees differ in their abilities and that many of them, through lack of proper job placement and training, lack the opportunity to make maximum use of their abilities.

The Human Relations Movement led by Elton Mayo, F.J. Roethlisberger, and William J. Dickson followed, focussing human resource management's attention on sociological changes that affected the attitudes and production of the workers. In the 1920s, the business and industrial world produced tycoons in enterprises who controlled the wealth and thinking in their spheres of influence. Commercial employees and industrial labor, and even government leadership, were cowed into quiescence by their nature and power. The interests of labor in organization did not exert any force to counteract the autocratic nature of management. This condition remained until the first quarter of the 20th century, when labor agitation started being felt in lowered production and its detrimental economic results. The human relations movement taught that active participation of workers in decision-making through membership in committees, suggestions systems, and increased face-to-face dialogues can increase productivity.

By the end of World War II Human Resource Management had come of age, and its contributions to production efficiency had become more widely accepted. There was increased emphasis upon personnel research and the growing strength of organized labor. Training programs were organized to help managers and supervisors to better understand their subordinates. The National Laboratory for Group Development Sensitivity conducted courses to develop a greater awareness of the reactions of others to managers. This was the Era of the Behavioral Sciences and Group Dynamics, wherein behavioral sciences were applied to solve management problems.

STUDY/REVIEW QUESTIONS

1. What is the difference between the art and the science of management? Explain.
2. Explain the different functions of management.
3. What is human resource?

SUGGESTED ACTIVITIES AND ASSIGNMENTS

1. List all the Filipino values that interplay in the different functions of management. analyze whether these values are helping or hindering the attainment of management's objectives.
2. Interview three managers whom you know and ask them to define

human resources management in the Philippine setting.

3. Visit the Human Resources Department or Personnel Department of a firm and ask them to explain to you their Human Resources Program.

NOTES

[1]Leon C. Megginson, *Personnel and Human Resource Administration* (Illinois: Richard D. Irwin, Inc., 1977).

[2]Herbert J. Chruden, Arthur W. Sherman, Jr., *Personnel Management* (New York: South-Western Publishing Company, 1968), p. 12.

[3]Gril, Curtis, Ling, *The Management of Personnel Relations* (Homewood, Illinois: Richard D. Irwin, Inc., 1965), pp. 21-23.

REFERENCES FOR FURTHER READING

Andres, Tomas D. *Understanding Filipino Values: A Management Approach.* Quezon City: New Day Publishers, 1981.

_____. *Management By Filipino Values.* Quezon City: New Day Publishers, 1985.

Martinez, Esdras T., Pacita A. Abasolo, & Crispiniano P. Carlos, Jr. *Management: Theory and Practice.* Manila: GIC Enteprises & Co., Inc., 1972.

Sison, Perfecto S. *Personnel and Human Resource Management.* Manila: Rex Book Store, 1981.

2

HUMAN RESOURCE MANAGEMENT IN THE PHILIPPINES

HUMAN RESOURCE MANAGEMENT in its primitive form existed in the Philippines long before the colonial period. The natives took the necessary steps to have strong, well-developed and well-trained human resources as security against the forces of nature and of man and as a formidable defense against marauders and invaders. No wonder, when Ferdinand Magellan tried to dominate the islands Lapu-Lapu, a human resource manager, was able to form a strong force that defeated the royal army of Spain. Every datu at that time was mindful of his duty as a human resource manager.

Human Resource Management as a specialized and systematized branch of management is a relatively new field in the Philippines. Its development is primarily a post-war phenomenon resulting from the increasing complexity of business operations, the number of government regulations and labor laws promulgated, the growth of labor unions, and the influx of new concepts in management. Scientific personnel management in this country began in the early 1950's.[1] The growth of personnel management as a discipline in the Philippines has been slow but steady. There was hesitancy in accepting the personnel department as a significant part of a total business organization. Top management had to be convinced that the organization needed a personnel department to handle, among other functions, employer-employee relations. The enactment of labor laws such as the Minimum Wage Law of 1951, the Industrial Peace Act of 1953, the Blue Sunday Law of 1953, and the Medical and Dental Treatment Act 1954, spurred the organization of personnel department.[2] There was a dearth of qualified personnel men with clear ideas as to their own role in the management hierarchy. These were the factors which had to be overcome before the personnel department was accepted and recognized as a distinct part of the organization.

The Personnel Management Association of the Philippines (PMAP) has pioneered and given impetus to institutionalizing personnel management. During its formative years, some of its activities were bringing personnel managers together to discuss common problems and find possible solutions for an individual company's problems and working to have the personnel function recognized as a significant, though not yet an equal, cog in the wheel of management. This was understandable in the fifties and early sixties when Philippine corporations were more concerned about finance, plant facilities and marketing. Personnel programs, if there were any, were informal. The people manning the small personnel departments performed clerical tasks. They hardly had a say on policies regarding recruitment, hiring, promotion or termination.

Since its organization in 1956, PMAP has gained prestige and is now generally recognized by private firms and governmental agencies as the exponent of personnel management development in the Philippines.

In 1971, the association established the Institute of Personnel Management (IPM) as its arm for the professional development of personnel managers. As the training arm of PMAP, IPM has been effective in clarifying and identifying the role of the personnel manager in the organization. The Institute has trained a good number of personnel managers of many corporations.

Human Resource Management in the Philippines has come a long way. Today it occupies a distinct position in the corporate structure. Personnel relations being an area of management directly concerned with people—often mentioned as the greatest asset of organizations—the job of the personnel manager has become one of the most sensitive positions in the company. The government has started to tap the resources of many personnel managers through PMAP in formulating policies and they are invited to committee hearings on matters affecting business and industry. This was the case in the planning and development of the Labor Code before it was finally approved on November 1, 1974.

Human Resource Management has come of age in the Philippines, ready to move on to the next decade.

Prospects of HRM in the Philippines

The present thrust of Human Resource Management in the Philippines in centered on manpower development. Developing human resources is a priority. The shift in government policy towards reliance on labor-intensive technologies in agriculture and industry shows the growing appreciation of the vital role to be played by the country's vast human resources.

Spearheading the government programs for training human resources is the National Manpower and Youth Council. One of its tasks is coordinating and evaluating the Manpower Development efforts of both the government and private sectors. Other government agencies involved in non-formal programs for human resource development are the National Science Development Board, University of the Philippines Institute for Small-Scale Industries, Civil Service Commission, and others.

The private sector is encouraged to participate more actively in the country's human resource development program. The Labor Code of the Philippines provides for industry boards to undertake manpower development programs to suit the requirements of specific industries. Tax deductions are offered to private firms who undertake training, retraining, apprenticeship, and management development programs.

The Philippine Society for Training and Development (PSTD) is the professional organization in the Philippines devoted exclusively to the education, development and expansion of skills and standards of the training profession. It regularly conducts forums for ideas and problems related to manpower training and undertakes studies and research so as to become more effective in meeting training and development needs of the Philippines. During November 7-12, 1979, the Philippines was the venue for the 8th International Training and Development Conference with the Theme: "Human Resource Development Horizons in the Eighties and Beyond".

Recent Trends in Human Resource Management

Human Resource Management is not new; businesses have always "managed" their manpower. What is new is the serious attention given by a growing number of companies to planning for their human resources.

One of the two recent trends in this area is taking more

responsibility for managing human resources out of the hands of the personnel specialist and putting it into the hands of the line manager. The other trend is increasing opportunities for the human resource specialist to contribute directly to the profitability of the organization.[3]

Human Resource Management today is moving rapidly in the following directions:[4]

1. Having a more important role in the management of the business;
2. A shift in emphasis from packaged "personnel programs" to staffing systems to fit the specific needs and objectives of the individual company;
3. Having responsibility for developing the organization rather than just maintaining it (that is, emphasis on planning and developing the company's human resources as opposed to emphasis on keeping records);
4. More direct involvement with the top management of the organization in deploying and developing its human resources.

There is an increasing awareness that the effective utilization of human resources is a chief element in the overall management of the organization.

Dr. Herbert Henems, director of the Industrial Relations Center at the University of Minnesota, and one of the most respected members of the work force management profession, outlined the following necessary changes:[5]

1. Push more of the personnel and industrial relations function back into line management where it belongs; help line supervisors do a better job of managing people.
2. Do micro-work force planning for the whole organization.
3. Rediscover employees; push motivation to the forefront.
4. Organize personnel and industrial relations departments around expected goals or outcomes (rather than along functional specialities).

There is a growing recognition that the job of managing human resources is the responsibility of *all* managers. Human resources must be effectively managed to achieve organizational goals and at the same time provide opportunities for individual growth in the organization. Increasingly, managers are finding it important to develop a planning framework within which decisions regarding staffing, allocation of employees within the organization, and the conservation and development of manpower are made.

Four basic world-wide trends in business which may serve as predictors of substantial and forthcoming changes affecting Human Resource Management are the following:[6]

1. The development of a service economy,
2. the emergence of a knowledge society,
3. the transformation of society into a concerned humanistic one, and
4. the emergence of youth culture.

Several changes are influencing the movement from traditional personnel administration to Human Resource Management:[7]

1. The changing concept of the individual in management thought,
2. the changing attitudes and expectations about work held by growing numbers of employees,
3. the changing structure of the work force, and
4. the external pressures on organizations affecting employment policies.

With the advent of behavioral sciences, modern management has come to consider employees as reservoirs of talents and skills, and research findings indicate that employees have a strong interest in achieving personal success through their work and want to contribute to the success of the organization.[8] In particular, there seems to be a changing concept of success among workers. Employees increasingly emphasize the importance of self-fulfillment on the job and opportunities for personal development.

With regard to the composition of the labor force, more and more knowledge workers are joining it because of the changed technology. The trend seems to be for the labor force to steadily become a white collar workforce. Growth is occurring in the professional, management, technical, clerical and service occupations. In addition, the level of education of the workforce is rising, and more and more knowledgeable workers are joining the workforce.

Management will face increasing pressures and regulations from external sources with direct impact on its personnel policies and practices. For example, we have in the Philippines labor code and amending decrees, as well as letters of instruction and implementing regulations issued by the Secretary of Labor and Employment, the Employees Compensation System, Maternity Leave amendments, and

Social Security amendments.

In the service economy, wherein more and more activities, both in the public and in the private sector, will take the form of providing services rather than manufacturing consumer goods, more people will be involved in processing, analyzing, and adjudicating transactions covering these durable consumer goods than in their actual production. In developed countries, automation will take over work done by humans. White collar workers will increase, and more managers, supervisors and foremen will be required.

Demand for better techniques in managing the knowledge workers will also be heavier. A knowledge worker may be likened to a complex data processor whose creative system is primarily concerned with problem-solving. His needs are security, social relationships, esteem, autonomy, and self-actualization. The manager must cooperate with his workers so as to identify and resolve problems and objectives which may be simultaneously personal and corporate.

Finally, the new breed of Human Resource Managers will be concerned with matters of high importance and with contemporary issues such as company policies, human asset accounting, management of managers, quality of work life, and total mobilization of human resources to meet corporate goals. As a result of the changes and pressures described above, many organizations are responding with new approaches in managing human resources. Emphasis on human resource planning in organizations is increasing.

Today's Human Resource Managers must use preventive research instead of simply waiting for problems to occur. Four cardinal points concerning personnel activities warrant the attention of policy makers:[9]

1. Personnel administration as a concept and function is undergoing vast modifications.
2. A comprehensive personnel resource system contributes substantially to the various organization work systems and also significantly affects economic performance, institutional welfare and employee realizations.
3. Personnel management is increasingly able to make contributions to vital organizational decisions, performance and accomplishments.
4. Of necessity, personnel management is moving into higher levels of professional activity; matters confronting it are increasingly complex and sensitive, and its tools, appropriately, have grown more sophisticated.

STUDY/REVIEW QUESTIONS

1. What factors led to specialized and systematized Human Resource Management in the Philippines? Explain each factor.

2. What are the prospects of Human Resource Management in the Philippines?

3. Enumerate the recent trends in Human Resource Management in the Philippines.

SUGGESTED ACTIVITIES AND ASSIGNMENTS

1. Analyze our Philippine History and indicate instances of positive human resource management of Filipino leaders like that of Lapu-Lapu in Mactan.

2. Interview the head of one of the professional associations in personnel administration on the current trends in human resource management practices in the Philippines.

3. Write a position paper on what the role of human resources management should be in the total development of Filipinos.

NOTES

[1]Perfecto S. Sison, *Personnel Management* (Manila: Personnel Management Association of the Philippines, Inc., 1973), p. 20.

[2]Quintin S. Doromal, "Personnel Management in the Philippines: Retrospect and Prospect," PMAP 20th Anniversary Convention, Convention Bulletin, 1978.

[3]Lawrence A. Klatt, Robert S. Muralick, Fred E. Schuster, *Human Resources Management: A Behavioral System Approach* (Illinois: Richard D. Irwin, Inc. 1978), p. 15.

[4]Ibid. pp. 15-16.

[5]Ibid, p. 17

[6]Davis Keith, *Management for the Future* (McGraw-Hill, June 1978).

[7]James A. Craft, Symposium on HRM, March 1975

[8]Elpidio C. Jimenez, "Human Resource Management: Concepts, Contents, Practices and Trends", 15th National Conference, PMAP, Nov. 322-24, 1978.

[9]Elmer H. Burack & Edwil L. Miller, "The Personnel Function in Transition" 15th PMAP National Conference, Nov. 22-24, 1978.

REFERENCES FOR FURTHER READING

Andres, Tomas D. *Management by Filipino Values.* Quezon City: New Day Publishers, 1985.

Keith, Davis. *Management for the Future.* U.S.A.: McGraw-Hill, 1978.

Klatt, Lawrence A. et al. *Human Resources Management: A Behavioral System Approach.* Illinois: Richard D, Irwin Inc., 1978.

Sison, Perfecto S. *Personnel and Human Resources Management.*

PART TWO

HUMAN RESOURCE MANAGEMENT AND THE CORPORATE ORGANIZATION

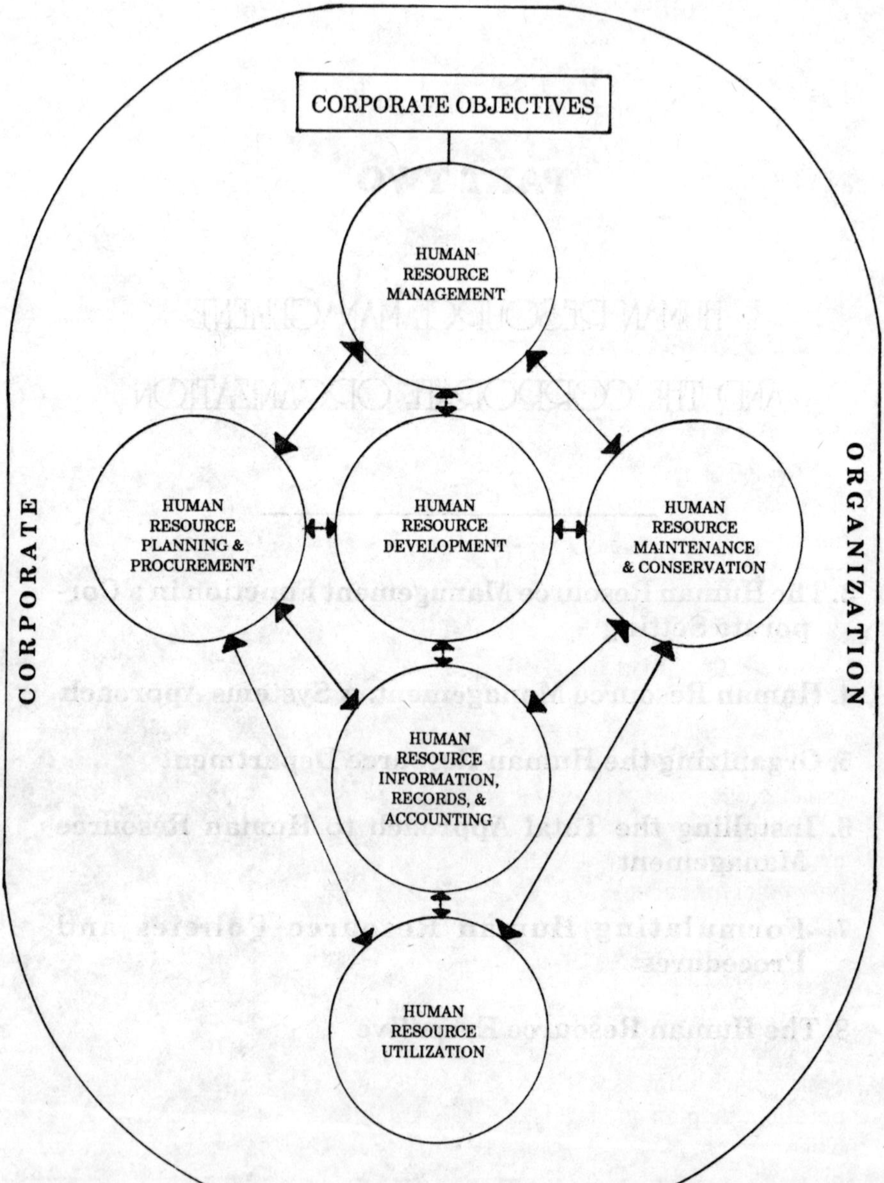

Human Resource Management and the Corporate Organization

3

THE HUMAN RESOURCE MANAGEMENT FUNCTION IN A CORPORATE SETTING

HUMAN RESOURCE MANAGEMENT as a corporate challenge moves from the traditional though necessary function of maintaining harmonious relationships between employees and management, into a role that supports organizational goals and also individual employee aspirations.

The human resource unit has faced a long uphill struggle for recognition of its ability to contribute to organizational goal attainment. In the past, Human Resource executives were frequently excluded from the corporate planning process or else planning for the most effective use of human resources was at best, haphazard.

The primary task is to put the importance of human resource management into its proper perspective--as a basis for performing all personnel functions.

The Corporate Setting

The need for planning is usually determined by top corporate executives, with final authorization resting with the president of the corporation. A plan is simply a predetermined course of action. Once objectives are stated, four basic elements are involved in the planning process. They are:[1]

1. An evaluation of present conditions which should show where change is needed or will be forthcoming, even without planning.

2. A time dimension since the planning process is related to time. This encompasses short-run and long-run plans.
3. Data collection. A segregation problem caused by a preponderance of extraneous data exists at this point. A judgment must be made as to the quality of data.
4. A degree of importance must be allocated to each plan. At higher levels of management, plans are usually broad in scope, growing narrower as they move downward in an organization, allowing some variance of interpretation by operating personnel.

In any planning process, the head of each department must formulate plans in relation to his specific department, participate in formulating company-wide plans and assist other departments in formulating their plans. Top management has both the authority and the responsibility to see that the planning process is properly coordinated.

Human resource managers are responsible for efficient utilizing of human resource. This should place them in an important position relative to top management.

The following hypotheses explain the cause and effect relationship between the utilization of human resources and productivity of an organization, and the derived employee satisfaction:[2]

1. An organization's performance and resulting productivity are directly proportional to the quantity and quality of its human resources.
2. While employee performance must be evaluated in economic terms of efficiency and effectiveness, it can be best achieved through recognizing and enhancing the human dignity of each employee.
3. The quantity and quality of human resources can be effectively increased through education, training and personal development.

The Human Resource Department should have information in the following areas:[3]

A. Designation of Key positions in the organization
    1. Incumbent
    2. Potential Replacements
B. Salary Schedules
C. Evaluation Reports
D. Work Force Information
    1. Separation rates

2. Skills inventory
3. Recruiting
   a. Sources
   b. Costs
   c. Time required
4. Job designations and wage rates

E. Ratio of personnel staff to work force
F. Information concerning union-management relations and predictions in this area.

The Human Resource Department should be a major factor in planning for and utilizing scarce resources in specialized skills. It should have the data that can be used to level out the peaks and the valleys of production to provide more stable employment and to effect various economies by such action. For example, costs can be lowered and company atmosphere and morale greatly improved by minimizing crash hiring and training programs.

Human Resource Departments should be used as separate planning units to enable them to keep personnel policies consistent throughout a company. The Human Resource Department's awareness of employees' reactions to various changes by management helps it adopt a "planned change" strategy to prepare for reactions to proposed innovations. The Human Resource Department must be included in any planning process. It must carry out the planning activity so as not to restrict future options but rather to prepare for future possibilities. Line departments must be made aware of the assistance available to them through the Human Resource Department. It should be able to show top management that structure problems must be solved before there can be improvements in management and employee relationships.

Human Resource executives must measure the human organization in order to keep higher management advised as to the state of the organization. They must view themselves as links between government and their company.

Human resource planning must parallel structural planning. The shift that has occurred regarding personnel activities has changed the personnel manager from being merely administrator of company regulations and policies regarding employees to being a manager of the human resources "assets" of the firm.

Some of the changes which will drastically affect the human resources of a company are the following:[4]

A. Internally
   1. New Departments
   2. New business
   3. Expansion of some existing functions
   4. Contraction of other functions
   5 .Increased turnover and transfer of personnel
   6. Increased decentralization and divisional autonomy
B. Externally
   1. Employees changing employers more frequently
   2. Changes in the skills mix of the work force
   3. More stringent employment and safety laws
   4. Higher expectations of workers at all levels
   5. Increased union emphasis on job security and extended benefits.

These factors in turn will cause constant changes in the corporation's need to focus on such human resources concerns as: the number of people affected, types of skills needed, working relationships between people and departments, forms of compensation and rewards, appropriate organizational structures, and methods of motivation and control. This leads to the following changes:[5]

1. Realizing that the HR function plays a strategic role by linking its skills and activities with the business plans of the organization.
2. Providing information about the human assets of the firm for action-taking purposes of line management and staff specialists.
3. Automating the retrieval and analysis of personnel information centrally and locally.
4. Developing performance measures for the human resource management activities carried out by both the department and line management.
5. Creating new incentives for the proper use of human resources; a continuing search for talent internally and externally and the replacement of less talented people.
6. Using individual performance appraisal methods to improve and maintain performance, not simply to record it, especially by relating it to rewards and job training.
7. Treating evaluations of potentials in individuals as indicators for developmental training.
8. Offering meaningful career planning and counseling at all levels.
9. Evaluating the structural relevance of the whole organization and

its components as their roles change so that the structures fit the work, not just a chart.

10. Increasing the ability to create and staff non-traditional organizations (e.g. matrix structures).
11. Being more sophisticated in the design and programming of compensation and benefit packages.
12. Providing training designed to have lasting effect on the current and future business plans.
13. Researching and testing innovative human resource programs and methodologies.
14. Increasing communication with the personnel functions of other corporations and community agencies for more effective intake and out-placement of people to mutually even out excesses and deficiencies.
15. Helping managers and employees to put their energy on tasks, not conflicts, interpersonal communication, group problem solving, and conflict resolution.
16. Removing the blockages that prevent the success of special programs within; for example, Batarisan Out-of-School Youth Skills Training Programs.

Clarity of vision and committed top executive leadership are essential for insuring that employees are as much a part of strategic planning as capital. The following considerations have an important bearing on the success and speed with which effective Human Resource Management can be implemented:[6]

1. *Top Management commitment is the key.* Top management must understand that effective human resource management is a significant element in the firm's overall corporate strategy. This commitment should be e videnced by the Human Resources executive being positioned among the most senior executives in the company. He should be expected to play a major role in top executive debates regarding business plans and corporate strategy.
2. *Credibility and cooperation must be won.* Even with top management backing, the Human Resources VP must still gain credibility for himself and his organization by wholeheartedly assisting in the realization of corporate and division operating objectives.
3. *Piecemeal improvements must often precede wholesale restructuring.* Fixing the most troublesome individual aspects of the

current personnel systems first may facilitate the ultimate reorganization.

4. *Human Resources Staff Skills must be upgraded.* Most staff members are likely to need new skills and perspectives.

5 *Human Resource Management is likely to require a considerable reorganizing of the personnel staff.* They must become responsive to strategic and operating priorities.

Human Resource people should operate as participating members of the management team. They should become more involved as participants in overall organizational decisions which affect the total business such as being called in to discuss with top management the advisability of establishing a new high-level marketing position, or whether to build a new plant in an outlying community.

STUDY\REVIEW QUESTIONS

1. What are the four basic elements involved in the planning process of a corporate organization? How does each of these elements affect human resource management?

2. Enumerate the changes which will drastically affect the human resources of a company. Explain each.

3. What considerations have an important bearing on the success and speed with which human resources management can be implemented in a corporate organization? Explain each.

SUGGESTED ACTIVITIES

1. Interview a president of a corporate\organization on how the corporation\organization prepares its corporate plan.

2. Identify the socio-politico-economic changes happening in the Philippines and explain how these changes affect the human resource management on a national scale.

3. Get hold of an organization's corporate plan and tell whether or not the plan reflects the human resource management's vital role.

NOTES

[1]A. Thomas Hollingsworth & Paul Preston, "Corporate Planning: A Challenge for Personnel Executive" (15th National Conference PMAP), Nov. 22-24, 1978.

[2]Leon C. Megginson, *Personnel & Human Resources Administration* (Illinois: Richard D. Irwin, Inc., 1977).

[3]Hollingsworth & Preston, op. cit. p. 4.

[4]Arthur J. Daltas, Howard M. Schwartz, "Towards Human Resource Management" (Cambridge: Center for Organization Development Inc., 15th National Conference, Nov. 22-24, 1978), p. 1.

[5]Ibid, pp. 2-3.

[6]Ibid, pp. 4-5.

REFERENCES FOR FURTHER READING

Andrés, Tomas D. *Understanding Filipino Values: A Management Approach. (Quezon City: New Day Publishers, 1981.*

_____. *Management by Filipino Values.* Quezon City: New Day Publishers, 1985.

Megginson, Leon C. *Personnel & Human Resources Administration.* Illinois: Richard D. Irwin, Inc., 1977.

4

HUMAN RESOURCE MANAGEMENT: A SYSTEMS APPROACH

THE HUMAN RESOURCE SYSTEM is a unique subsystem of a business because it operates upon all the other subsystems.[1] It is the principal subsystem because whatever affects the business as a whole also affects the human resource system.

The inputs into the human resource system come from the larger business system in the form of business objectives. The organizational subsystem, one of the major parts of the human resource system, is concerned with modifying the work environment. It deals with the organization as a whole and consists of various subsystems such as the staffing and organizations structure, the appraisal and reward system, the labor relations system and the organizational development system.

The second major part of the human resource system focuses on the individual as a subsystem. This involves individual development through such means as communication, motivation, leadership and appraising.

The outputs of the human resource system are individual and organizational performance. Individual performance results in need fulfillment, growth and development; and organizational performance leads to productivity, maintenance and growth. These two outputs should be coordinated so that both may accomplish the organizational plan.

It is the responsibility of all managers to manage human resources in the business system. All are responsible for the development, maintenance and performance of the human resource system. In the construction of a human resource system, management must determine how many people with what skills will be required over a number of years. Total human resource cost must be estimated and trade-offs between capital equipment and human resource must be evaluated. Management must also consider human resources in its evaluation of the company's assets.

The process of structuring the human resource system so as to develop, modify and ultimately achieve company objectives is called organizational planning. This process specifies integration of the existing framework, guiding principles of technology, and the overall goals of the firm. It sets a target for organizational change, especially regarding structure and staffing. Its primary purpose is to divide the organization into manageable and efficient units and to provide proper integration for these units, according to predetermined business objectives.

Once management has carried out its organization planning, it is ready to take systematic steps to match the needs of its plans with human resources. This process is called human-resource-needs planning. The specific activities of organizational planning: are review of proposed organization changes, preparation of job descriptions, preparation and maintenance of organizational charts and manuals, analysis of the basis for grouping functions and analysis of goals of organizational units. Systematic steps must be taken to have the right people in the right quantity at the right time, performing activities which give the individual and the organization maximum benefit. An essential element of this planning is anticipating future human resource needs. Equally important are work force inventories. Given inventories of the present human resource needs along with turnover rates, Human Resource planners can arrive at an estimate of Human Resource planners can arrive at an estimate of Human Resource needs.

Organization planning and human resource needs must be integrated with all parts of the human resource system and must be conducted within the constraints of such outside developments as the labor market and legislation. The development of organizational capabilities is achieved by a subsystem of the human resource system--the human resource development system. This system is composed of line managers, the Human Resource Manager and the training and development director and staff. The inputs processed are the employees of the company.

The approach to organization planning depends upon the standard of effectiveness one chooses to use, that is, one which provides the best way for accomplishing organizational goals with the human resources available.

Effective human resource management requires a comprehensive programming effort which in turn necessitates an awareness of needs. A monitoring and interpretative capability can result in a vital input of information which will assist a human resource systems effort.

David L. Austen of the National University of San Diego, California advanced the concept of three main categories of personnel work as corresponding to three systems: Value-centered systems, data-centered systems and power-centered systems.[2]

The Value-Centered Systems have three major areas of effort: (1) leadership development systems, (2) career development systems (3) motivation systems. The person managing these areas is called a value systems manager. He examines from a value-centered viewpoint the standard structure of employment, compensation, employee relations, benefits, training-development, compensation, and health and safety to see exactly what value base lies beneath the traditional way of doing things. The manager thus demonstrates awareness of human values as he interviews and selects applicants, The employment function is restructured as part of a larger, more value-oriented frame of reference. Furthermore, the pay plans, benefits and promotion policies will have to be integrated into the organization's motivation systems.

The Data-Based Systems have three major areas of effort: (1) Organizational Needs assessment, (2) Value analysis and decision-making, and (3) Communication Systems. An organization must collect and evaluate information about its past performance and its present and future needs. Organizational needs assessment combines the duties of manpower planning, salary surveys and employee relations policy creation. Closely allied to needs assessment is the more basic question of what needs are to be assessed, by whom, and for what human or corporate purpose. If a Human Resource Manager adds to this the question of what kinds of decision-making methods a company uses, or does not use and some understanding of why this is so, then the Human Resource Manger is on his way to making a meaningful contribution to the management of a company.

Another vital function of the data systems manager is to extract from Communication Theory better ways of achieving:[3]

1. A clearer identification of the many styles of management used by his or her company, and the effects of innovativeness on these styles.
2. A better understanding of the supportive or the undermining

effects of the company's communication methods, particularly on the hourly employees;

3. More awareness of how to foretell success or failure of a communication effort, particularly in terms of the compatibility, communicability or complexity of a new idea.
4. Greater sensitivity to various ways of looking at target population (the ones your are trying to influence) and whether their acceptance of an innovation is an individual choice or is a collective choice (one requiring the agreement of the group before an individual can choose), such as group auto insurance, or is an authoritative choice such as those rendered under collective bargaining agreements.
5 .Some knowledge of different kinds of target populations:
   a. Creators of innovations
   b. Adopters of innovations such as legislation mandating smog control devices on automobiles.
   c. Implementors of innovations
   d. Users of innovations, such as patients taking a new drug prescribed by a doctor, or a foreman using MBO techniques.
6. Some familiarity with the various ways of structuring the problem of communication. Lots of interesting research data are available describing communication as a diffusion process evolving through the five stages of awareness, interest, trial adoption, evaluation and final adoption.

The third facet of the systems approach to human resource management requires knowledge of and experience with power. The Power-Based Systems have three main areas of effort: (1) the management of conflict, (2) the management of facilitation systems, and (3) the management of company control networks. This system is under the control-system manager whose authority and area of expertise cut across all personnel fields and extend into every important area of human resource activity. One of the key functions of the control-systems manager would be to familiarize himself with the relevant literature, extract from it the insights that it contains and use this new awareness to examine the behavior and the policies of the company.

Another function is the creation and administration of facilities systems. Human resource problems in the fields of internal pay equity, benefit plan administration, accident prevention, grievances and employment placement are all fertile fields in which to apply the principles of facilitation. The entire disciplinary policy of an organization

MANAGERIAL FUNCTIONS

	Employment	*Compensation*	*Employee Relations*	*Benefits*	*Employee Training & Supervisory Development*	*Health & Safety*
I. Value Systems Manager						
1. Leadership Development	Recruiting Interviewing	Pay policies Job descriptions	Promotions Transfer	Tuition refund	Employee selection Program creation	Examinations Treatment
2. Career Development	Testing Selection		Terminations Performance Evaluation	Leave of absence		
3. Motivation Systems				Plan creation		
II. Data Systems Manager						
1. Organizational Needs Assessment	Manpower Planning Advertising	Job evaluation Salary surveys	Policy creation Benefit surveys	Plan creation Benefit surveys Cost analysis	Needs identification Program analysis	
2. Value Analysis & Decision Making Systems						Data analysis
3. Communication/ Diffusion Systems						
III. Control Systems Manager						
1. Conflict Manager	Placement	Internal Equity Cost analysis	Discipline Grievances	Plan administration	Program administration	
2. Facilitator Systems			Turnover analysis EECC Discharges			Accident prevention & investigation
3. Gate-Keeping						

could be re-examined from the principles of group dynamics or transactional analysis.

Gate Keeping Systems permit or deny access to information. The control-system manager must seek out and identify rules being followed which fill a void created by management. He must know who are following them, and what effects these have on the company.

STUDY/REVIEW QUESTIONS

1. What are the elements of the human resource management system?
2. How is human resource management related to organization planning and development?
3. Explain the three main categories of personnel work as corresponding to value-centered systems, data-centered systems and power-centered systems.

SUGGESTED ACTIVITIES AND ASSIGNMENTS

1. Interview the head of Organizational Planning and Development of a corporation/organization and find out what human resources management system they have.
2. Ask some employees of a corporation about the different activities they have in their company such as seminars, workshops, etc. to enhance their skills, knowledge, attitudes, and values.

NOTES

[1]Laurence A. Klatt, Robert G. Murdick, Fred E. Schuster, *Human Resource Management: A Behavioral Systems Approach* (Illinois: Richard D. Irwin Inc., 1975), pp.11-12.

[2]David L. Austen, "Must the Past Be Prolonged? or, Why Can't We do Things Differently?" 15th PMAP National Conference, Nov. 22, 24 1978.

[3]Ibid, 8.

REFERENCES FOR FURTHUR READING

Andres, Tomas D. *Organizational Development For Productivity in the Philippine Setting.* New Day Publishers: Quezon City, 1983.

_____. *Management By Filipino Values.* New Day Publishers, 1985

Klatt, Laurence A. et al. *Human Resource Management: A Behavioral Systems Approach.* Illinois: Richard D. Irwin Inc., 1975.

5

ORGANIZING THE HUMAN RESOURCE MANAGEMENT DEPARTMENT

MANAGEMENT if effective, comes only when each person knows exactly where he stands and what his duties are. When two or more persons combine their efforts in a definite way, and for a given purpose, there is an organization. Thus, any relationship between persons is a basic element in the design of an organization. The two chief principles of organization are *functionalization*—that is, the grouping of managerial activities according to kinds of duties—and *coordination* of key activities.

The most effective means of achieving coordination of various activities is the establishment of key jobs, so located as to prevent the holders of these jobs from interfering in other areas of authority. The responsibility and authority of each individual and of each organizational unit must be clearly defined and understood by every person involved. The most practical way is to reduce these points to a written organization chart specifying distinctly the limits to which authority extends and the groups of persons and types of jobs for which each one is responsible.

The Human Resource Management Department to be established should possess the following characteristics: balance, flexibility, and adjustment to personnel. The organizational structure is balanced when each function is allocated capital and personnel commensurate with its contribution to organization objectives.

Defining The Human Resource Management Department's Functions

There are certain basic functions all managers perform: *planning, organizing, "staffing", leading* and *controlling*. These represent what is often called the "Management Process". "Staffing", almost tantamount to human resources management, is the function which focuses on activities like recruiting, selecting, training, compensating, appraising and developing.

There are three types of authority in organizations: line, staff and functional. *Line authority* consists of the right or power to issue orders to subordinate personnel and to take disciplinary action against them for the violations of these orders or for other just causes. Line authority can be exercised only over subordinates in the chain of command and not horizontally over persons in other departments of the structure. *Staff authority* actually is not authority at all in the strict sense of the word because it does not provide any specific right to direct, issue orders, or to discipline others. Instead, it involves merely the capacity to provide assistance, advice or service to others. *Functional authority* involves the right to issue orders that pertain to the performance of a particular function but it is not as binding as line authority since it does not carry the right to discipline others in order to enforce compliance. Functional authority may be exercised over individuals throughout the organizational structure.

The Human Resource Manager with his Department carries out these three authorities through these main functions. *First*, he exerts line authority in his own unit and implied authority elsewhere in the business organization. He exerts functional, coordinative authority to ensure that the personnel objectives and policies of the organization are coordinated and carried out. He provides various staff services to line managers such as assisting them in personnel hiring, training, evaluating, rewarding, promoting and imposing discipline on employees in all levels.

There are two conceptual approaches to the human resource function.[1] One approach reflects an attitude that the human resource function must rely on formal organization authority to be effective. This approach involves heavy administration of traditional service areas such as salary administration, benefits, policy, etc. The second approach, supported by Jeff Moony, is based on the concept that authority is derived from competence and the influence developed through successfully assisting follow managers. This second approach reflects the fact that responsibility for human resources is dispersed throughout the entire organization.

There are several content changes in the human resource work that can be described as follows:[2]

1. *Enlargement of traditional personnel activities.* The cornerstones of personnel are employment, training and development, job evaluation, and wages and benefits. The most obvious change is the application of personnel procedures to knowledge workers and managers so that techniques of employee selection have been enlarged to include the selection of managers, professional workers and technical workers. There has been a shift away from the technique or recipe approaches to selection and movement toward a heavier research orientation and discussions of policy implications in selection. In the area of training, emphasis is not only on skills training but also on development of technical, professional and managerial personnel, especially in the area of decision making and human relations training.
2. *Refocusing traditional personnel activities.* There is more interest in gaining expertise managing in employment, training, compensation, and benefits.
3. *New and emerging personnel activities.* Planning is becoming an important feature of the personnel function. Staff and recruitment planning occur at the organizational level. Career planning and new assessment approaches are emerging in the personnel field. New knowledge areas and functional undertakings include the motivational-behavioral aspects of virtually all programs, group approaches in development and career planning.
4. *Personnel Information Systems: Analysis and Integration* Information about labor market conditions, technical trends, and occupations plus all manner of information about internal operations (job, available people resources, business developments, new technologies) form the critical data base for modern human resource management. Human resource specialists must be familiar with the tools, methods, and concepts of research and statistical analysis and must be able to apply these procedures to data.

The Human Resource Department's job is to serve management, not employees. In turn, employees are served best when managers grasp what they themselves can do to further their goal of successful operations, perhaps by improving the work place, communication, job design, and relationships with employees. Human Resource Management should help managers to incorporate concern for employees into operating plans, not to do it for them. Human Resource function should invest heavily in development of expertise in areas of managerial concern such as benefit administration, labor law and negotiation, salary surveys and job classification, safety laws, performance appraisal systems, training needs analysis, employment law, screening and testing.

In order to make sound contributions to organization decisions, human resource people need to develop expertise that managers will find useful in achieving worker motivation and productivity, organization structure, and managerial performance. Human resource people should deal in trends versus individual cases. Let's say, human resource people show line managers that a sick leave problem is part of a bigger pattern, or that the boss' ineptness at handling a case is just one symptom of general poor performance. Human resource people should base advice on research and evaluation, rather than on opinions and platitudes.

Human resources management therefore includes many functions. Although the details of implementation differ among organizations, the general benefit of human resource management is much the same among the more progressive organizations. Likewise the scope and application of Human Resources Management functions vary with the

1. Size of the firm
2. Nature of the business or industry
3. Complexity of operations
4. Qualifications of the personnel staff
5. Attitude and support of top management
6. The company's relation with the union
7. State of the labor market
8. Prevailing economic conditions in the area
9. Presence or absence of competition

The following are the major responsibilities of the people in the Human Resources Management Department:[3]

1. Developing and administering human resource policies and programs.
2. Assisting Line Management in measuring the level of morale and taking steps to improve situations which lead to employee dissatisfaction; The human resource people, therefore, have to

provide assistance to line management in dealing with human resource problems. Such assistance may be provided thru:

a. Employment recruitment, selection, hiring and placement.

b. Determination of skills available in the work group

c. Employee counseling

d. Employee benefits and services

e .Medical and hospitalization facilities

f. Safety rules and accident prevention

g. Employee suggestion system

h. Labor relations problems

3. Evaluating Human Resource Performance in the following areas:

   a. Merit rating

   b. Employee opinion service

   c. Study and analysis of statistical data related to personnel.

4. Coordinating Personnel Activities. The Human Resource Department undertakes or shares operational responsibility for interdepartmental programs in personnel areas where coordination can be best be achieved by some degree of centralized administration. Such areas include:

   a. Employment—recruitment, selection, hiring, placement and separation from the service.

   b. Training of supervisors and employees.

   c. Fringe benefits.

   d. Wage and salary administration—setting salaries and wage rates.

   e. Health and safety—including accident prevention and the promotion of good health among personnel.

   f. Miscellaneous employee services.

5. Job Evaluation and Classification and Salary Administration. The Human Resource Department evaluates the jobs in the firm through job analysis and job evaluation. It recommends classifying of jobs and establishing a sound wage and salary structure. It then administers the firm's policies governing wages and salaries. It aids labor relations people in handling wage disputes. It incorporates such concepts as fringe benefits, commissions, bonuses, profit-sharing, and other forms of employee remunerations.

6. Forecasting — This denotes predictions of phenomena which may affect business plans. Careful forecasting helps executives select the right objectives and chart the routes of progress.

7. Programing — This is a recent development that consists of

detailed planning. A program is an explicit statement of steps to be taken toward an objective. In developing a program, the Human Resource department must anticipate the what, who, how. and when of action.

8. Scheduling — Detailed schedules are needed so that objectives will be met at their proper deadlines.
9. Budgeting — a budget is a device for both planning and controlling the activities within a business for a given period of time. In order to arrive at the over-all total budget, each unit prepares its particular budget by requesting its subdivisions to prepare their respective budgets.
10. Procedures — this responsibility of the personnel department means the prescribed ways of doing something, or a standard method by which work is performed. They provide a means of checking when expected events do not occur and constitute an important part of the training of new employees.
11. Making intelligent use of human resources by creating more productive jobs. More people may be employed by reducing the capital cost per worker e.g., rather than have three lines operating one shift, it should be one line operating three shifts.
12. Proper planning and competent supervision. Fuzzy planning with no clear objectives, compounded with incompetent supervision will waste human resources.
13. Training the workers adequately.
14. Being concerned with the health of the workers.
15. Provision of recreational facilities and opportunities.
16. Structuring work assignments so that employees will find them at least interesting and if possible, challenging.
17. Compensating the workers fairly and making certain that the fairness of the compensation is not merely a unilateral judgement of the management.
18. Giving the workers an adequate sense of security.

STUDY/REVIEW QUESTIONS

1. What are the functions of the Human Resource Management Department? Explain each.

2. Explain this statement: "Human Resource's job is to serve management, not employees."

3. Enumerate the major responsibilities of the people of the Human Resource Management Department.

SUGGESTED ACTIVITIES AND ASSIGNMENTS

1. Visit the Human Resource Management Department of a Company and interview the HRM/Personnel Manager on the functions of the Department.

2. Identify the Filipino values that exist in the HRM Department of a Company and analyze whether such values are positively or negatively affecting their functions.

NOTES

[1]Jeff Mooney, "Jeff Mooney Comments on George Odwine's Article" 15th PMAP National Conference, Nov. 22-24, 1978. p. 1.

[2]Edwin L. Miller & Elmer Burack, "The Emerging Personnel Function", 15th PMAP National Conference, Nov. 22-24, 1978.

[3]Dalton Mcfarland, *Management Principles and Practices* (New York: The McMiller Co., 1959), p. 130

REFERENCES FOR FURTHER READING

Martinez, Esdras T. *Human Resources Management.* Manila GIC Enterprises & Co., Inc. 19__

Mcfarland, Salton. *Management Principles and Practices.* New York: The McMiller Co., 1959.

Sison, Perfecto S. *Personnel and Human Resources Management.* Manila: Rex Book Store, 1981.

6

INSTALLING THE TOTAL APPROACH TO HUMAN RESOURCE MANAGEMENT

HUMAN RESOURCE MANAGEMENT is dedicated to developing ways of bringing out the best in people in work organizations so that they can contribute their most towards corporate goals and at the same time enhance opportunities to achieve their personal life goals.

Of all the resources needed in any endeavor the human resource is usually the most critical. Like all other resources, human resources must, therefore, be effectively managed, that is, properly allocated and efficiently applied.

Human resource management is inevitably a line management responsibility. However, the Human Resources Manager must provide active support and involvement in achieving organizational and people effectiveness. It is, therefore, important that the human resource approach be comprehensive and flexible enough to meet the expanding staffing needs of the company. Human resources managers are expected, in varying degrees, to perform the following functions: job descriptions, manpower planning, recruitment, testing, selection, compensation, personnel relations, training and retirement. They should take the initiative in fitting an open job slot with the best possible person, work towards establishing an environment beneficial to the organization and see that he himself is involved in the management of the organization.

The Human Resources Unit should be directly involved in the organization's internal response to policy decisions. This constant communication between management and human resources produces close ties so that manpower planning, recruiting, selection, etc. can be affected in direct conjunction with the overall plans of the organization. There should be direct and constant communication between any local unit of the organization and the head of the Human Resource Management Unit so as to make personnel aware of subtle changes in the needs of the organization and to enable the Human Resources Manager to communicate management's feelings, attitudes and priorities to the employees.

The Human Resources Manager and his staff must be chosen just as carefully as one might choose the head of Finance or Marketing units. Jobs must be perceived by both management and the Human Resources Unit in a setting that includes the work environment as well as the organizational environment.

Several recent modifications in the human resource area, will greatly influence the work and the environment in which the Human Resources Manager will operate. They are the following:[1]

1. Within organizations there will be structural modifications and creation of new jobs built around manpower planning, manpower forecasting, career planning, and manpower information systems.
2. There will be emphasis upon forecasting an organization's human resources needs as well as assessing the qualifications of the present work force. The Human Resources Manager must become more sensitive to what operating managers find to work best.
3. Re-examination of the human resources program for maintenance functions and also for the development of a more comprehensive scheme to translate the corporate or institutional plans and objectives into future quantitative and qualitative manpower requirements are necessary.
4. The Human Resources Manager will be called upon to assist top Management in the effective utilization of human resources and all the capabilities of the human resource function. The Human Resources Manager must become increasingly oriented toward growth and efficiency of the organization instead of merely administering traditional personnel activities. This will mean greater emphasis upon planning the future organization and its personnel requirements, identifying and selecting personnel to meet these expected needs, developing and utilizing the organization's human resources, and assessing and rewarding performance.

The Organization of the Human Resources Management Unit

The organization of the Human Resources Management Unit should fit needs and conditions within the company it is to serve. The size of the company, the geographic location of its units, the nature of its operation, the caliber of its work force are some of the factors in organizing the unit.

Take the following steps:

1. *Evaluate the present management system and organizational structure.*

   There are three basic types of structure around which the functions of an enterprise may be organized. These three types include the functional, the line, and the line-and-staff structures. The *functional type* of structure is intended to provide personnel with the opportunity to achieve minimum functional specialization. In this type of structure, each manager has authority over the personnel within all other departments with respect to their performance of the function for which he is responsible. The *line type* of organization structure permits a clear line of authority to be maintained from the highest to the lowest level within the structure. The *line-and-staff type* of structure combines both the line and the functional structures. The line departments are those that are concerned directly with the accomplishment of the objectives of the enterprise, while the staff departments provide assistance in those more specialized areas that the line managers do not have time to master.

2. *Ascertain top management's philosophy on human resources.* Human Resource Management philosophy is influenced by prior experiences, education and background, corporate philosophy, changing environment, basic assumptions about people and the need to motivate subordinates.

3. *Gain top management's support.* It is essential that top management commitment be obtained very early in the program. The company's philosophy toward human resources must be ascertained, and the availability of funds and other resources required must be determined.

   There should be a clear statement of the human resources manager's authority to carry out the human resource program.

4. *Determine functions.* Write down the functions aimed at achieving the objectives of the particular unit. These functions are

embodied in the Human Resource Management Program which must contain the activities of the Human Resources Management Unit.

5. *Prepare a functional chart.* The functions of the unit are next grouped into separate units such as recruitment, employment, etc. Draw the functional organization chart of the department to show the mutual relationships of the units.
6. *Write the job descriptions, job specifications, and job work performance standards.* Clearly define for each function or group of functions the duties to be performed and the responsibilities of the job, and indicate the corresponding title for each position. Indicate the duties involved in each position and the time to be spent for each task to show its relative importance. Determine for each job the qualifications of personnel needed and list these qualifications in the job specification. Give titles or other identifying descriptions to each position or job.
7. *Select the best qualified applicant for the job.* Choose people on the basis of their qualifications as indicated in the job description, job specification and job work performance standard.
8. *Train and develop the Human Resource Staff.* The Human Resource staff and employees must be given orientation on company and department policies and rules. They should be gradually trained in all Human Resource functions so as to have a wholistic approach to their job.
9. *Assess the human resources management needs of the company.*

   Design a survey-questionnaire to assess the Human Resource Management needs of the organization and obtain top management approval of the questionnaire, the distribution procedures and the overall model of the assessment program.

   After top management has approved the information-gathering questionnaires and the procedure for their distribution, it is preferable for each functional vice president to distribute the instrument to his subordinate division managers at an appropriate meeting so that instructions can be clarified.

   Tabulate the responses to the questionnaires and analyze the data. Brief top management with summary data. Brief functional and divisional managers with detailed information about human resources needs in order to effectively relate these needs to the objectives of the organization.
10. *Interact with management.* The Human Resource Manager and his staff should begin a series of discussions with top manage-

ment, functional managers and division managers. At this stage different viewpoints must be reconciled, a commitment must be made for follow-through and problems identified and dealt with. These meetings should result in the integration of Human Resource meeds with the needs and objectives of the organization. Consideration must be given to budget constraints, new assignments and work load changes.

The end result of these joint deliberations is a statement of Human Resources needs of each organizational element.

11. *Design and formulate a total and comprehensive Human Resource Program and Policies and prepare its budget.*

    The Human Resources Manager and his staff then translate the Human Resources needs into a Human Resource Management program and budget. The peso cost of the HRM program must be translated into a proposed Human Resource budget. Specific items in the HRM program are adjusted (advanced, delayed, deleted) to fit the pesos available. However, an overall view of where the organization is in regard to Human Resource Management and where it wants to go now exits.

12. *Implement and administer the human resources program and policies.* At this stage, the department is ready to start business. The Human Resources Manager must initially exercise close supervision over his staff to see that they strictly follow established procedures in the Human Resource programs.

13 .*Evaluate the effectiveness of the human resource systems and programs.* After a reasonable period of operation, the human resources department's performance should be evaluated. The operation of the system should likewise be re-examined from time to time. Certain changes in forms and procedures can make the handling of functions more effective.

14. *Undertake improvements.* The Human Resources Manager must not hesitate to make such changes if they will improve the program and the system.

The Human Resource Management Program

Good human resource management depends upon forming and implementing sound programs. A good Human Resource Management Program should meet the organization's human resource needs in order to attain organizational objectives.

HUMAN RESOURCES DEPARTMENT ORGANIZATION

Human Resources Manager

Human Resources Planning & Procurement

-Manpower Planning
-Manpower Inventory
-Manpower Audit
-Job Analysis
-Job Description, Job Specification, Job Work Performance Standard
-Recruitment, Interviewing, Testing, Placement, Hiring
-Employment, Reassignments, Terminations, Retirement
-Statistical Analysis
-Manuals
-Systems & Procedures
-Policies
-Morale Surveys
-Organizational Development

Human Resources Development & Training

-Pre-Employment Training
-Employees Orientation and Induction
-Rank & File Development and Training
-Supervisory Development
-Middle Management Development
-Executive Development Program
-Pre-Retirement Development Program
-Athletic & Recreational Program
-Socio-cultural Program
-Career Planning and Development Program
-Guidance & Counselling Program
-Assessment Center and Promotion

Human Resources Conservation

-Appraisal of performance
-Wage and Salary
-Wage and Surveys
-Benefits Program
-Employee Classification and Re-classification
-Occupational Health and Safety
-Awards
-First Aid
-Medical Facilities
-Health Program
-Treatment and Medical Services
-Pensions
-Profit Sharing
-Publications
-Grievances
-Suggestion places
-Collective Bargaining agreement
-Labor Relations
-Associations

Human Resources Information System & Services

-MIS
-Security
-Plant Administration
-Insurances
-Canteen and Cafeteria
-Janitorial Services
-Services Cars
-Parking
-Miscellaneous

A Human Resource Management Program consists of a series of activities intended to carry out the human resources management policies of the organization in order to realize the objectives of the company. A Human Resource Management Program defines (1) the objectives, (2) the policies and procedures, and (3) the means of carrying out the varied human resources management functions. It prescribes a step-by-step procedure in carrying out the objectives of the organization.

Since human resource management is utilized on all levels, it permeates the whole organization. A well-planned human resource program achieves a good employer-employee relationship and results in a more efficient business operation. It is an instrument for promoting company-wide harmony in human resource management relation; hence, its objectives must be preventive rather than curative.

Human Resource Objectives

Human resource objectives for any organization must include five points:[2]

1. Provide stable employment, equitable compensation, desirable working conditions, and opportunities for advancement for employees in return for their skill, care, effort, dependability, and teamwork.
2. Provide a climate conducive to the development of each employee in accordance with his needs, interests, desires, abilities, and willingness to take on additional responsibility.
3. Manage the human resource to insure continuing vitality and growth of the company while realizing a profit and providing opportunities for public service.
4. Provide enlightened leadership to insure maximum work satisfaction for each employee in a decentralized environment.
5. Define clearly for each individual the responsibilities of his position to enable him to make his best c ontribution to overall organization goals.

Below is an example of composite balanced human resource objectives:[3]

1. Reduce employee turnover from 57 percent to 37 percent per year.
2. Develop and install an hourly job evaluation program.
3. Overhaul the exempt salaried compensation program.

4. Review, audit, and improve employee services.
5. Establish a system for each identification of management potential.
6. Initiate and implement a new approach to manager development.
7. Improve communication with employees.
8. Develop and implement a maintenance training program.
9. Develop and implement a new system for making rapid work force adjustments up and down.

If the objectives of a Human Resource Program are to be achieved, they must be made part of appropriate policies that will help assist management in decision-making with regard to human resource.

Policies

Policies are guidelines in performing given functions. To set guideposts for line management in managing the human asset is a vital part of the human resources managers responsibility. To insure consistency of action by all managers, policies are decided upon. They are formulated and recommended for approval by the executive office so as to provide for equitable treatment of all employees and to communicate top management's major philosophy, values and attitudes.

Among the most relevant human resource management policies are those relating to compensation, vacations, holidays, fringe benefits, severance pay, promotions, and education assistance.

The Human Resources manager must make all managers in the organization fully aware of their accountability for the human resources entrusted to their care. He must provide them the training, along with simple, workable procedures—the tools and techniques to assist them in discharging this responsibility.

Procedures

Workable procedures must also be established by the human resources manager in order to ensure consistency. Each manager in the organization must learn all the human resource procedures such as those regarding grievances, promotions, transfer, or wage adjustments, in order to prevent oversights that might be detrimental to the best interests of either the employee or the organization. However, procedures must not be reared as ends in themselves nor as excuses for failure to take needed action. They must be treated as means to an end.

Budgets

Financial support through the budget makes the program meaningful. A budget, which is a financial estimate of future needs, arranged on an orderly basis for a definite period constitutes both a financial plan and control for expenditure.

Areas Covered by a Human Resource Management Program

A good Human Resource Management Program covers the following activities:

1. *Employment of competent Employees* — Manpower planning and recruitment, interviewing, testing, indirection, placement, transfer, merit rating, promotion, training, counseling and separation of employees.
2. *Safety* — Provision of safety standards, mechanical safeguards, safety engineering, accident investigation, safety rules and safety records and statistics.
3. *Employee Relations* — Matters related to collective bargaining, wage and salary administration, grievance systems, medical and dental services, labor-management relations, morale studies as well as records and statistics. Such activities strengthen employee morale. Line Managers appreciate programs that establish a better understanding between all managers, between supervisor and subordinate, between departments, and between supervisor and rank-and-file employees. They want programs that help an executive to recognize deficiencies in his own performance and instill in him a desire to eliminate them; programs that reveal operating problems beyond the control of a particular department or executive--problems that demand action from top management for proper solution. They welcome programs that uncover men of ability whose talents might otherwise have been ignored, and they encourage interdepartmental transfer of competent personnel. Managers welcome especially programs that give them keener insight into their responsibility for training

employees and appraising their abilities, that stress an executive's obligation to advise and counsel his subordinates and help them so that they may develop their talents fully.

4. *Employee Research and Standards* — This includes job analysis, job description, evaluation, work performance standard, grading, wage analysis, labor market surveys, organizational planning, employee manuals, personnel audit and human resource accounting. Human resource management must be able to present in accepted statistical form data on the various programs and activities of the organization which can be presented in percentages and ratio. Graphs and illustrations such as human resource strength projections can show rate of turn-over, rate of tardiness and absenteeism, conversion of income rates, rate of accidents, expenditures for WCC; the effect of the safety program on costs, ratio and cost of employee benefits, manpower losses due to non-production time because of absenteeism, tardiness, maternity leave, sick leave, vacation leave, accident leave, or other calamities, projection of manpower r equirements, and expenditure for SSS and Medicare.
5. *Employee Services* — This includes recreational plans, insurance plans, pensions, profit-sharing plans, and miscellaneous services.

Implementing Successfully the Human Resource Management Program

The Human Resource Manager and his staff must be genuinely and sincerely interested in their work. They must know the business and the internal as well as the external interfaces of the business, including the politics obtaining in the company and relate their Human Resource work to it.

Aside from obtaining the full support of top management in Human Resource Management, they must know the people least or most interested in supporting the programs. The Human Resource Manager should develop a master plan with priorities; then he should start with the program least likely to be rejected and really make good at it. He should not introduce programs likely to disrupt operations or put managers on the defensive, even if he feels the program is proper. He should be of help to departments rather than be a "pain in their necks." He should get the cooperation of line supervisors and employees.

The success of the Human Resource Management Program can be measured by the degree of employee satisfaction with their jobs, by their improved performance, by the employees' friendly attitude and respect for their employer and by the increased competence and motivation of the workers.

STUDY/REVIEW QUESTIONS

1. What are the distinct modifications in the human resource area which have significant influence upon the work and the environment in which the Human Resources Manager will operate? Explain each.
2. Enumerate the different steps in organizing the Human Resource Management Unit.

SUGGESTED ACTIVITIES AND ASSIGNMENTS

1. Write a position paper on the proper approach of installing a Human Resource Management Unit in companies in the Philippines. Have in mind the Filipino psychology of both employer and employees.
2. Make an abstract of two articles or books wherein Filipino values are related to Human Resource Management.

NOTES

[1]Elmer H. Burack, Edwin L. Miller, "The Personnel Function in Transition", 15th PMAP National Conference, Nov. 22-24, 1978.

[2]Robert L. Desatnick, "Innovative Human Resource Management, U.S.A.": American Management Association, Inc., 1972, pp. 27-28.

[3]Ibid., pp.40-41

REFERENCE FOR FURTHER READING

Andres, Tomas D. *Management by Filipino Values*. Quezon City: New Day Publishers. 1985.

Chruden, Herbert J. et al. *Personnel Management.* Cincinnati: South-Western Publishing Company, 1968.

Yoder, Dale et al. *Personnel Management and Industrial Relations.* Englewood Cliffs, New Jersey: Prentice-Hall, Inc. 1982.

7

FORMULATING HUMAN RESOURCE POLICIES AND PROCEDURES

THE POLICIES of top management give direction to the activities and set the limits within which action is to be pursued. Policies are formulated by management even before an organization opens for business in order to guide the line manager or supervisor on the scope of his activities, authority, and responsibility, and it enable him to arrive at sound decisions. The importance of policy is reflected in the oft-repeated statements of employees and management: "Our policy is . . . ." "We need a policy on. . . ." "What is our policy on this?"

Company policies then are broad guides for action. They define the responsibility of supervisors and managers in their jobs. Since policies are statements of how it wants to run an organization, management rightly expects strict adherence to them. Policies indicate the best method of conducting any portion of work at hand. They assist in employee problem-solving and decision-making.

Human Resource policy is a plan of action that serves as a guide particularly in matters related to employee selection, hiring and firing, fringe benefits, training and development, evaluation, promotion, emotion, transfer, wages and salaries, grievances, discipline, medical care, hospitalization and retirement.

Classification of Policies

Policies are classified as "general" or "specific" according to the amount of detailed description contained in the statement. General policies might apply to the entire organization and then be defined by an implementing policy statement for a specific department or division.

Policies may be grouped as to *origin;* as to level in the organization and as to *functions* or activity.

1. *As to origin*
   a. Imposed policies are those required by the government such as laws, rules, procedures and administrative orders.
   b. Appealed policies are formulated when a subordinate endorses to his superior matters not covered by the existing policies. The decision or instruction given to the subordinate becomes an appealed policy and will serve as a guide on matters of similar nature in the future.
   c. Originated policies are those originated by the Board of Directors or top executives for the guidance of all parties: the stockholders, management members, customers and employees.
2. *As to level in the organization:*
   a. Basic policies. These are policies formulated at the start of the business, but they may be amended to cope with changing conditions. They are broadly stated and serve as guides for all.
   b. General policies. These policies are used by middle management. They consist of specific guides in line with the basic policies.
   c. Department policies. These policy statements are intended to guide those in lower management in carrying out the general policies and eventually the basic policies of the organization.
3. *As to functions or activity groupings:*
   a. Human Resource Policies
   b. Financial Policies
   c. Production Policies
   d. Sales Policies

The Need for Human Resource Policies

Human resource policies are valuable in fixing definite objectives for the organization and in providing strong coordinating influences that tend to hold the organization together. Carefully developed policies are vital to the management of human resources because each person is sensitive to any difference in the treatment, no matter how slight, that he may receive as compared with other persons. Policies promote uniformity of action and prevent conflicting decisions, especially as regards labor matters. They tend to eliminate errors, red tape, and inconsistencies in action and prevent unfairness in handling individual cases. One thing that will impair employee efficiency and morale most quickly is for the boss to display favoritism when making decisions, such as those relating to promotions, vacations, schedules, wage increases, assignment of overtime, or infractions of rules. Human resource policies give employees a greater sense of security by enabling them to know what treatment to expect. Managers also can act with a greater degree of confidence in resolving problems since they have a basis upon which to make and to defend their decisions.

Desirable Human Resource Policies of an Organization

1. The Organization believes it is good business to promote good employee relations. The most important assets of the organization are capable and satisfied employees.
2. Applicants for employment will be considered solely on the basis of fitness, ability and desirability for the work at hand.
3. An employee of the Organization, through either initial appointment or promotion will have to undergo probation from a minimum of three months to a maximum of six months.
4. The Organization shall pay fair and equitable compensation in accordance with the principle of a "fair day's pay for a fair day's work". The Organization shall maintain leadership in compensation in comparison to the usual industry rates.
5. Good employee benefits will be offered to meet the needs of the employees.
6. Working conditions will be constantly improved in accordance with good community practice.
7. It shall be the policy of the Organization to recognize outstanding work and unusual progress and development.
8. Promotions will be made with proper consideration as to ability, merit and length of service. It is Organization's policy to fill all vacancies wherever possible by the promotion or transfer of present employees.
9. The company Union will be recognized as an organization that is endeavoring to improve the social and economic status of those it represents. The company or Organization will deal with its of-

ficers and those they represent sincerely and considerately and on a business-like basis with a view to developing the greatest mutual confidence and respect.

10. Contracts which the Organization has entered into with the Union on hours of work, rates of pay, and other conditions of employment will be administered strictly in accordance with the intent of their provisions.

Guidelines for Effective Human Resource Policy Formulation

The Human Resources Manager represents management in administering, implementing and interpreting human resource policies. Frequently, he is confronted by new and terrifying responsibilities, challenges and demands in terms of understanding and the proper utilization of human resource policy. Thus, he must know how a policy is made and administered.

Company policies are based on historical events, the present situation, or anticipated future needs. They must be issued by top management, which is responsible for making major policies that are by their nature company-wide in application. Minor policies, better known as rules and procedures, are usually formulated by minor executives or department managers and upon the professional competency of its human resource staff to formulate and to enforce policies that it may approve. In formulating human resource policies, the Human Resource Manager and his staff must insure that these policies are compatible with current business conditions, collective bargaining trends, and government regulations.

A policy may be formulated thus:

1. Top management may formulate and issue it. When the top executive is presented with a problem, his decision becomes a policy, The result is an originated policy which is usually broad in scope and may be detailed or specific.
2. Policy may also be formulated by a committee, the board of directors or the key men in the organization. When a problem calling for a policy decision arises, the group meets to analyze the problem against criteria, values, objectives, or other expected outcomes. The views of those at the meeting are presented as clarifications, amendments, or possible solutions. They then decide on what seems to be the best solution. If their decision is signed and promulgated by the top executive, the statement

automatically becomes a policy which the subordinates are expected to follow.

3. Certain practices, procedures, actions, and precedents that have been consistently followed for some time, crystalize into policies.
4. Memorandums which the top executive issues for the guidance of his subordinates on certain matters can be sources of policy. A decision made by a top executive on a particular problem is also a policy statement on that subject. The result may be an appealed policy because a subordinate appeals to his supervisor for guidance. The latter's memorandum or circular is often the statement of what the subordinates are required to do henceforth regarding a similar problem.
5. Administrative orders and procedures or contract specifications are called imposed policy. Policy formulation, may also be dome by the lower levels of the organization and communicated upwards to top management which has the exclusive authority to promulgate it.

Human Resource policies are usually formulated by the Human Resource Managers, and then submitted to top management for approval and release. The Human Resource Manager may, however, issue rules and procedures for implementing human resource policies.

Characteristics of Good Human Resource Policies

1. *Policies should reflect objectives and plans.*

   If a policy does not further plans or make objectives more attainable, it has not done its job. No manager should ever say: "There's no good reason why we do it, it is just our policy."
2. *Policies should be consistent.*

   An ineffective human resource program would surely result if the wage and salary program is based upon both a policy of human resource maximization and one of compensation's minimization.
3. *Policies should be flexible.*

   While many policies are, in effect, permanent, it should never be assumed that policies are laws engraved on stone. If goals, premises, or major plans change, policies can likewise be expected to change to meet the new situation.

   To be flexible as the situation changes is not to be casual in application. If current policies reflect objectives and if plans are consistent, they should not be regarded lightly or disregarded on slight pretext. It is sometimes impossible to make a policy to meet all conditions. But if a policy must be disregarded often, probably it is not sound, is not applicable, or too tightly circumscribes a manager's area of discretion.

4. *Policies should be distinguished from rules and procedures.*

   The correct separation of these three types of guidelines is admittedly difficult, but it is important to good planning, workable delegation of authority, and even good human relations. Some companies carefully distinguish between policies and procedures in their manuals by printing them on paper of different colors. It also helps to point out the policy to which each procedure is related.

5. *Policies should be in writing.*

   If policies are to be heeded, they should be written. The difficulty of communicating intentions and desires is reduced by precise communication in writing. Putting policies in writing is the best way of putting them to work.

6. *Policies should be taught.*

   Written policies must be explained, interpreted, and taught. What people do not understand they cannot use correctly and are likely to distrust. Issuing a written policy is not enough. Questions regarding it must be answered and subordinates must comprehend its goals and why it was developed.

7. *Policies should be controlled.*

   There should be a regular and careful review of company policies to see whether they are up to date, reflect goals and plans, are consistent and flexible, are distinguished from rules and procedures, are understood, and whether they hamper the manager's legitimate activity.

8. *Policies should be stable.*

   If policies are to serve as guides to action, they should not be changed frequently. Careful study should go into formulating policies.

9. *Policies should be consistent within the company at all levels and departments.*

10. *Policies must be sincere.*

    Policies are public pronouncements of the philosophy of the company. The wording of policies should include real intentions; otherwise, they become meaningless writings on paper.

11. *Policies must be realistic.*

Present conditions must be considered if policy statements are to be implemented.

Policies put into formalized written statements are called policy statements. Human Resource policy statements can be announced through Employee Handbooks, Company Magazines or publications, memoranda and circulars, company Bulletin Boards and meetings or conferences. Human resource policies must be dynamic in nature and must change in accordance with the conditions affecting them. HR policies must be integrated closely with policies relating to other functional areas.

It is the responsibility of line management to carry out human resource policies with assistance from the human resource manager .

Sometimes human resource policies are not implemented because of ignorance of proper procedure in carrying them out with fairness, lack of an officer to monitor their implementation, or lack of uniform and consistent application, or because of impracticality of the policy itself owing to changed or changing conditions and failure of management to amend it.

Ziegher has suggested the following as important guides for creating effective policies:

1. *Flexibility.* A policy must strike a reasonable balance between stability and flexibility. Conditions change and policies must change accordingly.
2. *Comprehensiveness.* A policy must be comprehensive enough to cover any contingency. The degree of comprehensiveness depends upon the scope of action controlled by the policy itself.
3. *Coordinative.* A policy must provide for coordination of the various subunits whose actions are interrelated without exact coordinative direction being provided. Each subunit is to pursue its own goals. The ultimate test of any subunits activity should be its relationship to the policy statement.
4. *Ethical.* A policy must conform to ethical behavior which prevails in society.
5. *Clarity.* A policy must be written clearly and also logically. It must specify the intended aim, define appropriate methods and delineate the limits of freedom of action permitted to those who are to be guided by it.

The ultimate test of a policy is whether the intended objective is attained. If the policy does not lead to the goal, it should be revised; thus policies must be subject to continual reexamination.

Uses of Policies

1. To inform the public, customers, and others of the philosophy of management of an organization for their guidance in dealing with the organization.
2. To serve as a guide on labor relations.
3. To enable executives to make decisions or take action on matters under their jurisdiction.
4. To justify the actions of executives on problems presented to them for decision.
5. To provide uniformity and consistency in action.
6. To enable executives to delegate more routine matters to their subordinates.

STUDY/REVIEW QUESTIONS

1. What is a human resource policy?
2. What are the different classifications of policies?
3. Why is there a need for human resource policies in an organization?
4. What are the steps in forming a human resource policy?
5. Enumerate the uses of a policy.

SUGGESTED ACTIVITIES AND ASSIGNMENTS

1. Make a list of Filipino values which a company should consider in formulating a human resource policy.
2. Secure a Personnel Policy Manual of a Company and identify the policies which are not in consonance with the Filipino idiosyncrasy and values.
3. Write a position paper on a government policy related to a human resource.

REFERENCES FOR FURTHER READING

Andres, Tomas D. *Understanding Filipino Values: A Management Approach.* Quezon City: New Day Publishers, 1984.

Angeles, Conrado P. et al. *Principles of Personnel Administration.* Quezon City: R.M. Garcia Publishing House, 1981.

Sison, Perfecto S. *Personnel and Human Resources Management.* Manila: Rex Book Store, 1981.

Ziegher, Raymond J. *Business Policies and Decision Making.* New York: Appleton Century Crofts, 1966.

8

THE HUMAN RESOURCE EXECUTIVE

MORE AND MORE the work of the Human Resource Executive is being recognized today as one that is as vital to the success of the organization as that of the production, finance and marketing executives. Hence, there is a need for human resource managers to be fully prepared for high quality performance in their jobs.

The Human Resource Executive should be a member of top management. He must help determine what policies, programs, practices, and approaches will contribute most to the objectives of the organization. He must be responsible to all levels of management for the most effective utilization of the human assets. He must make a major contribution to the development of the organization's short-term and long-term objectives while seeing to it that each employee develops his potential to the fullest extent. He must go beyond the traditional role of the personnel manager and act as a catalyst as well as business effectiveness consultant.

The Human Resource Executive must respond effectively to the organization demands for improved employee performance. He must also respond to employee demands stemming from such recent developments as better education of the labor force, changing demographics of the labor force, changing levels and types of work-related expectations, quality of work-life issues, and increasingly complex governmental policy issues. Furthermore, the Human Resource Executive must rationalize the work and purposes of Human Resource Management in all sectors on the "maçro and micro-levels" to harmonize with the goals of government as well as to meet the requirements of the growing work force and national population. He must see to it that the management of human resources in his organization is not only related to development goals, but also to the ethos of the nation. That is, the human resource management formulas must meet the criteria of relevance and utility, responsiveness to socioeconomic and political realities, and the people's growing sense of national identity.

Functions of a Human Resource Executive

The Human Resource Executive must occupy a position that reports to the president. His broad function is to formulate and implement policies and plans to insure the most effective planning, recruitment, selection, development, and compensation of the organization's human resources; contribute to the development of the organizations long-range and short-term objectives by initiating and implementing employee relations practices which will encourage each employee to realize his personal goals, while maximizing his contribution to business effectiveness; provide for the resolution of management problems and the realization of opportunities through innovative approaches to human resources management.[1]

The Human Resource Executive administers those parts of the human resource policies and programs entrusted to him. He sees to it that all labor laws and government orders are properly carried out. He gives guidance and counselling to employees. He coordinates all activities concerning human resources. He negotiates labor contracts and attends negotiations with labor unions. He trains and develops the organization's human resources through a comprehensive training and development program. He stimulates better employees' point of view to the management. He influences people to cooperate toward some goals which are desirable for both the organization and the employees.

The Human Resource Executive has the following principal responsibilities:[2]

1. Formulate and recommend human resource objectives for inclusion in the organization's overall objectives.
2. Show the potential contribution of good human resource management to organizational objectives.
3. Identify management problems that can be realized through improved effectiveness in human resource management.
4. Formulate, recommend and implement employee relations

policies designed to improve individual productivity, job satisfaction and profitability.

5. Make managers aware of their full responsibilities in the management of human resources entrusted to them.
6. Provide the necessary tools, techniques, and methods which foster the development of a business climate conducive to employee development.
7. Establish the necessary procedures for human resource recruitment, selection, utilization, motivation, development and compensation. Insure that these are incorporated into every manager's job performance evaluation.
8. Develop and staff the employee relations functions to provide for innovative approaches to labor and union relations, personnel practices and services, training and development, communication, community relations, benefit plan development and administration, and problem solving.
9. Serve as a catalyst and business effectiveness consultant in initiating and implementing new approaches to human resources management.
10. Aids in interpreting management policies to employees and employees' point of view to management.
11. Advise and assist management in the promotion of sound employee-management relations as well as relations with the union.
12. Assist line personnel such as the foremen, supervisors and department heads in implementing human resource policies and programs.
13. Assist individual employees in solving problems which affect their general morale and efficiency.
14. Attend to government and public relations concerning employees.

Qualifications of a Human Resource Executive

The demand for human resource executives/managers is expanding and will provide career opportunities for many individuals who are interested in this challenging type of work.

Age. A seasoned Human Resource Executive must be at least thirty years old. A certain amount of maturity is required for such a delicate job. Furthermore, it is doubtful if anyone under 30 years of age could have acquired the qualifications and experience needed for such a job.

Education. A Human Resource Executive must have at least a minimum of a bachelor's degree, preferably in psychology, the behavioral sciences, business management, or communication. If possible, he should have a master's degree and/or even a doctoral degree in business/educational/public administration, the behavioral sciences, or psychology.

He should be proficient in psychology, and have knowledge of labor laws, economics, statistics, humanities, safety, sociology, English, Filipino or any predominant dialect of the employees, industrial engineering, communication and labor economics. Psychology deals with the mind and with human behavior in relation to physical and social environment. A Human Resource executive needs psychology to meet problems with regard to personnel relations, placement, morale and motivations, grievances, accidents, tardiness, absenteeism, training, counseling and other operational functions of the manager. Economics treats of production and distribution of wealth. The human resource management involves the human element in this production and distribution of goods and services for profit. The Human Resource Manager's knowledge of economic principles is needed in matters involving wages, insurance plans, retirement and pension plans, profit sharing and other fringe benefits.

A Human Resource Manager must have a working knowledge of the various laws affecting employee-employer relationships. He must know the rights and privileges of the worker as provided in the labor and social laws such as the eight-hour labor law, workmen's compensation acts, women and children laws, social security system articles, and other national laws.

Sociology treats of the origin and evolution of human society, the progress of community or social groups and the laws controlling human institutions and functions. A knowledge of sociology would be valuable to the Human Resource Executive.

Research is the systematic investigation of phenomena and Statistics is the science that deals with the collection, tabulation, and classification of quantitative data. It is a tremendous asset for a Human Resource Executive to have a good knowledge of statistical analysis and interpretation and the ability to report and present such data clearly in concise language. Familiarity with research methods and techniques will enable him to be accurate in his human resource management. Industrial engineering enables the Human Resource Executive to establish standards for judging performance and developing financial incentives.

The Human Resource Executive must have a broad background in such disciplines as psychology, sociology, philosophy, law and economics, if he is to:

- Effectively engage in planning
- Design the structure of relationship of people and organizations
- Motivate workers to work willingly and productively
- Wield control in the light of organizational goals
- Recruit, select, and place qualified personnel
- Initiate personnel development plans
- Reconcile individual, social, and organizational needs.[3]

To succeed in all these tasks, he must have considerable creativity and imagination, learn to handle conflict situations and to resolve them, reconcile freedom with discipline. To improve human relationships and to foster effective team functioning—tasks which the organization expects him to perform—the Human Resource Executive must also be aware of changes in Managerial styles. He must keep in mind that there is no single encompassing theory of management. There can only be a variety of ways in which policies and programs are designed. The Human Resource Executive must be a chance agent, an innovator and creator, a settler of conflicts and an entrepreneur.

It is beneficial for the Human Resource Executive to participate in seminars and other special courses like those concerning pollution, wages, compensation, public relations, labor laws, and current problems and recent trends in personnel. He must also know modern management tools and techniques such as organization, information systems, accounting and finance, business planning, and controls. He must be particularly well-versed in personnel management tools and techniques such as job evaluation, compensation, manpower planning, union relations, training and development.

The Human Resource Executive may specialize in a specific task such as training and development; however, it is recommended that he be broadly trained. A Human Resource Executive must have communication skills, both written and oral and inter-personal competency. He must have training in organizational development (OD) so as to have a complete understanding of the systems view of organizations and the role of conflict.

Experience. A Human Resource Executive must have successful employment experiences in his background that are related to the human resource field. Ideally, a candidate for a Human Resource Executive position has had at least 10 to 15 years of progressively more responsible, successful assignments as human resource personnel specialist, supervisor, and manager in an organization whether it be business, educational, ecclesiastic, public, government or private. His assignments must have included actual exposure and participation in organizational planning and manpower planning, management systems, personnel and union relations, recruitment, compensation and benefits, policy formulation and administration, applied behavioral sciences, manpower inventories, orientation, induction and training, preparation of position descriptions and job evaluations and establishment of performance standards and personnel practices.

The Human Resource Executive candidate must demonstrate skill in the following areas: in identification and resolution of real management problems, in employment, discipline and discharge, promotion, transfer, counseling, speaking and in writing clearly, concisely, and effectively; in leading, as demonstrated by the ability to build an effective team, in identification and implementation of innovative approaches to the solution of employee relations. He should be able to demonstrate that he can talk sensibly and authoritatively on at least 75% of subjects like the following: Behavioral Sciences, Business planning/Forward planning, Career Development, Complaints and Grievances and Discipline. Labor Legislation, Management by Objectives, Management Succession Planning, Manpower Planning, Motivation and Morale, Organizational Planning and Organization Development (OD), Pensions, Personnel Records, Recruitment and Selection Practices, Retirement Packages, Salary Structuring and Reviewing, Trade Unions, Training and Management Development, Training Needs Analysis, and Counseling.

A Human Resource Executive must be an efficient corporate planner and follow personnel human resource policies throughout the organization.

He must be able to work using modern technology, like computers. He must understand organizational structures and organizational behavior and should be able to show to top management that organizational structure problems must be solved first before there can be improvement in management-employee relationships. He must be able to show that Human Resources services and programs assist in increasing output rather than disrupting it.

Personal Characteristics. The Human Resource Executive's success is dependent upon more than his education and experience. Much depends on his personal characteristics, such as flexibility and adaptability, high energy level coupled with good health, dynamic leadership ability, creativity, with a need to achieve, service orientation, sensitivity and concern for others and ability to relate with equal effectiveness to top managers as well as rank-and-file employees.

Other required personal characteristics of the Human Resource Executive are: good mental health, a sense of humor, ability to communicate with others, patience, and a high degree of objectivity toward other individuals. Above all, he must be a man of integrity, courage, justice, honesty, and circumspection in order to earn the respect of both management and employees.

STUDY/REVIEW QUESTIONS

1. What are the functions of a Human Resource Executive? Explain each.
2. Enumerate the principal responsibilities of the Human Resource Executive.
3. What is the most important qualification of the Human Resource Executive in an organization in the Philippine setting? Give your reasons why such is the most important qualification.

SUGGESTED ACTIVITIES AND ASSIGNMENTS

1. Make a list of the positive Filipino values which a Human Resources Executive must have in a company in the Philippine setting.
2. Make a comparative study of the qualifications of a Human Resources Executives of a stable company and of an unstable company. Indicate similarities and differences in their values systems and traits.

NOTES

[1]Robert L Desatnick, *Innovative Human Resource Management,* U.S.A.: American Management Association, Inc. 1972, p. 26.

[2]Ibid. pp. 26-27

3 Geronimo Z. Velasco, "Human Resources Management: The Emerging Corporate Challenge", 15th National Conference, Personnel Management Association of the Philippines, Nov. 22, 1978.

REFERENCE FOR FURTHER READING

Andres, Tomas D. *Understanding Filipino Values: A Management* Approach. Quezon City: New Day Publishers, 1984.

Desatnick, Robert L. *Innovative Human Resource Management.* U.S.A.: American Management Association, Inc., 1972.

Sison, Perfecto S. *Personnel and Human Resource Management.* Manila: Rex Book Store, 1981.

PART THREE

HUMAN RESOURCE PLANNING AND PROCUREMENT

---

9. Organization and Management of Jobs

10. Human Resource Planning

11. Human Resource Procurement, Selection and Equipment

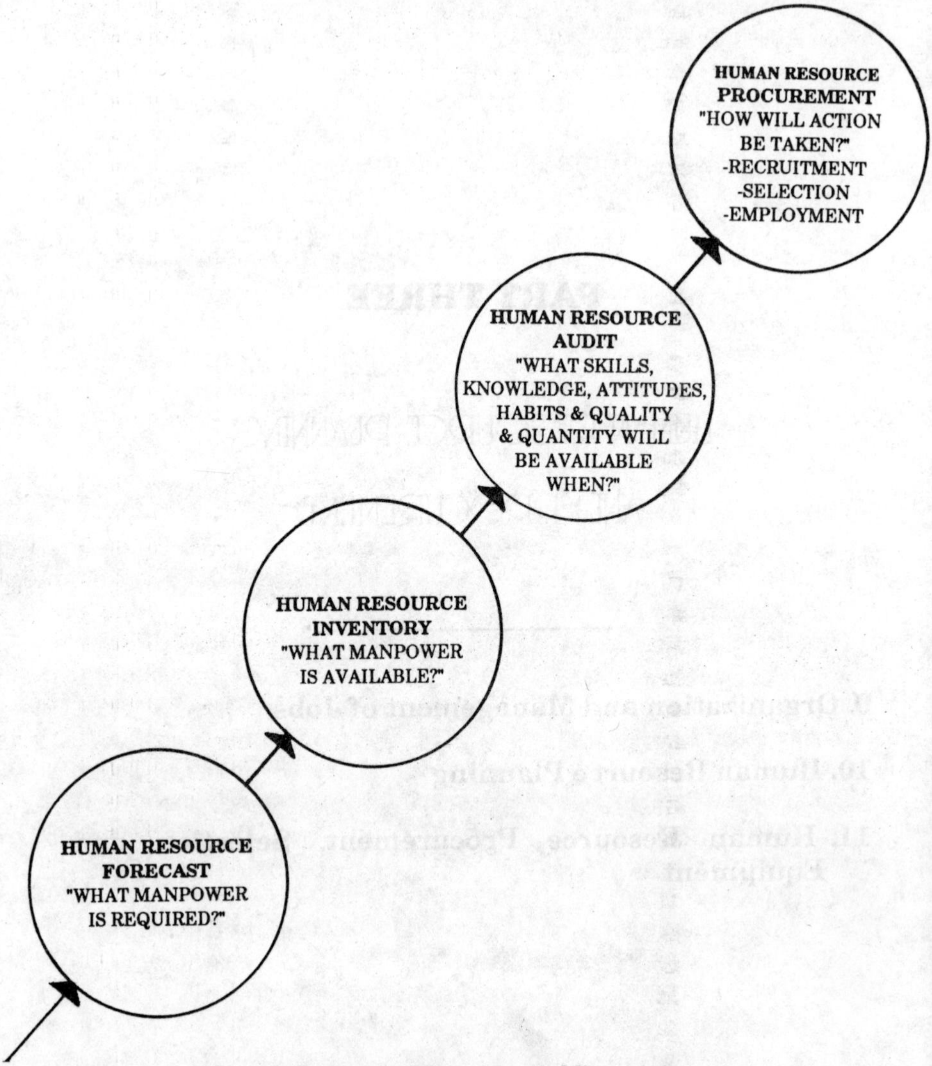

Human Resource Planning and Procurement

Human resource planning and procurement is needed by companies for their own survival. Effective human resource planning means analyzing an organization's manpower needs under changing conditions and developing the activities necessary to satisfy these needs. Ideally human resource planning is included in the earlier stage of corporate planning.

Human resources need to be considered in the context of long-range strategic planning.

9

ORGANIZATION AND MANAGEMENT OF JOBS

UNDERSTANDING the different jobs in an organization is essential. Each employee should render the maximum contribution he is capable of making. For him to be able to do so, the tasks must be divided into jobs that can be performed effectively and also provide a source of satisfaction to the persons who are assigned to them. The task of establishing the duties and responsibilities and standards for each job within an organization, therefore, is a most important function of human resource management.

The job is the smallest unit into which the activities of an enterprise are divided. Jobs that are similar in terms of the work performed and the qualifications that they require of employees may be grouped into families known as *occupations*. The portion of a job that is performed by an individual employee is called a *position*.

The job serves to define the activities of the organization that an employee is to perform. It provides the means for dividing and assigning the authority and responsibility that must be exercised by the incumbent job holders. Furthermore, it is the basis for selecting and training employees, for evaluating their performance, and for determining the rate of pay.

The Design of Jobs

Job design means specification of jobs according to content, methods, and relationship with other jobs in order to satisfy technological requirements as well as the social and personal requirements of the job holder.

Jobs can be divided into two categories:

1. those with physical environment and physiological requirements, and
2. those with organizational, social, and personal requirements.[1] Responsible autonomous job behavior indicates desirable individual-organizational-technological relationships in productive organizations.

Responsible behavior means:

1. acceptance of responsibility by the individual or group for activities required to complete the product or service,
2. acceptance of responsibility for rate, quantity, and quality of output and
3. recognition of interdependence of individual or group on others for effective progress of a cycle of activities.

Similarly, autonomous behavior encompasses:

1. self-regulation of work where the job is an assignment having inputs, facilities and outputs,
2. self-evaluation of work content and performance,
3. self-adjustment to changes required by technological variability, and
4. participation in setting up of goals or objectives for job outputs.

Jobs can be classified into two types:

1. Those whose content and structure reflect interaction with personal and technological requirements and
2. Those whose characteristics reflect interaction with personal and organizational requirements.

Job content is made up of a number of kinds of tasks and their interrelationships. Many of these tasks are specific illustrations of the need for the development of a work role which provides comprehensiveness, that is, the opportunity to perform all tasks required for completion of a product or process and at the same time imposes the responsibility and confers the authority for self-direction and self-regulation.

Analysis of Jobs

Job Analysis means determining by observation and study the nature of a specific job. It determines the tasks which comprise the job and the particular skills, abilities and responsibilities required for its successful performance.

There are three parts essential to the analysis of any job:

1. the job must be completely and accurately identified;
2. the tasks, duties and responsibilities, and work performance standard of the job must be completely and accurately described;
3. the requirements the job makes upon the worker for successful performance must be indicated.

The following are the steps in doing job analysis:

First Step: *Organization's Policy.* Obtain top management's support simultaneously. If the program is to be successful, the cooperation of the other departments must be obtained by the Human Resource Department. For this program it is recommended to hire a job analyst with a high degree of analytical ability and writing skill to complete job data and prepare the job descriptions, specifications and work performance standards.

Second Step: *Questionnaire.* This method, which requires employees, supervisors, or both to accomplish the questionnaire, is logical since employees are familiar with the minute details of their jobs, and with proper guidelines they will provide data that are more than adequate.

The job analyst designs the questionnaires, and distributes them to the employees through their supervisors. After completing a questionnaire, the employee submits it to his supervisor who then checks the accuracy of data furnished.

Third Step: *Interviewing.* With proper question-guides, trained job analysts can obtain more complete and accurate job information through interviews. One or more employees on each job should be interviewed for reasons of accuracy and employee acceptance. It is advisable to discuss the data thus gathered with the supervisors and other employees in order to insert modifications where they are needed, and to obtain general approval. The steps are:

1. Explain purposes;
2. Discuss desired method for obtaining factual data;

3. Secure cooperation;
4. Obtain lists of all jobs in the unit concerned with titles and numbers of workers in each;
5. Discuss the nature of work and details of a job;
6. Obtain recommendations of the most desirable employees to observe during the course of the study on the basis of efficiency and willingness to cooperate with the analysts.

Fourth Step: *Observing the Employees at Work.* Some details of job performance, which may have been missed by the two previous methods cited, can be obtained through observation. This approach works best when the work cycle is short and manual operations are perceptibly prominent. The following are guidelines in observing employees at work:

1. Note carefully each operation performed;
2. Make certain all observable operations have been noted;
3. Check for specific items to be included in the Job Analysis Schedule;
4. Record working conditions, tools, equipment and materials used;
5. Question worker about those operations which are not observable and obtain from him an estimate of the percentage of time used in each operation performed;
6. Review the notes concerning the job elements with the worker and ask for suggestions.
7. Review observations and notes with the immediate superior of the worker observed;
8. a) Determine if the job has been thoroughly covered;
   b) Obtain estimates of percentage of time for each operation;
   c) Ascertain what specific tools are furnished by the worker and by the company;
   d) Obtain information for relating the job to other job sections.

Fifth Step: *Writing the first Draft of the Job Description, Job Specifications and the Job Work Performance Standards.*

After a job is analyzed, the data about it are gathered, summed up, and recorded. The *job description* is the written statement covering the duties performed, the responsibilities involved, and the relation of the job being studied to the other jobs in the company. The *specification* is the determination of the personal qualifications which the worker must possess. The *job work performance standard* are criteria by which the worker's performance will be evaluated. The job position title is the name that indicates the functions of the job.

A job specification consists of the following:

1. Job Requirements
   a. Educational Requirements
   b. License Requirements
   c. Experience and/or Training Requirements
   d. Knowledge Requirements
   e. Skills Requirements
   f. Attitude/Habit Requirements
2. Physical Requirements
   a. Physical exertion
   b. Working Conditions
   c. Hazards

A job work performance standard consists of the outputs/results a job position must deliver and the quality and the average time/period required per work.

In writing the job descriptions and specifications and job work performance standards, the following are guidelines:[2]

1. The statements should be terse and direct, using the simplest wording possible.
2. All words and phrases which do not contribute to the description should be omitted.
3. Each sentence should start with a functional verb, present tense, with the implied subject being the worker holding the job.
4. Emphasis should be given on the skill involved and to the particular tools and equipment used.
5. Full capital letters should be used to spell out any job letters appearing in the description. The names of all departments, special equipment, and similar items should have the first letter of the words capitalized.
6. The term "occasionally" should be used to describe those duties performed "once in a while", and the term "may" should be used to described those duties which are performed only by some of the workers.

Sixth Step: *Have Division/Department/Section Head Review and Approve the first Draft.*

1. Allow all supervisors concerned to review and edit the

original draft;

2. Revise draft on basis of comments, changes and criticisms suggested by the reviewers.

Seventh Step: *Panel Discussions on the revised semi-final draft.*

After all pertinent data have been consolidated on all jobs of a certain section/department/division, the final job description, job specification and work performance standard should be discussed for further revision, if needed, by a panel preferably consisting of the Human Resources Managers and the superiors of the unit involved.

Eight Step: *Finalization.*

1. Review the semi-final draft on the basis of comments, changes, and criticisms suggested by members of the panel;
2. Obtain written approval of contents from top management before final typing;
3. Arrange for typing the completed analysis of the final draft (5 copies); two to be retained in the Human Resources Management Department's files and one copy to go to the Employment/Recruitment Office, another to the offices of the unit involved.
4. Submit Manualized Report to units concerned.

Uses of Job Analysis

The job analysis serves as a guide in the recruitment, selection, placement, and counseling of employees. Furthermore, it serves as a good basis for evaluating or classifying jobs so that workers can be compensated equitably on the basis of the skills required and the complexity of duties and responsibilities involved. The bases of the job evaluation are the job description and job specifications.

The job analysis serves as a tool in promotion and transfer along lines determined by the duties, responsibilities, job requirements and working conditions. It is also an important tool in employee counseling and in the settlement of grievances since a job analysis indicates the duties and responsibilities inherent in the various positions in the organization.

The job analysis enables management to institute corrective measures against working conditions that are unnecessarily hazardous, unpleasant, or unhealthy. It is a big help to supervisors, providing them

JOB DESCRIPTION

Class No.	Job Title	Salary Range

JOB SUMMARY

STATEMENT OF DUTIES

BASIC RELATIONSHIP

Reports to	Supervises

JOB SPECIFICATIONS

Qualifications Guide	Education	Licenses Secured/Examinations Passed
	Experience	Length of Company Service
Responsibillity		
Physical Demands		
Hazards		
Working Conditions		
Equipment Used		

with precise and detailed descriptions of the jobs under their jurisdiction, and guides them in establishing production standards, simplifying work procedure, and improving methods.

The job analysis helps in determining training needs of an employee and in standardizing job titles according to functions required.

STUDY/REVIEW QUESTIONS

1. Explain what a job design is.
2. Enumerate the different steps in making a job analysis.
3. Give two important uses of job analysis in Philippine companies.

SUGGESTED ACTIVITIES AND ASSIGNMENTS

1. Secure a job description, job specification, and a job work performance standard from any organization or company and evaluate them.

2 .Interview an employee and ask him the uses of a job description in his work.

3. Make a list of Filipino values that influence the organization and management of jobs.

NOTES

[1]Louis E. Davis, "The Design of Jobs," *Industrial Relations*, VI, No. 1 (October 1966), 21-45.

[2]Herbert J. Chruden & Arthur W. Sherman, Jr., *Personnel Management* (Chicago: South & Western Publishing Company, 1968.)

[3]J.L. Otis and R.H. Leukart, *Job Evaluation*, 2nd ed. (Englewood Cliffs, New Jersey: Prentice-Hall Inc., 1954) pp. 247-276.

REFERENCES FOR FURTHER READING

Chruden, Herbert J. et al. *Personnel Management.* Chicago: South & Western Publishing Company, 1968.

Martinez, Esdras T. *Human Resources Management.* Manila: GIC Enterprises & Co., Inc., 1979.

Otis, J.L. et al. *Job Evaluation.* Englewood Cliffs, New Jersey: Prentice-Hall Inc., 1954.

Sison, Perfecto S. *Personnel and Human Resources Management.* Manila: Rex Book Store, 1981.

10

HUMAN RESOURCE PLANNING

TODAY HUMAN RESOURCE planning and procurement is not a choice left to the goodwill of top management, a luxury of profitable companies, or a fringe benefit of large organizations. It is a "must," a requirement of the economic system, the competitiveness of the market, and the changing environment.

Traditionally, personnel people have been concerned with day-to-day clerical operations and routines involved in hiring, transferring, and laying off people, filling out forms, and explaining the benefit package.

Today, a human resource executive should have immediately available a survey of the organization's human resources in depth. This should be in the form of a manpower inventory that details each employee's education, experience, specialized training, salary history, and career interests, as well as performance appraisals and ratings of promotability and potential. The manager can then match manpower availability with current and anticipated needs with regard to expansion, new markets, new technology, changing business conditions, and governmental and labor relations. With systematic manpower planning, manpower development can go on continually and not be curtailed in bad times. The commitment by top management to such a program will help insure a supply of qualified replacements for jobs vacated by planned transfers and promotions.

Effective human resource planning is a process of analyzing an organization's human resources needs under changing conditions and developing the activities necessary to satisfy these needs. It is essentially a two-step process. The emphasis is on techniques or systems to be applied. The forecasting of needs allows determining of priorities and allocating of resources to where they can do the most good. Analysis of needs leads to program planning. The planning approach defines human resource needs in relation to the organization's overall needs and defines a strategy to satisfy them. In this way, individual development, training programs, recruitment, compensation and other activities become integral parts of a dynamic process.

Staffing includes planning and budgeting by successive levels of management. In some companies human resource planning is done at an early stage in the planning cycle. Human resource needs must be considered in the context of long-range strategic planning. Time should be provided to allow advance planning for staffing, related career development and organizational changes. Analysis and planning of work activities, organizational changes, and specific job requirements are increasingly important in forecasting.

In the Philippines, human resource problems on the national plane fall into two general categories:

1. Those related to underdevelopment of skills, knowledge, and talents of persons in the labor force, and
2. Those related to underutilization of their capabilities.

Human resources are the ultimate wealth of a nation. Capital and natural resources are passive factors of production. Human resources are the active agents who accumulate capital, exploit natural resources, build social, economic, and political organizations and carry forward national development.

The importance of human resource planning is more evident when we consider the changes within the next two decades as revealed by the Population, Resources, Environment and the Philippines' Future (PREPF) study team:

- Urbanization will raise the age of entry into the labor force but also lower the age of retirement.
- Opportunities for leisure will widen for an increasing proportion of the labor force.
- The growing number of female workers, especially in the urban areas, will pose a challenge to employment.
- The narrowing of child-bearing years will facilitate entry or re-entry of married females into the labor force.
- Young people are likely to remain single longer, and to establish households in "non-family" situations.
- Urban environments are likely to suffer more owing to overcrowd-

ing, pollution, and inadequate drainage, among other things.
- The level of educational attainment may go higher but the quality of education may not.
- Non-formal educational schemes are likely to proliferate to compensate for deficiencies in parental education.
- Income inequality is not likely to be reduced without positive government intervention.
- Workers are likely to be even more collectively organized and represented.

Human resource management, like any area of management, is concerned with the optimum utilization of people. It starts with human resource planning.

Human Resource Planning: Definition and Scope

Human resource planning is the process by which a company ensures that it has the right number and kind of people, in the right places at the right time, doing the things for which they are economically most useful. It is a method for determining future human resource requirements and developing action plans for meeting them. Thus a human resource plan should be prepared at the same time that overall corporate plans are being formulated since they affect each other.

Human resource planning should involve every phase of a company. It must evaluate the current performance levels of individuals and predict their potential. It must provide for career management or charting, and provide systems, forms, grades, and charts for matching job requirements with skills available. It encompasses everything that concerns people--cost, morale, leadership, productivity, forms of compensation, and conservation of the resource. It provides for the total human input required by the company and assures a planned return for their cost.

Basic Approaches to Human Resource Planning

Human Resource Planning at the company level will be concerned with the following:

1. The human resource needed to assist the company and each

operating unit in meeting its production targets.

2. An inventory of available human resources within the firm and outside the firm.
3. The identification of gaps in matching the human resource supply with demand.
4. The preparation of programs for increasing productivity, growth and development of people.
5. Systems and procedures that will enhance the utilization of human time and potential.
6. Furnishing the environment necessary to attract and retain productive people.

Objectives of Human Resource Planning

Human Resource planning determines gross manpower needs and translates these into talent and skill requirements.

The specific goals of human resource planning are the following:

1. Standards regarding replacements. For some companies replacement must be available for 90 per cent of the jobs at least 45 days before needed.
2. Employee turnover. For some companies, turnover should not exceed 15 per cent for one year.
3. Cost limits on payroll and employee benefits. Such costs for some companies will not exceed 68 per cent of total operating budget of the company.
4. Number of people involved and types of training expected. For some companies at least 90 per cent of all employees are engaged in some form of training.
5. Evaluation of job performance. In some companies, job performance reviews are conducted for 95 per cent of all jobs.
6. Opportunity for job performance review. In some companies employees are assured of a job performance review and an interview with their supervisors at least once each year.
7. Percentage of promotions that should occur each year. For some companies at least 20 per cent of all employees will be promoted or experience some form of job enlargement.
8. Goals for training supervisors. In some companies each year 90 per cent of all supervisors will engage in formal training designed to improve leadership skills.
9. Measurement and improvement of productivity levels. In some

companies, productivity will be monitored and increased at least 5 per cent.

10. Communication of employees benefits. Some companies focus employees' attention on the cost of benefits and their advantages.

Basic Stages of Human Resource Planning

First Stage: *Analysis of the current human resource situation.*

This analysis will reveal data on the human resource currently employed and also the human resource position of the company in relation to the national economy, particularly the labor market. The basic question is "Where are we (with regard to the human resource guideposts) now? Are we getting to where we want to go? Are there difficulties or problems?" Human resource problems may surface in the light of desired corporate goals. A clear understanding of these goals is fundamental in the planning process. We may have such objectives as:

a. Optimum use of human resources
   1. provision of high level manpower for critical occupations
   2. provision of highly trained or skilled manpower
   3. channeling of manpower to more productive uses

b. Conservation of human resources

These objectives may be used as gauges in identifying problems. Desired allocation of manpower is viewed against present levels of distribution. Desired levels of productivity are viewed against actual levels of productivity. Deviations that may be revealed in such comparison will be take-off points in planning out a strategy.

The nature, extent, and pattern of these deviations must then be analyzed. Why do such deviations exist? When do they happen? What are causing these deviation?

Some deviations may be related to:

a. Demographic profile — The census of population classified by geographic area, sex and age levels, levels of education completed, occupations and sectoral distributions.

b. Sectoral employment profile — data on employment by occupation, by industry, and volume of production by industry classified by geographic area. Employment on education and training terms will also be desirable.

c. Labor Force — data on the labor force classified by sex, and age, sex and employment status, education and/or training.

d. Employment hours and earnings — employment figures by economic activity; hours worked weekly or daily, hourly or weekly earnings by economic activity by occupation.
e. Forecast of economic conditions — Directions, pattern of investments, planned productivity by section by geographic location, individual or sectoral growth plans, and foreign trade will be vital inputs for manpower forecast. "How many people will be required, in which industry or sector and in what occupation?"
f. Non-economic conditions — Assumptions and forecasts of political and natural events.

A very useful tool in analyzing the current human resource situation in a company is the *Human Resource Inventory* or stock-taking of the firm's employees; it seeks to establish how many of what do we have? This inventory should be assembled piece meal in the various segments of the company.

The basic element of a Human Resource Inventory is a straightforward head count. It would require updating-at weekly, monthly or other intervals of time and may be done:

1. By department;
2. By branch - by: location, pay, sex, age, employment status, length of service, job classification, qualifications.

Simple analyses of the information compiled in the inventory may be made. Examples are:

1. Analysis of payroll, category/salary level:
   a. by age bands;
   b. by length of service;
   c. by sex.
2. Analysis of age bands:
   a. by length of service;
   b. by sex;
   c. by occupation or job classification

A Human Resource inventory must include a detailed analysis of individual skills and abilities--a Skills Inventory. It is the total human resource which is significant. It should report skills and abilities of all kinds and at all levels.

The objectives of a Skills Inventory are:

1. To tell professional and technical skills being employed or

available for future employment in the firm.

2. To reveal what skills are immediately or readily available and by so doing to reveal what skills are not available.
3. To reveal what recruitment is necessary to provide the required skills.

The content of a Skills Inventory is information concerning each employee on:

1. Education and formal qualifications;
2. Foreign language proficiency;
3. Work experiences;
4. Skills that can be practised competently
5. Additional skills

The three main functions of a Skills Inventory are:

1. To provide a continuing census to assist in planning and forecasting.
2. To give ready access to data that will be needed by the Recruitment Department.
3. To assist in matching men to jobs within the company.

The second tool to be used in human resource planning in a company is the Human Resource Audit. This seeks to answer the question: "What has been and, is happening, to our human resources?" This examination regarding the total manpower environment has three major aspects:

1. the internal environment of the company
2 .the environment of the industry, and
3. the environment of the national economy as a whole.

The Human Resource Audit seeks to answer the following questions:

1. What is the picture of starts and terminations this year? last year? over the past two years? five years?
2. What is the picture of absences?
3. Which types of labor is difficult/easy to recruit?
4. What is the picture of salary and age distribution?
5. What are the trends in the labor market for the skills we need?
6. Why do people leave us to work elsewhere?
7. What is the demographic pattern over a 5-, 10-, 15-, mile radius?
8. Is a government policy on housing or other, developments going

to increase the labor force in the area?
9. What are our performance standards?
10. What does training cost us in terms of time, effort and money?

From the Human Resource skills Inventory and its Audit, can be deduced in broad terms for any particular skill, the following factors of input:

1. Recruitment from outside the Company;
2. Lateral transfers (not involving promotion) into different skill category within the company;
3. Vertical transfer (promotion and upgrading) such as completion of apprenticeship.

Similarly, the following factors of outflow:

1. Wastage
   a. Voluntary wastage comprises-resignations due to marriage, pregnancy, change of residence, immigration, change of job, early retirement or an unhappy personal relationship.
   b. Involuntary wastage comprises-death, retirement, and dismissal.
2. Lateral Transfer.
3. Vertical Transfer.

Second Stage: *Forecasting Human Resource Requirements*

It is necessary to have an indication of future development in order to plan out necessary steps now. There are two considerations:

1. What is the manpower demand for specific types of manpower at given periods of time to perform various roles?
2. What is the best employment profile to be used for future trends?

The most important step in forecasting human resource requirements is to identify what is to be forecast. This requires the drawing of a forecasting model which would attempt to do three things:

1. Define categories of Skill in terms of kind or amount;
2. Identify each type and level of job; and
3. Identify those self-contained units which request separate quantitative human resource forecasts.

Where sub-units exist within an organization it will be necessary to make separate forecasts for each sub-unit.

Further, there should be explicit definitions of skill categories as follows:

1. Managerial;
2. Technical;
3. Professional and administrative;
4. Manual or operatives;
5. Manual/operative supervisory;
6. Clerical and office;
7. Clerical and office supervisory

Clear recognition of skill levels is necessary. For example, the skill category manual/operative might be on three levels, namely:

1. skilled;
2. semi-skilled;
3. unskilled.

Third Stage: *Forecasting Human Resource Supply*

The total stock of human resources at any given time is the population count. For practical purposes, this has to be narrowed down to the labor force, that is, those who, at a given time, have had work, are looking for work, and are fit to work. Past trends, patterns, and expected developments will give us a picture of future manpower supply.

An important element in the forecasting of labor supply concerns how many will leave. Wastage analysis and labor turnover may statistically be foreseen by the known rate of retirements and voluntary wastage. It should be noted that length of service is a useful indicator of leaving. To forecast movements within the company resulting from promotions and transfers, it is necessary to assess the potential of employees. Availability of training resources will also affect the future supply of labor and so will trade union attitudes and payment policies.

In any unit of a company there will be frequent changes in the mix of skills. Thus, the human resource planner must identify the dynamic factors of skills inputs to and outflows from that particular unit. These factors will determine employees and the type of skills which will be available in the future. Some of the inputs and outflows may be the results of movement of staff from one branch or location to another within the company (internal transfers); others may represent recruitment from outside or losses to other organizations (terminations).

Fourth Stage: *Reconciling Human Resource Requirements and Supply Forecasts*

When viewed side-by-side, both human resource requirements and supply forecasts may reveal gaps which exist between employment and the labor force; between occupations employed and occupations not employed; between employee educated and/or trained and those not educated and/or trained. We can compare these gaps at the beginning of the forecast period with the same in the intervening period. Are the gaps growing? Are they narrowing? The nature of each gap must be described. What are the causes of these gaps?

The main processes to find the answers are: assessment of performance of present work force, identification of possible discrepancies and imbalances compared with production targets, and identification of possible causes for such imbalances and deviation. Take for example the problem of unemployment at the national level.

Fifth Stage: *Operationalization or Action Process*

Once a problem has been identified and its cause pinpointed, we must assess the resources, consider priorities and set a target. Specific action plans or blueprints for bridging the gap between the forecasts and inventory are made. These include determining who should invest, how, and who will train the prospective employees and for how long.

On the human resource demand side, it is generally believed that unemployment can be reduced through more investments. Where not enough investment is available, altering the factor mix or rendering existing capital more labor intensive may be resorted to.

On the supply side, where rapid population growth causes increasing entrants into the labor force, training of human resources for export can be a solution.

Whichever side the human resource planner attacks, he must set objectives, and translate them into quantifiable targets. Details of operations include:

1. Identification of alternatives to solve the identified problems.
2. Pinpointing specific problem areas such as work environment, management policies, etc, or manpower shortage, etc.
3. Identification of programs to carry out alternatives.
4. Designing these specific programs.
5. Implementation of the programs.

A very important step in manpower forecasting is identifying what is to be forecast. Such forecasts must concern three things: define type and level of skills, identify each type and level of job, and identify self-contained units that require separate manpower forecasting.

Sixth Stage: *Evaluation and Re-planning*

The three basic loops in the planning and development cycle are:

1. *Planning loop* — Planning sets objectives and classifies them. Objectives are priorities, weighted and ranked. They spell out functions and imply certain standards to ensure their achievement. They also imply financial requirements, resources and constraints in achieving objectives.
2. *Programming loop* — Programming translates objectives into operational terms. Specific actions and appropriate structures, standards and targets are set into motion.
3. *General Feedback or Evaluation loop* — Evaluation of accomplishment in both planning and programming is done. Programs are evaluated in terms of conformity with set program targets and standards. Results form the bases for replanning and reprogramming.

Evaluation should be able to assess a plan's effectiveness. Results are fed back to the planning loop.

How to Establish Human Resource Planning in the Company

A human resource planner can start by designing and installing a total corporate human resource planning system intended to produce annual and long-term corporate human resource plans.

Another approach is by formalizing certain existing human resources activities, with the expectation that these may later become building blocks for an integrated human resource planning system.

A third approach is to analyze and solve specific human resource problems, and furnish human resource planning assistance on a project basis.

The following are the steps for an integrated strategy for establishing Human Resource Planning:

1. Assess the organization's receptivity to changes in the areas of human resources. Who are the most interested and which units of the organization are most and least likely to support a human resource planning program?
2. Identify the human resource planning needs and problems of the organization.
3. Formulate the objectives and scope.
4. Determine the time horizon of the human resource plan. Should

it be tied to the annual operating budget?

5. Delineate the respective roles of the corporate staff in administering the plan.
6. Consider how to enlist the support and involvement of top management in human resource planning.
7. Identify the key interfaces in the company such as persons responsible for long-range planning, business research, and organization planning.
8. Outline in principle the design of the human resource planning process, for top management approval.
9. Prepare a formal, detailed implementation plan, including provision for program reporting.
10. Develop methods of monitoring the plan, in order to evaluate the accuracy and practicality of the forecasting and planning process and to check whether recommendations are acted upon.
11. Plan for later revision and improvement of the plans.
12. Institutionalize the planning process, to make its place secure within the management system.

Forecasting Short-term Manpower Requirements

There are seven steps in forecasting short-term manpower requirements. They are as follows:

1 .Find out what your department is scheduled to produce in the next week, month, or quarter, or as far ahead as you can determine.
2. Calculate how much this work schedule means in terms of total man-hours. You can do this by getting an estimate from the time-study, industrial engineering, or planning and scheduling department, or other man-hour data from cost accounting.

   Where jobs are machine-controlled, make your estimates based upon:

   a. How long the machine will take to do each job--allowing for breakdown, idle time, etc. and;

   b. How many hours are needed to run the machine.
3. Convert your totals to man-hours and divide by 8 to see how many man-days it will take you to complete your schedule for the period you have selected.
4. Divide the total man-days by the number of working days during the period to find the number of operators you will need.

5. Check how many indirect people you will need to service the required number of operators during the period.
6. Add the number of operators (direct labor) to the number of indirect people to get the total need.
7. Make allowances for absences. What is the average number of days absent per month of the employees in your department? What is the total number of man-days a month that your employees lose?

STUDY/REVIEW QUESTIONS

1. What is the nature and scope of human resource planning?
2. Explain the basic approaches to human resource planning.
3. What should be the objectives of human resource planning in organizations in the Philippines? Explain the rationale of your answer.
4. Explain the basic stages of human resource planning.

SUGGESTED ACTIVITIES AND ASSIGNMENT

1. Go to the Ministry of Labor and Employment and find out what steps have been taken to perform human resource planning on a national scale.

2. Go to a Philippine corporation and find out what steps have been taken in human resource planning on a corporate scale.

3. Secure human resource planning forms used in any organization or company and criticize them.

4. Make a list of Filipino values that influence organizations in the Philippines to implement human resource planning.

REFERENCES FOR FURTHER READING

Andres, Tomas D. *Human Resources Training and Development.* Quezon City: New Day Publishers, 1980.

_____. *Management By Filipino Values.* Quezon City: New Day Publishers, 1985.

Martinez, Esdras T. *Human Resources Management.* Manila: GIC Enterprises & Co,. Inc,. 1979, pp. 78-91

Work Bank, "The Philippines: Priorities and Prospects for Development, 1960."

11

HUMAN RESOURCE PROCUREMENT

NO ORGANIZATION should underestimate the importance of proper human resource procurement. To be considered adequate, a Human Resource Management Program must be designed to attract the best applicants for the job, develop them into efficient workers and make them loyal employees.

Recruitment methods vary from one company to another. A company as large as Philippine Refining Company uses sophisticated recruitment methods like retaining executive placement outfits, e.g., John Clements; recruiting in schools and universities, placing large sized ads in the leading dailies, etc.

Small companies, on the other hand, cannot afford these expensive methods and must employ simpler procedures like smaller want ads, referral from friends, etc.

Recruiting Competent and Motivated Human Resources

Recruitment is the securing, through planned and systematic effort, of the right quantity and the right quality of people needed to meet present and future manpower requirements. It is the process by which prospective applicants are induced to apply to the company in order that their qualifications for present and anticipated vacancies can be evaluated through sound screening and selection procedures.

In human resource procurement, the first consideration is the recognition by management of the need for sound policies and procedures on recruitment, selection, and hiring the best candidate for every job.

Standard policies and procedures on recruitment are needed in order:

1. To define the recruitment and employment function
2. To establish approval of procedure for recruitment
3. To indicate the requirements to be met prior to management approval.

Some of the general policies, authorities, and responsibilities for human resource recruitment are the following:

1. Wherever vacancies arise whether in existing or newly-created positions, prior consideration should be given to filling vacancies from within in order to maximize the abilities of present human resources.
2. Candidates for any position should be selected solely on the basis of satisfying the hiring standards and job specifications.

   Hence, hiring standards and job specifications should be established by the requisitioning manager concerned, with the assistance of the Human Resource Management Department.
3. Staff movements within the Organization should assist in employee development and provide advancement opportunities for those with potential and proven performance.

   The Human Resource Management Department is responsible for identifying employees and officers with development and advancement potentials.

   Consequently, an Annual Manpower Review should be established to enable the organization to determine the availability of well-prepared and qualified personnel for the present as well as long-term future requirements.
4. Within the approved salary range for a position, the requisitioning Head and the Human Resource Management Department shall recommend the salary to be offered to a selected candidate.

In planning a recruitment, hiring and placement program, Management should define its overall objectives. Various forms must also be designed to explain the needs of the company.

The responsibility for recruitment, and hiring of employees in big companies is usually assigned to a Human Resource Management Department or an agency which assists the line supervisors or depart-

RECRUITMENT PRACTICE

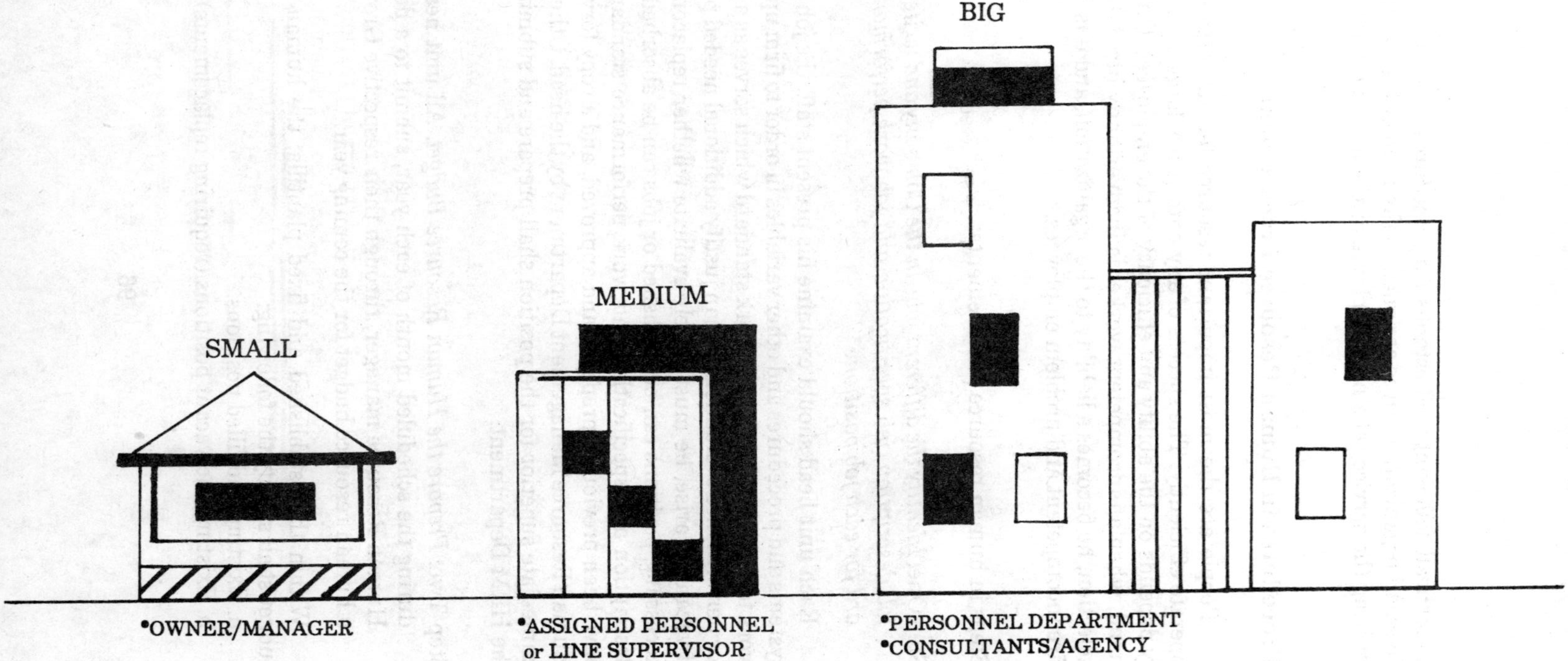

ment head, following well-established procedures of selection. However, in small organizations, it is assigned to the head of the department requiring the services of a new employee or the line supervisors.

Procedures in Human Resource Procurement:

People are the most important resource for any organization to operate efficiently. The success of any enterprise, large or small, chiefly depends on the ability and efficiency of the employees. On the other hand, when an incompetent worker is inadvertently hired due to poor selection, he becomes a liability to the organization, and it is difficult to fire incompetent and problem employees.

Steps in human resource procurements:

Step One: *Identify the different jobs in the Company and write down the job description, job specification and job work performance standard for each job position.*

Each unit head should examine his present staff, the job contents, systems and procedures and other variables in order to firm up his exact work force. Having a definite work standard which serves as a yardstick for performance evaluation, he can justify additional needed personnel. If vacancies arise, he must closely evaluate whether replacements are necessary, positions can be abolished or jobs can be absorbed. The job description and specification and work performance standard should have been previously prepared and approved, and a copy forwarded to Human Resource Management Department by the head. Otherwise the immediate superior for the position shall prepare and submit them to the HRM Department.

Step Two: *Prepare the Human Resource Budget.* All unit heads shall, during the scheduled month of each year, submit to a designated Human Resource manager, through their respective Group Head, a human resource budget for the coming year.

Within the established and fixed plantilla, the human resource budget shall specify the following:

a. Existing and filled positions.
b. Existing and vacant positions (requiring replacements)

c. Previously approved new positions to be filled.
d. Proposed new positions (requiring approval): number of additional personnel, the hiring month per position, job description and proposed salary range for new positions if not yet classified in the established salary structure, and the justification relevant to work program/objectives for the year.

The Human Resource Management Department shall review, recommend and submit the Human Resource Budget to the president who in turn shall submit it for the approval of the Executive Committee and finally the Board for inclusion in overall operating budget.

The approved manpower budget shall serve as the basis for recruitment as well as the authority to hire.

Step Three: *Make requisition for employees.*

Upon approval of the human resource budget, all requisitions for personnel on regular payroll, whether replacements or additions, shall be submitted through the respective group head, to the Human Resource Management Department for implementation.

Step Four: *Recruit qualified applicant*

On receipt of Personnel Requisition, the Human Resource Management Unit shall recruit the qualified applicant for the position.

As a general principle, opportunities for the vacant position must be open to all who qualify regardless of the source fro which they come.

If the company has the in-breeding policy of recruitment, the Human Resource Management Department shall determine from the inventory of manpower and positions, present staff who may be considered as possible candidates. If someone from within qualifies for the job, HRM Department shall secure the approval of the candidate and his immediate Superior including the respective Group Head. Should favorable approval be obtained from the Group Head, HRM Department shall endorse the employee's records to the requisitioning head or Group Head for consideration.

A firm date for the release to the requisitioning unit or group of the selected candidate shall be secured by HRM Department from the candidate's Group Head. HRM Department shall advise the candidate and secure his agreement of the move and the exact date and the salary being offered, whereupon HRM Department issues the necessary papers to effect the transfer.

Should no candidate from the present staff qualify for the vacancy, Human Resource Management Department shall forward to the requisitioning unit Test Results and Interview Evaluation of qualified candidates previously secured and processed. The requisitioning head shall make the final selection of a candidate from among those endorsed by HRM Department.

Should no candidate qualify from those previously screened and processed, HRM Department shall determine the most productive external sources of qualified applicants. Some external sources of labor are persons who apply in person, who answer advertisements, or are recommended by schools, colleges or universities, or employment agencies/recruiters.

Let us study the different sources of applicants:

Newspaper Ads. The never-ending task of human resource recruitment for new and old companies, large and small, has made the Classified Ads of newspapers the prime source of manpower procurement. The advantage of the classified ad is the nationwide exposure of the company in need and the great numerical response it generates. The basic disadvantage, however, is difficulty in selecting qualified applicants owing to the avalanche of responses. It takes a longer time to get the right applicant for the job because of the intricate process involved in hiring, like filling up of application forms, interviews, psychological examinations, etc.

Referrals. Recommendation by friends and relatives has these advantages:

1. The recommendee immediately becomes a known person to the prospective employer.
2. It eliminates the long process of selection from a big number of applicants.
3. Once hired, the recommendee is bound to perform very well lest it would be embarrassing to his "padrino".

There are also some disadvantages to this:

1. At the outset employer is under undue pressure to accept the recommendee especially if the referral comes from a relative or a very close friend.

2. Once accepted and the employee is later found to be inefficient, the employer finds it difficult to fire the inefficient worker.
3. The area of choice is limited.

Placement Bureaus of Colleges & Universities

Placement bureaus of universities and colleges are among the best sources of manpower. Aside from being FREE, they shorten greatly the tedious procedural aspects of hiring. In some companies, all they do is send the "specifications" of the prospective employee they need. The placement bureau sends them three applicants with the corresponding bio-data and evaluation for every job requirement.

Ministry of Labor and Employment Offices

Since companies are required to submit to the Ministry of Labor and Employment a regular listing of their manpower requirements, the public placement offices may be tapped for procurement purposes.

Private Employment Agencies

Except for the initial fees—approximately 10% of the employee's salary—these agencies may provide *gratis* the properly screened manpower.

Dehiring Companies

Dehiring companies do not yet exist in this country. In United States some executives are engaged in "recycling of corporate officers." The basic concept of dehiring companies is the creation of a better atmosphere before, during and after the recycling of an executive and his eventual placement in some other company where his services are most needed. These dehiring companies are a more sophisticated version of our private placement agencies. They consider only executives who are good performers who for retrenchment or personality conflict reasons alone are being recycled. This could be a prime source of procurement, especially for multinational companies.

Step Five: *Issue application forms*

A Preliminary Interview is conducted to eliminate those applicants who clearly do not meet the job specifications. Application forms are issued to those applicants who seem to meet the requirements. These forms give important information on the applicant and his suitability for the job applied for.

Step Six: *Receive the applicants*

A rapid appraisal of the applicants will eliminate the undesirable. Then a more rigid screening is done.

The Human Resource Management Department should be prepared to provide information about the organization and current job openings and to assist with the completion of application form. The Department should arrange schedules for interviews, tests, and other steps in selection.

Step Seven: *Administer the employment tests.*

The major objective of Personnel Testing is to determine the probable effectiveness of an individual in the job and how much satisfaction he can get from the job. Applicants for a certain position should be given a battery of tests so as to reveal their fitness for the job-through interests, intelligence, emotional make-up, and adaptability.

The more tests are given to an applicant, the more the HRM Department can evaluate competence, probable performance, and an individual's personality.

Personnel tests fall in four categories: the intelligence test; the Aptitude test which measures specific abilities in performing a job; the Interest test which measures an individual's interests and attitude about a job, and the Personality test which measures the temperament of an individual and his motivation.

The HRM testing staff makes a close analysis of the requirements of the job so that they can prepare the right type of tests. The tests should reveal educational attainment, training and experience, age and sex, and lastly, the qualities or traits of the person to be hired. The HRM staff then prepares an Analysis and Interpretation Report based on the test results, primary interview, and bio-data of the applicant. After a careful analysis of these three sources, the HRM Department then can arrive at a decision as to who will be recommended for a final interview and placement decision by the requisitioning department head.

Take the case of a Company which employs mostly clerical staff and salesman. A standard testing program can be followed in this manner:

1. Intelligence tests:
   a. SRA Adaptability Test
   b. Culture, Fair Intelligence Tests (Non-Language)
2. Aptitude and Ability Test:
   a. Short test of Clerical Ability specifically: Business Vocabulary
3. Interest Test:

a. Thurstone Interest Schedule

4. Personality Test:
   a. Survey of Interpersonal Values/Survey of Personal Values; and for salesmen, tests to be administered are the same as the above except No. 2 which will be replaced instead by the Sales Series, specifically on Test of Sales Aptitudes.

Some basic testing guidelines are the following:[1]

1. Use tests as a supplement.
2. Validate the tests in your organization.
3. Analyze all your current hiring and promotion standards.
4. Keep accurate records.
5. Beware of certain tests.
6. Begin your validation program now.
7. Use a Certified Psychologist.
8. Remember that test conditions are important.
9. Avoid invasions of privacy.

Some companies employ work sampling for employee selection. This involves choosing several specific tasks that are crucial to performing the job the HRM Department is recruiting for. The applicant's performance on these tasks is used as a predictor of their performance on the job. For example, several people familiar with the job of automotive mechanic analyze the previous work experience of the automotive mechanic applicant. These experts list all possible tasks (like "overhauling") that automotive mechanics would be required to perform. For each task the candidate will be asked to indicate frequency of performance and to evaluate its importance to the job. The experts then, discuss the applicant's differences, and decide on two crucial matters: "use of tools" and "method of work." Next, the experts choose several tasks that are crucial in automotive mechanics. These tasks have to "make sense" as regards the applicants' prior work experience and "use of tools" and "method of work."

In this case, four tasks may be selected to be described: disassembling of an engine from a body; disassembling a cylinder head cover and cylinder head, disassembling a rocker arm and disassembling the crankshaft from the engine block. Next, these four tasks will be broken down into the steps needed to complete them. Each step will then be analyzed to determine the different ways each step could be accomplished. Some approaches will be better than others; therefore, the experts will give different weights to different approaches. Next, the applicant will be required to perform each of the steps. A test administrator watches the applicant and checks the approach the applicant used. The final step is to determine the relationship between the applicant's score on his description of procedure and his actual performance on the job. Once HRM staff is sure that work sample and description predict job success, they can begin using them for selection.

Nine Factors Involved in Estimating the Aptitude of an Individual for Average, Satisfactory Work Performance:

G — Mental - Intelligence. The ability to "catch on" or understand instructions and underlying principles. Ability to reason and make judgements.

V — Verbal - Ability to comprehend language, to understand meanings of whole sentences and paragraphs. To present information or ideas clearly.

N — Numerical - Ability to carry out arithmetic processes quickly and accurately.

S — Spatial - Ability to think visually of geometric forms and to comprehend the two dimensional representations of three dimensional objects. The ability to recognize the relationships resulting from the movement of objects in space. May be used in such tasks as blue-print reading and in solving geometry problems. Frequently described as the ability to "visualize" objects of two or three dimensions, or to think visually of geometric forms.

P — Form Perception - Ability to perceive details in objects, or in pictorial or graphic material, to make visual comparisons and see slight differences in shapes and shadings of figures and width and lengths of lines.

Q — Clerical Perception - Ability to perceive pertinent detail in verbal or tabular material. To observe differences in copy, to proofread words and numbers, and to avoid perceptual errors in arithmetic computation.

K — Motor Coordination - Ability to coordinate eyes and hands or fingers rapidly and accurately in making precise movements with speed. Ability to make a movement response accurately and quickly.

F — Finger Dexterity - Ability to move the fingers, and manipulate small objects with the fingers, rapidly or accurately.

M — Manual Dexterity - Ability to move the hands easily and

skillfully. To work with the hands in placing and turning motions.

Step Eight: *Investigate the Applicant's background and personal references.*

The HRM Department must verify statements made by the applicant by means of telephone calls, letters of inquiry or sending information forms to his former employers, teachers, or individual references, or making use of the services of the credit information bureaus. Some companies employ a polygraph (lie detector), a device attached to the applicant's hand and/or arm, which records involuntary physiological responses as the individual answers questions about his former employment, subversive activity, prior arrests, and other areas believed to be important.

If the telephone is used in checking references, the following are the guidelines:[2]

From your record, can you tell me when he started with your firm and when he left the company?

What was his job classification with your company, and what were his duties?

How would you rate his job performance in terms of work volume and work quality?

Did he receive any promotions or demotions while with you?

As his supervisor, what did you find was the most effective way to motivate him?

Be sure to obtain the applicant's consent to being checked, especially with respect to his present employer.

Most companies obtain this consent in the form of a question incorporated in the application form to be answered in the affirmative or the opposite.

Step Nine: *Interview the Applicant*

No company hires an applicant without making an interview of some kind. Special emphasis is placed on abilities which can not be adequately evaluated through pencil and paper tests. Some firms even interview applicants several times. The last interview is called hiring and placement, or employment interview.

The employment interview gives the HRM staff the information necessary to describe an applicant accurately as to his probable performance. It helps also the applicant to see the advantages of employment in a certain organization. The employment interview should follow certain procedures.

Basically, there are two types of employment interviews: the initial and the evaluation interview. The initial interview eliminates unqualified applicants and interests qualified applicants in employment. It is conducted at the beginning of the selection sequence and results only in a tentative decision. Initial interviews last between fifteen and thirty minutes. The most effective way to conduct this kind of interview is the screening approach—that is, the interviewer asks the applicant make or break questions that tell him whether the applicant meets the bed rock qualification of the job. To do this, the interviewer must have ready a set of questions to which certain answers will disqualify the applicant immediately.

A few examples of such questions are:[3]

"What are your salary requirements?"

"Can you work overtime?"

"Do you have a driver's license?" (for a chauffeur's position)

"Do you type?" (For a typing position)

If the applicant qualifies on these critical questions the HRM staff then explores briefly his education and full-time experience. He may then explore briefly his attitude. Broad open-ended questions such as these are effective:

"What is there about selling that appeals to you?

"What makes you feel that you would do well in clerical work?"

If at this point, the applicant looks like a good prospect, an appointment for testing and evaluation interview can be arranged.

The evaluation interview is done to provide a through review of the applicant's qualification so as to enable the interviewer to make a final decision. It usually lasts thirty to sixty minutes.

The major interviewing styles are the patterned and the non-directive. The patterned interview style, used in the initial interview, follows a predetermined outline of questions carefully designed to reduce variability in the information obtained from the interview. The information is recorded on a preprinted from and its data are classified, tabulated and used to build standards with which the responses of many applicants can be compared.

In the non-directive open-ended interview, the HRM staff uses comprehensive questions and encourages the interviewee to take the lead in covering the information relevant to the job. Both the patterned and non-directive interviewing styles are used in the evaluation interview. For a managerial position, the style will tend to be more non-directive while in the clerical, production, and sales positions, the styles will be more patterned.

The basic purposes of the interview are to find out the following:[4]

1. *Personal Qualities.* Personal qualifications required in the position: physical appearance, health, dress and grooming, voice quality, diction, vocabulary, poise, alertness, and aggressiveness. Most of these qualities are assessed by the interviewer's observations rather than by the applicant's answers to his questions.
2. *Academic Achievement.* Type of schooling, quality of grades, class standing, social activities, relationship with teachers, honors and awards, athletic accomplishments. Questions in this area can reveal an applicant's initiative, independence, reliability, intellectual competence, and emotional stability. Fruitful avenues to explore are the reasons why the applicant chose the schools he attended, the amount of advice he received while in school, the degree to which he financed his own education, and his personal appraisal of his scholastic achievements.
3. *Occupational Experience.* The applicant's technical competence as well as the level of responsibility and skill attained in previous jobs, and his reasons for leaving former jobs. Questions in this area should be directed at obtaining evidence of good judgment, initiative, drive and energy, and ability to assume responsibility.
4. *Interpersonal Competence.* The applicant's ability to get along with others. It is not enough to base judgment on the applicant's behavior during the interview. Specific questions must be asked about his family history, leisure-time activities, hobbies, and community interests.
5. *Career Orientation.* The applicant's career aspirations, his immediate and long-range goals, and his potential for advancement. Answers to questions in this area form the heart of a managerial applicant's qualifications.

The interviewer must follow certain guidelines to make the interview effective:[5]

1. He must know well the job to be filled and the qualities needed by the candidate.
2. He must be prepared for the interview, be attentive, empathetic, and genuine. He has secured adequate background information

on the applicant.

3. He must observe all reactions by the applicant.
4. He must show acceptance and interest. He schedules interviews when he has enough time. He puts the applicant at ease.
5. He must get private information and try to see the whole picture. He insures that interviews are held in private.
6. He mustn't put on an act, be defensive, become involved emotionally or be authoritative. He is aware of his own prejudices and tries to avoid their influence on his judgments. He avoids any suggestion of discrimination.
7. He must let the applicant talk and avoid leading questions. He adjusts the level of his language to the ability of the respondent and keeps control of the interview.
8. He must know how and when to close the interview. He records the facts during the interview, and impressions and judgments immediately thereafter.

The HRM Interviewer now writes the Interviewer's Report, which is a record to support a recommendation. The interviewer must cite and interpret evidence regarding the candidate's background or behavior that may be relevant in comparison with other candidates, real or imagined. The ratings are usually made on a five-point scale, ranging from favorable to unfavorable.

In writing the report, the interviewer balances the plus and minus factors against each other in making his final recommendations.

The interviewer's rating is based on the following factors:

1. Initial Impression. The candidate's appearance, manner, self-expression, and responsiveness. Does the candidate have neat grooming, a pleasing voice, good physique, proper dress and poise? The interviewer relates his initial impression to the requirements of the job for which the candidate is being considered.
2. Work Experience. How the applicant gets along with people. What in his experience enhances or diminishes his stature as a candidate?
3. Education. The interviewer writes down the versatility the candidate has demonstrated in his studies and in his extra-curricular activities. He evaluates the candidate's motivational and social values.
4. Early Years. A background is evaluated as good or bad only as it favorably influences the candidate's qualifications.

5. Present Activities and Interests. Do the candidate's present activities enhance or diminish his stature as a candidate?

Step Ten: *Match the applicant with the Job*

After completing all the previous steps in screening the applicants, the Human Resource Staff now decides who may become a gain or a loss for the company.

In making the decision there are three different ways: The *first* is the successive hurdles approach which selects only those applicants who successfully meet the established requirements at all hurdles. The *second* is the multiple correction approach which requires the applicant to go through the entire selection process in order that complete data may be obtained about him. These data are reduced to scores and combined. If the combined scores are above the level needed to qualify, the applicant is hired; otherwise, he is rejected. The *third* method is the discriminate analysis approach. This is a statistical approach which predicts success in alternative groups, relating an applicant's talents to organizational needs.

Regardless of which approach is used, there will be individuals who are rejected and must, therefore, be advised about it.

Step Eleven: *Make the Final Evaluation of the Applicant*

The final evaluation of the applicant is the total person with all his positive and negative traits and characteristics.

The HRM staff considers the following factors:

Can Do Factors

a) Appearance, manner
b) Availability
c) Education
d) Intelligence
e) Experience in the field (if applicable)
f) Knowledge of the product (if applicable)
g) Physical condition, health

Will Do Factors

Character Traits (Basic Habits)
Stability: Maintaining the same jobs and interests
Identity: Sincerity in his willingness to work; he is what he says he is
Perseverance: finishing what he starts

Ability: capability to adapt and to get along with others
Loyalty: identifying with employers
Self-reliance: standing on his own feet; making his own decisions

Leadership

Job Motivations
Need for income or desire for money
Need for security
Need for status
Need for power
Need to investigate
Need to excel (to compete)
Need for perfection
Need to serve

Basic Energy Level

Vigor
Initiative
Drive
Enthusiasm

Degree of Emotional Maturity

Freedom from dependence
Regard for consequences
Capacity for self-discipline
Freedom from selfishness
Freedom from show-off tendencies
Freedom from pleasure-mindedness
Freedom from destructive tendencies
Freedom from wishful thinking
Willingness to accept responsibility

Step Twelve: *Let the Requisitioning Superior or Unit Head Make the Final Selection*

After a careful evaluation of all applicants for a job the three or more qualified, as determined by the HRM staff are referred to the requisitioning superior or unit head for final selection. Usually the applicants are interviewed in the very office or shop where they will work, giving them a chance to meet their prospective superior and see their work place.

Below are some guidelines the HRM Executive can give to the requisitioning head in making the final selection:

1. *Set high standards of performance.* If opportunity for advancement is company-wide, then level of competence and performance must be of company-wide calibre.
2. *Hire employees with potentials.* To develop high level of performance, requisitioning head must hire people of high competence for career assignments. In starting people in each function, the head must not simply hire people who can do the job at hand, but those who have potentials to grow and if possible go up the ladder.
3. *Offer appropriate economic incentives and other rewards.* Compensation must be consistent with individual contributions, business results and competitive compensation practices. It would be better for the requisitioning unit and eventually for the company to maintain a small staff who are outstanding performers and highly motivated because they are highly paid than a large group which is less compensated. The compensation structure should encourage high performance.

Step Thirteen: *Let the Applicant Undergo Physical and Medical Examination.*

To make sure that the new employee is fit to work, to protect the firm from claims for disability or sickness, and to safeguard the older employees against possible contamination, the selected applicant is required to pass a physical and medical examination by the company physician. Likewise, the applicant will be required to submit such documents as:

a) Three (3) I.D. pictures;
b) Xerox copy of Transcript of Records or Diploma;
c) Xerox copy of birth or baptismal certificate;
d) Completed SSS Incoming Information Sheet;
e) Witholding Tax Statements;
f) Police and NBI Clearance;
g) Marriage Certificate (if married);
h) Board Rating and Board Certificate (if licensed);
i) Residence Certificate;
j) Tax Account Number

Step Fourteen: *Hire the Selected Applicant.*

When a candidate has passed all the requirements, the Human

Resource Management Department shall prepare the necessary papers such as:

a)Appointment papers
b)Absence control card
c)Company I.D. card

The HRM staff shall also discuss with the candidate the conditions for employing him, see to the signing of the employment contract by him, and the company official responsible for confirming appointments, and accomplish the permanent personnel records.

Step Fifteen: *Give the New Employee an Orientation and Induction about the Company.*

The Human Resource Management Department shall assist the requisitioning staff in an orientation and induction program as the recruit joins the Company. He will be briefed on the company history, objectives, rules and matters related to his job.

On the first day of employment the recruit is made to feel comfortable in his surroundings where he sees new faces with whom he will work.

The itinerary for the first day more or less includes the following:

1. A briefing on company history, objectives, policies, rules and procedures as well as issuance of the Employee Handbook, if there is any.
2. Introduction to his associates and subordinates.
3. A description of his duties and responsibilities.
4. A lead man is assigned whom the new employee may consult should he have problems.
5. An introduction to the company facilities and services and regulations for their continued use.
6. A briefing on what he should do when he is sick, involved in an accident, or has a complaint or grievance.
7. The new employee is made to try his job. First, the job is presented in detail and explained. Then, he is told to perform the operation. If he fails, he is encouraged to try again until he makes it. If he knows how to do it, he gets praise.
8. Before being dismissed from work for the day, the new employee reports to the Human Resource Executive so as to enable the latter to complete their proceedings and process all payroll deduction authorizations.

Step Sixteen: *Make a Follow-up on Placement*

The Human Resource Management Department now closely monitors the progress of the new employee, giving counsel to him when necessary. Formal evaluations may be made periodically to anticipate the problems before they become involved in inefficiency or serious loss.

There are several categories of employees and workers:

1. *Probationary.* Probation shall constitute the period during which an employee is observed and tried to determine his fitness for the job as well as his usefulness to the organization.

The probationary period shall not be more than six (6) months from the date the employee actually started working.

The standards under which he will qualify as a regular employee will be made known to the employee at the time of his engagement by the supervisor and/or department head concerned. His superior shall decide within six months if the employee deserves confirmation of his appointment to the position.

The unit head shall make the proper recommendation based on his observation and the report of the employee's immediate superior to the HRM Department which shall process the necessary papers and implement the recommended action.

Probationary employment may be terminated only for the following reasons:

a) For a just cause;
b) When authorized by existing laws;
c) When the employee fails to qualify as a regular employee in with reasonable standards.

If an employee does not meet the requirements of the job at the end of the six-month trial period, he shall be released from employment.

An employee who passed the probationary period will be so notified through an Employee Status Change Notice confirming his status from Probationary to Regular Employee.

2. *Regular* or *Permanent.* A regular or permanent employee is a person who, having passed through a probationary period of employment, is placed on the regular rolls of the company and is assigned to perform work directly related to the regular operations of the firm.
3. *Temporary.* A temporary employee is hired to perform work on a specified project, upon completion of which the workers'

employment is terminated.

4. *Contractual.* A contractual employee is hired on an individual employment contract basis.

Some clerical employees are hired on contractual basis to act as relievers for employees on maternity leave or to assist in the pressure of work on occasions during the year.

The HRM Department shall screen and evaluate all applicants to be hired on casual basis and those referred by service agencies. The HRM Department shall perform the recruiting function for all contractual employees, and coordinate with the divisions and groups in the Company as well as the agencies/institutions offering contractual services.

5. *Casual/Emergency Worker.* A casual employee is one who is hired for only a few days or a few months at a time to fill a gap in the absence of another employee, or to work during peak periods.

Some companies in the Philippines employ as casual or emergency workers students who are in their last year in college and who show promise of being potential candidates for employment.

Whatever may be the category of the employee or worker in the company may be, the HRM executive must encourage him to have freedom of discussion with his superiors as to work assignments, promotion opportunities, compensation, training, complaints, etc. Each employee should feel perfectly free to discuss such matters with (1) his immediate superior, (2) the Human Resource Management Department and/or (3) the boss of his immediate superior.

STUDY/REVIEW QUESTIONS

1. Why are standard procedures on employment needed in organizations?
2. What are the general policies, authorities and responsibilities in human resource recruitment and employment?
3. Explain the different steps in human resource procurement.
4. Identify the different sources of applicants.
5. Give reasons why selection is necessary in human resource procurement.

SUGGESTED ACTIVITIES AND ASSIGNMENT

1. Secure application forms from any organization and comment on them.

2 .Interview a recruitment officer of any organization and ask him how the Filipino values of *lagayan, pakikisama, bata-bata, padrino* system, and regionalism affect his work.

3. Apply for a job position in a company for which you are qualified and write a report about your experience.

NOTES

[1]Gary Dessler, *Personnel Management: Modern Concepts and Techniques* (Virginia: Ruston Publishing Company, Inc.m 1978), pp. 116-118.

[2]Richard H. Magee, "Reference Checking—Objectives and Techniques," *Personnel Journal,* Vol. 43, No. 10 (November, 1966), pp. 551-555.

[3]Felix M. Lopez, "The Employment Interview" (Rosylin, New York: Felix M. Lopez and Associates).

[4]Ibid, p. 4.

[5]Stone, C.H. and Kendall, W. E., *Effective Personnel Selection Procedures* (Englewood Cliffs, New Jersey: Prentice Hall, Inc., 1956).

REFERENCES FOR FURTHER READING

Andres, Tomas Quintin D., Pilar Corazon B. Ilada-Andres. *How to Land A Job, Be A Model Employee and Be A Top Earner.* Makati: St. Paul Publications, 1984.

Sison, Perfecto S. *Personnel and Human Resources Management.* Manila: Rex Book Store, 1981.

Stone, C.H. and Kendall, W. E. *Effective Personnel Selection Procedures.* Englewood Cliffs, N.J.: Prentice-Hall, Inc., 1956.

PART FOUR

HUMAN RESOURCE DEVELOPMENT AND MANPOWER TRAINING

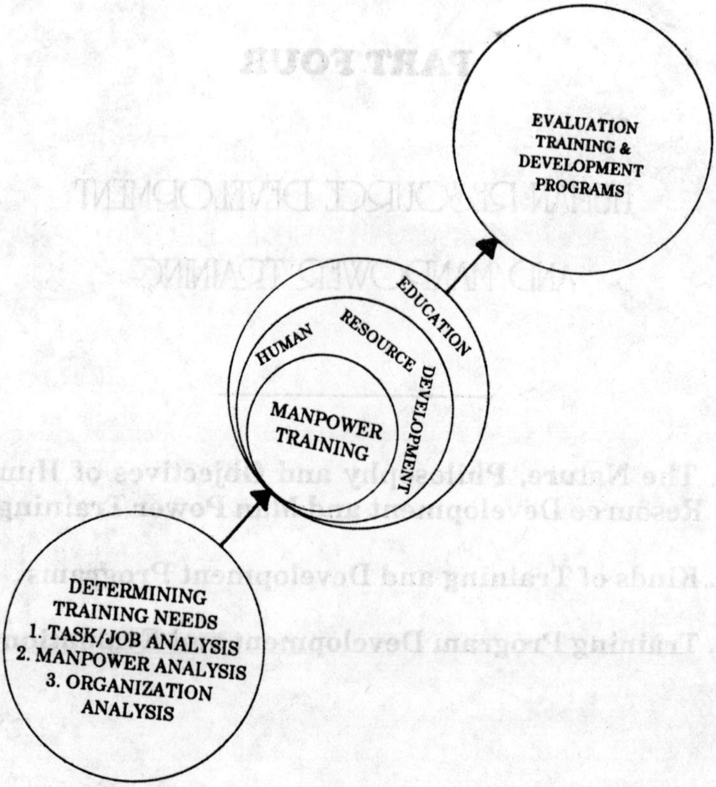

Human Resource Development And Manpower Training

The people an organization has procured must be trained, developed, and educated. The continued growth and stability of an organization depend upon the quality and adequacy of its human resources. It is, therefore, desirable that its employees and officers be developed to the optimum level of their potentials.

12

THE NATURE, PHILOSOPHY AND OBJECTIVES OF HUMAN RESOURCE DEVELOPMENT AND MANPOWER TRAINING

NO COMPANY nor organization can survive unless it grows. The growth of manpower is the key factor for the success or failure of many an organization today.

HRD Philosophy

Human resource development and manpower training is founded on four principles:

First, human beings have the capacity for growth. Everyone in an organization has the ability to grow and should strive constantly in this direction in order to sustain the growth of the company.

Second, every individual has unique value. Thus, each one is a person in his own right, different from all others, and is capable of innovative contributions.

Third, an employee's interest and organizational objectives can be integrated. The objectives of an organization with regard to human resource development are the following:

1. To motivate members to strive to increase their contribution to the organization;
2. To attract and retain competent members; and
3. To achieve maximum values from the employee's work in return for training and development costs incurred.

On the other hand, the employee's expectations are the following:

1. Equitable manpower development treatment;
2. Opportunities for deserved advancements, promotions, or transfers;
3. Favorable work situations in which maximum contributions can be made, and
4. Being kept informed on training matters affecting him.

The achievement of both the company's objectives and the employee's interest is possible. Growth of an organization depends upon its human resources. Conversely, the morale of the members of an organization is at its highest when their basic need for security and recognition is met.

Lastly, human resource development and manpower training is an investment that will yield a considerable return.

What is Human Resource Development?

Human Resource Development is defined by Nadler as a "series of organized activities conducted within a specified time and designed to produce behavioral change".1 There are three different types of activities included in this definition of HRD: Training, Education, and Development. Their relationship is illustrated in Figure 1.

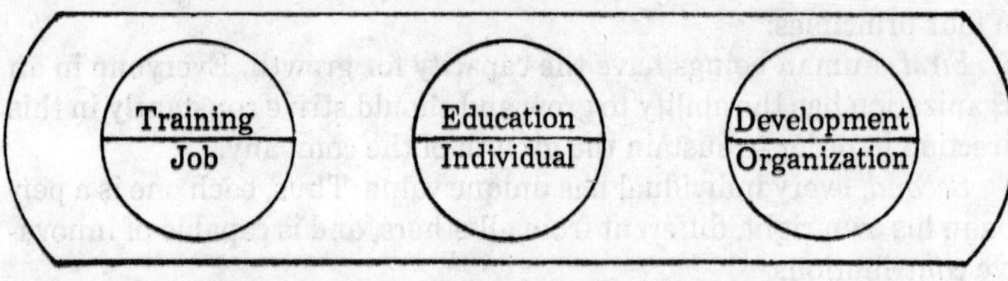

Kinds of learning experiences within the HRD function:

Job. Learning experiences enable the employee to function more effectively on his job. This is generally termed as training.

Individual. Those learning experiences designed to prepare the individual for a future but fairly well-defined job may enable him to move to the new job within a reasonable period of time. This we call education.

Organization. Learning experiences designed to open the individual to new jobs and performance patterns based on possible future direction of the organization fall under the term development.[3]

The three components of HRD are essential to the success of the organization and to development of human potential. Thus HRD includes not only the training, education, and development work carried out in an organization on behalf of its employees, but also that variety of HRD activities being carried out for non-employees such as work study, cooperative education, apprenticeship, and training activities carried out for customers and users of an organization's products.

Human Resource Management (HRM) has two specialties:

1. Human Resource Utilization (HRU) which includes recruitment, selection, placement, appraisal and compensation; and
2. Human Resource Development (HRD) which includes the learning experiences which contribute to individual and organizational effectiveness.[4]

"Human Resource Management" (HRM) and "Human Resource Administration: (HRA) are newer terms replacing the older term, "Personnel Management" to help identify the expanding role of the profession—to include a set of functions of greater importance in the management of organizations than has traditionally been assumed by personnel managers.

Organizational Development:

OD is a modern approach to the development of an organization through planned change using knowledge and techniques from the behavioral sciences. It attempts to integrate individual needs for growth with organizational goals and objectives.

Human Resource Development and manpower training are tools to attain organizational development for effectiveness.

Objectives of HRD

Companies engage in human resource development and manpower training for three reasons:

The *first* reason is to prepare for positions left vacant, thus providing left vacant, thus providing continuity for the smooth operation of the company.

The *second* is to prepare employees to perform newly-created duties and responsibilities brought about by changes in an organization's objectives, structures, laws, policies, and new technology.

The *third* is to improve the ability of employees to perform present or future duties more effectively.

Maximum utilization of human resources is the main purpose of HRD. Manpower training prepares people to function well, willingly and with understanding of their jobs. It develops an attitude of willing cooperation between employees and management. It also develops comparable skills and understanding in management so that they may secure full cooperation from each other and their subordinates.

The ultimate objective of HRD is to achieve organizational effectiveness. Thus, development and manpower training are closely related to the OD process. The objectives of OD:[5]

1. Improvement in organizational performance as measured by such indexes as profitability, turnover, innovation and share of market.
2. Improvement in the organization's adaptation to its environment, including the willingness of members to face up to organizational problems and their effectiveness in consistently reaching creative solutions to those problems.
3. Improvement in such internal behavior patterns as interpersonal and intergroup cooperation, the level of trust and support, owning up to feeling and emotions, openness and completeness of communication, and widespread participation in the planning of organization strategy.

Benefits of HRD

Despite the many benefits that can be expected from human resource development and manpower training, many variables influence business activities and organizational development.

James E. Barett in his "The Case for Evaluation of Training," an article he wrote for *Business Horizons* and in an editorial of *Business Week* in a 1962 issue emphasized the following advantages of HRD:

1. Reduced supervision, for the trained employee is one who can supervise himself.
2. Reduced accidents, since more accidents are caused by

deficiencies in people than by deficiencies in equipment and working conditions.

3. Increased organizational stability and flexibility which sustain the company's effectiveness despite the loss of key personnel through the creation of a reservoir of trained replacements.

The many benefits that can be expected from training and development are:

1. Training helps employees to learn their jobs quickly, economically, and effectively.
2. Existing employees can improve their performance and keep up-to-date in their specialized fields.
3. The standard of work required by the Company is more likely to be achieved and maintained if employees are well-trained.
4. A greater volume of work can be expected from trained staff, because they work more rapidly and they make fewer mistakes.
5. A reduction in work errors benefits a Company in two ways. First, management can spend more time in planning and development activities instead of correcting errors often involving overtime, are eliminated.
6. Labor turnover among new staff, if caused by ineffective learning and inadequate training can be reduced.
7. Retention of staff is an advantage to a Company only as long as the skills and knowledge of its employees contribute to the Company's operations. By retaining staff, new abilities replace obsolescent expertise.
8. Training in sage working practices reduces accidents, benefiting both the employees and the company.
9. A company needs a flexible work force to operate efficiently when staff members are absent. Training increases staff versatility by widening their range of expertise to include related jobs.
10. A company with a reputation for providing good training tends to attract better applicants.
11. Employees are less likely to become frustrated and leave if opportunities for further training and development are available within the company.
12. Employees increase their contribution to the Company if proper training is given to them.
13. In terms of cost reduction, efficient training procedures may contribute in the following manner:
    a. Reducing the time required to bring the unexperienced

employee to an acceptable level of job proficiency.

b. A reduction of the costs of extra materials and supplies due to excess waste and defective products.

c. A reduction of the costs of managing personnel regarding turn-over, absenteeism, accidents, grievances and complaints.

d. A reduction of the costs of servicing customers is achieved by improving the flow of goods and services to the consumer through well-trained personnel.

e. A reduction in the general overall costs of administration is created by building a wholesome climate which motivates each employee toward achieving the major goals of the organization.

f. Reduction of Machine maintenance cost.

g. Reduction of supervisory burden.

h. Reduction in grievances.

14. Improvement in method and system of work performance.
15. Improvement in quality.
16. Improved versatility.
17. Encouragement of promotion within industry.
18. Improvement of communication.
19. Improvement in morale.
20. The development of supervisors in giving clear orders.

Human Resource Development and Manpower Training, also offer social and personal benefits. The advantage to society of having a well-trained national work force is very real. Without sch expertise, the high standard of living of technology-based societies would not be possible. Furthermore, those who have been trained are more valued in the labor market. This provides them with a higher standard of living, higher status, a greater degree of job security, better promotion prospects, greater job satisfaction and recognition as well as personal satisfaction.

A word of caution with regard to this matter. HRD may create some problems if it is not integrated into the policies and operations of the Company. It is insufficient to provide first-class training opportunities without also recognizing that the training adds to employees' market value. In order that the benefits of training accrue to the company bearing the cost of the training, the company must pay attention to the broader context of an integrated personnel and total operating policies, making remuneration, prospects for promotion and physical working conditions equally attractive as those offered by competitors.

The Cost of Investing in HRD

After discussing the gains a company can derive from investing in HRD, the next logical question to be answered is: "What costs are involved in HRD?"

The true cost of human resource development and manpower training to a company is not the financial expenditure incurred—that is the money costs—but the opportunity cost involved. We can use as a better measure of HRD costs the opportunity which a company foregoes without HRD rather than its accountancy procedure. In other words, we may spend one hundred thousand pesos on HRD and Manpower training, but if, in not having training, we lose the opportunity to make five hundred thousand pesos, then the opportunity costs of training is five hundred thousand pesos, then the opportunity costs of training is five hundred thousand pesos. However, since measures of opportunity costs are hard to establish, this approach is not practical for a business organization trying to identify training costs.

Another approach in identifying the costs involved in HRD and manpower training is to identify two kinds of costs. They are as follows:

1. The learning costs - the costs incurred while employees learn their jobs such as payments made to employee while learning on the job, the cost of materials wasted, sales cost or incorrect decisions made as learners practice, and the cost of reduced output caused by the slowing-down effect which learners have on the people with whom they are working.
2. The training costs - the costs incurred such as part of the manager's salary for the time he spends in coaching his staff, emoluments of training officers, instructors and their supporting staff, the capital and running costs (lighting, air-conditioning rates) of a training center, training aids such as projectors, films, handouts, books, programmed learning texts, and payments of fees to consultants, institutions and other outside bodies.

Since expenditure on training is only justified if it reduces the costs of learning, the relationship between learning costs and training costs should both be minimized.

Characteristics of a Successful HRD Effort:

In order to ensure a successful Program, the Company's HRD effort must be:

1. *A planned, organized and systematized undertaking.* It is not a disjointed series of activities or haphazard, crises action/reaction trial-and-error approach.
2. *An organization-wide undertaking.* This means that the strategies and content of any HRD program/activity must reflect and be within the context of the Company's social, behavioral, functional and technical systems and environment.
3. *Managed and supported from the top by the president*, executives, managers and supervisors who are committed to the change being sought via the HRD efforts.

The Primary Objectives of HRD in a Company

1. To structure and implement a company-wide HRD scheme by systematizing training and development activities of various groups and making a critical analysis of training needs of the employees at all levels.

2. To provide expertise to line management in designing, conducting and evaluating training and development programs.

3. To structure a career planning and development scheme that will identify stage with potential and arrange a succession s chedule for certain key jobs.

4. To undertake personnel researches that will provide data and insights into the manpower structure, motivations and similar areas of concern.

5. To facilitate internal communication between management and employees through internal programs and activities that will facilitate predetermined communication areas (e.g. identification of company goals, upward communication relations with staff, employee motivation and the like).

How HRD Influences Organizational Effectiveness

HRD achieves organizational effectiveness through planned organizational development (OD). Organizational development focuses on the totality of the organization rather than the parts; it integrates the elements of people, structure and technology into a p roductive and effective unit.

Organizational development uses group processes to focus on the whole philosophy of the organization in order to bring about planned change—of beliefs, attitudes, structures, and practices—to influence the operation of a management function in order to enhance total effectiveness.

The managed change efforts follow this systematized approach:

- A model of what should be at a designated time is drawn up.
- The *What is,* the present organizational situation is objectively assessed—situation audit; an analysis of strengths and weaknesses.
- Discrepancies between the actual and what should be are identified so that development steps can be taken leading to a model of where the Company plans to be.

Organizational development consists of the following:[6]

1. Organizational analysis - determining where in the organization training emphasis can and should be placed. It is the study of the entire organization. Indexes that may be used in organizational analysis include labor costs (direct and indirect), quality of goods or services, and employee morale.
2. *Operation Analysis* - determining what training is needed if an employee is to perform a task, job, or assignment effectively. Operation analysis focuses on the task or job regardless of the employee performing the job. Indexes that may be used here include data obtained from observing employees at work, such as is done in making a job analysis.
3. *Man Analysis* - determining what skills, knowledge, or attitudes an individual employee must develop if he is to perform his job in the organization. Man analysis focuses o the individual in his present position and in possible future positions and may include units produced, cost of producing audits, absenteeism, tardiness and accidents; setting up of steering, correcting and controlling mechanisms so that the ideal model may be approximated.

Organizational effectiveness in a Company depends on:

1. The formal structure of the organization (structural).
2. The nature of jobs and systems employed (technological).
3. The behavior of people within the organization (behavioral).

The structure is based on functional definitions translated into an operational system and processes that depict relationships among structure, work and people. Herein are the formal authority and reporting relationships, span of management control and hierarchal levels, planning and control systems, organizational policies and procedures, and the organization's strategic objectives.

Technological considerations are jobs and work procedures as well as technical resources, productivity indicators, standards of performance, wage and salary systems, and the reward/punishment system.

Behavioral dimensions focus on the human recourses as regards their knowledge, attitudes, skills and practices as these are related to their jobs and the organizational norms and values. Social, organizational, and psychological considerations here would be the organizational value systems, individual role perceptions and values, individual and group needs and motivations, patterns of interpersonal and group relationships, level of trust, level of job satisfaction and the flow of communication up and down and feedback.

HRD Strategies

To create a climate of involvement and participation that promotes the individual's growth as a person and as a professional, the following strategies are identified as they relate to the three dimensions of structure, technology and people.

The structural strategies which focus on the formal structure aims to facilitate organizational effectiveness through the following:

1. Delineation of authority and power that would streamline reporting relationships.
2 Analysis of leadership styles, formal and informal leadership patterns of behavior.
3. Behaviorally-based research that would be aimed at identifying how the people involved perceive experience of all the above-mentioned, realizing how perceptions of management are not the same as the perception of employees.

The *technological strategies* are those by which management provides the supportive environment related to the job which enhances employees' accomplishment. Frederick Herzberg, in his two-factor theory of job motivation, states the following.

1. Extrinsic or maintenance (hygiene) factors, namely: technical supervision, salary, job security.
2. Specific strategies such as job evaluation schemes, establishment of standards of performance, incentive schemes, wage and salary reviews, performance appraisal and counselling.

The behavioral strategy aims to influence individual and group behavior so that personal attitudes, norms and values harmonize with the organizational philosophy, objectives and values. This involves the following:

1. Training and development
2. Team building
3. Trust building through participative management
4. Resolution of conflicts and achievement of collaboration through effective communication and feedback.

The HRD Organization

Whatever form of structure of HRD Organization a Company may adopt, the main criterion to be satisfied is that the HRD Group contributes effectively to the running of the business.

Ideally the training officer or HRD manager reports to the executive vice-president or the chief executive of the Company. The reason is that HRD doesn't really belong to the Personnel Administration Unit, at least in a subordinate role. The strategies of administrative functions are different from those of HRD. Administrative strategies are bureaucratic, hostile, exacting, judgmental and punctual in the eyes of the employees while HRD strategies are humanistic, educative, proactive and beneficial to both employee and management.

Many organizations employ personnel managers and at the same time establish a HRD Department as a separate entity. This type of structure is common in medium-sized firms and in some very large organizations where the importance of training functions makes it necessary for the HRD manager to have direct access to the executive vice-president or the chief executive officer of the Company. Thus, HRD and the training function are separate from the personnel function.

The HRD Specialist and Practitioners

Human Resource Development while basically a young discipline, has gained increased importance in many organizations. The HRD specialist, called Human Resource Manager, Manpower Development Manager, Training Manager, training officer, training specialist or training director, assumes varied roles in accordance with the environment he will be working in. To be effective, he should be perceptive, creative, open-minded, cooperative, inquisitive, and intelligent.[7] He should be skillfull in human relations, communication, and have managerial, technical, analytical and conceptual competence.

With regard to educational background, the HRD Specialist should ideally have an undergraduate degree in one of the social or behavioral sciences such as psychiatry, general psychology, social psychology, education, political science, sociology, anthropology, business administration or public administration. He should have a working knowledge of many of these disciplines. It would also be helpful for him to have some knowledge of such technical disciplines as operations research, communications, general systems theory, information technology, finance, cybernectics, effekinesics, marketing, production, and finance.

The whole purpose of the mixed interdisciplinary approach is to give breadth and scope to the practitioner rather than a narrow specialization. The problems in training tend to be interdisciplinary in character. Broad knowledge and multiple skills are demanded of the HRD specialist if he and his training HRD staff, are to be ready for his six key roles:[8]

1. *Learning Specialist* – designing, developing, conducting and evaluating learning experiences.

2. *Training Administrator* – arranging training and employee development programs.

3. *Program Manager* – policy setting, planning, controlling and managing the various training and employee development programs.

4. *Consultant* – providing management and employee with advice and assistance.

5. *Career Development Specialist* – assisting in career development plans. However, this can be incorporated in his role as consultant.

6. *Researcher* – conducting research on learning activities.

STUDY/REVIEW QUESTIONS

1. Define Human Resource Development.
2. Give the philosophy of Human Resource Development.
3. Explain the three different kinds of learning experience within the HRD function.
4. Explain the two specialties of Human Resources Management.
5. What are the objectives of HRD?
6. What are the benefits of HRD?
7. What is the cost of investing in HRD?
8. Enumerate and explain the characteristics of a successful HRD effort.
9. What are the primary objectives of HRD in a company?
10. How does HRD affect organizational effectiveness?
11. What are the HRD strategies?

12. Give some guidelines in organizing an HRD in an organization.

13 .What are the duties, responsibilities and qualifications of a HRD specialist?

SUGGESTED ACTIVITIES AND ASSIGNMENT

1. Iterview a HRD Manager of an organization regarding the philosophy, objectives, organizational set-up and strategies of HRD in the organization.

2. Go to the National Manpower and Youth Council and find out what human resource development programs they have on the national level and regional level.

3. Write a position paper on the philosophy of human resource development in the Philippine setting.

NOTES

[1]Leonard Nadler, *Developing Human Resources* (Houston: Gulf Publishing Company, 1976) p. 3.

[2]Ibid.

[3]Leonard Nadler, "Implications of the HRD Concept", *Training and Development Journal* (May 1974) p. 4.

[4]Ibid, p. 3.

[5]Laurence A. Klatt et. al., *Human Resource Management A Behavioural System Approach* (Illinois: Richard Irwin Inc., 1978), p. 126.

[6]Herbert J. Churden & Arthur W. Sherman, Jr., *Personnel Management* (Chicago: Growth Western Publishing Company, 1958), pp. 201-202.

[7]Emmanuel V. Soriano, "The Future of Human Resource Development and the HRD Specialist" Keynote Paper No. 804, 8th International Training and Development Conference, Manila, Nov. 7-12, 1979.

[8]Dr. Gary B. Hansen, "Educating the HRD Practitioners of the 80's", Technical Paper No. 7934, 8th International Training and Development Conference, Nov. 7-12, 1979.

REFERENCES FOR FURTHER READING

Andres, Tomas D. *Management By Filipino Values.* Quezon City: New Day Publishers, 1985.

______. *Human Resources Training and Development.* Quezon City: New Day Publishers, 1980.

Nadler, Leonard. *Developing Human Resources.* Houston: Gulf Publishing Company, 1976.

Klatt, Laurence A. et. al. *Human Resource Management A Behavioral System Approach.* Illinois: Richard Irwin Inc., 1978.

13

KINDS OF TRAINING AND DEVELOPMENT PROGRAMS

TRAINING REPRESENTS a positive approach to the improvement of performance. But different people in different companies or organizations have different training needs. Thus the need for different kinds of training programs.

Apprenticeship Training Program

As one of the oldest formalized approaches to the training of individuals in a variety of skills, Apprenticeship Training includes classroom instruction as well as individual on-the-job training. It may take from two to six years to learn under the graduate or master craftsmen. Apprenticeship Training is well-developed in automobile companies and electrical manufacturers. It furnishes written agreements specifying the type of training to be given, the length of time of the apprenticeship, the hours to be devoted to training on the job and in the classroom and the wages of the apprentices.

Vestibule Training Program

Vestibule Training is advisable when a firm has to train a large number of employees in similar skills for positions in clerical or production work and when time is a factor and the work to be taught is relatively simple in nature. The length of training may be a few days or it may last several months. The learner is under no pressure. He can build his confidence at a pace natural for him. The firm is assured of uniform training done under ideal conditions with the best instructors available. This kind of training is usually established away from the actual workplace, although the same equipment, machines, tools and materials used in the training are used in actual production. It duplicates the regular work in almost every way except for the pressures.

Vestibule training programs are implemented in Insurance companies, Restaurant and Retail Food Store chains, and large Commercial Banks.

Orientation and Induction Training Program

Orientation and Induction is one of the most widely-used programs. It aims to have new employees learn as much as possible about the company in a short period so that they can easily adjust to the environment and become productive. This program teaches about the nature of the work environment,history of the company, terms of employment, wage and salary administration, policies and procedures, leaves, insurance, rules and conduct, etc. In some companies, major company executives speak to the new employees who are given plant and office tours.

One successful method used in some companies is the "buddy or padrino system" wherein the new employee is assigned to an older employee who is responsible for the new-comer until he becomes adjusted to his new position.

In some instances, a follow-up program is conducted after a time to determine whether a new employee has adjusted to his new job and whether any doubts or fears have developed in his mind.

Safety Training Program

The responsibility to develop a safety-conscious work force lies in the hands of a safety director or loss-control manager. This program is to be implemented by the line supervisors.

Co-Operative Training Program

Some colleges have co-operative training programs with local business firms. Practical training on the job is given to students. This training program can be used in various clerical occupations, manual trades, retailing, sales engineering, and technical jobs.

Dealer Training Program

In some companies, the training unit is called upon to render

technical assistance for their dealers. A Dealer Training Program may range from a one-day yearly meeting of dealers, where new products are displayed and explained along with new pricing policies to comprehensive programs of varying duration held both in the field, at regional training centers, and at the home plant and offices.

Dealer Training programs include both sales and mechanical training. A number of manufacturing companies such as appliance and automobile firms train technicians from dealers organizations, so that company products may be properly installed and serviced. Furthermore, dealer salesmen are trained in sales techniques.

Supervisory Training Program

In companies wherein promotion-from-written policy are strictly followed, first-line supervisors and potential first-line supervisors of the work force are trained on a released-time basis by a professional training unit. Training occurs both in training conferences and on-the-job. The number of sessions varies with the program being offered. The training program teaches supervisory techniques such as conference methods, performance rating, grievance procedures and handling problem employees. Communication, motivation, planning, organizing, leading and controlling are discussed.

Middle-Management Development Program

This Program aims to develop executives for responsibility of a broader nature. More often than not, managers in the Philippines have risen to their positions as a result of technical competence in a relatively narrow field of activity. The company feels that these men should get a broader business knowledge through a Middle-Management Development Program, either a formal one such as an MBA Program in Ateneo or La Salle or an informal program. When they return to their position, they are given an opportunity to demonstrate their newly acquired knowledge by carefully developed understudy-rotation plan. Each man is assigned to assist a major executive and is given a variety of administrative experience. Production and technical people are given marketing assignments.

Vocational Training

This provides the skills, knowledge, and attitudes required for employment in a particular occupation or field of economic activity.

Pre-Entry Training

Training in basic skills for immediate entry into the work environment is conducted here.

Basic Skill Training

This is the first stage of preparing the learner for a given task, job, occupation or group of occupations aimed at developing the fundamental attitude/knowledge/skill behavior pattern of specified standards.

Further Training

After basic skill training, further training is given to achieve recognized qualifications. It includes any or all of the following:

1. *Upgrading* – Training for supplementary skills and knowledge in order to increase the versatility of a worker or to improve his standard of performance.
2. *Updating* – Training to improve the performance of people in their occupation with respect to modern developments – new materials, tools, processes, etc.
3. *Refresher* – Further training in order to improve job performance. This also refers to training to regain skills and knowledge which may have been partly forgotten as a result of lengthy interruptions.
4. *Specialization* – Training given to deepen and broaden skills and knowledge for a particular task or aspect of a worker's occupation.
5. *Retraining* – Training for skills and knowledge required in an occupation other than the one for which the person was originally trained.

Accelerated Training

This usually refers to rapid-paced, condensed vocational training to fill immediate manpower needs.

Enterpreneuring Training

This refers to training schemes to develop persons for self-employment or for organizing, financing, and/or managing an enterprise.

Pre-Vocational Training

Training activities here are primarily for the youth and cover any and all of the following:

1. First introduction to work of a vocational character covering a range of activities;
2. Prepares the youth for choosing an occupation or a line of training;
3. Acquaints the youth with the different materials and tools, and elementary theoretical knowledge concerning a group of occupations;
4. Provides the youth with working methods and standards expected at work; and
5. Gives the youth basic knowledge about the contribution which they may make to the economic and social development of the country.

Instructor Training

This is aimed at developing the capacity to impart attitudes, knowledge, skills, and behavior patterns required for specific tasks, or group of related occupations.

Core Development

This refers to those programs which contribute to an employee's knowledge of the organization, the industry, and the procedures pertinent to his job. This includes on-the-job training, company orientation, Industry Educational Program, Functional Briefings, and Company Publications.

Technical Development Programs

These are aimed at increasing the incumbent's technical proficiency. They include on-the-job training, Manual Skills, Certification Exam Progress, On-Campus Programs, Industry Meetings, Professional Association Meetings, Vendor Schools, In-House Programs, Temporary Transfers, and Interdivisional Problem-Solving.

Leadership Development Programs

These are designed to improve leadership skills and include On-the-

Job Training, Management Supervisory, pre-supervisory training, on-campus programs and instructor's training.

Supplementary Development Programs

Activities which offer helpful experiences to employees are provided in these programs. They include among others oral communication, written communication, personal counseling, time management, community activities and interpersonal relations.

Salesmanship Training Program

This develops a salesman by giving him an orientation session on the company's products and the importance of service to customers, and teaches him to check the outside advertising, displays, and stock in stockrooms.

STUDY/REVIEW QUESTIONS

1. Explain the nature of the following training programs and give an example:
    a. Apprenticeship Training Program
    b. Co-operative Training Program
    c. Dealer Training Program
    d. Supervisory Training Program
2. Give the different activities involved in Further Training. Explain each.

SUGGESTED ACTIVITIES AND ASSIGNMENT

1. Secure a copy of a training program of an organization and criticize it.
2. Go to a training center and make a list of the training programs offer.
3. Participate in a training program and write a report about it.

REFERENCES FOR FURTHER READING

Andres, Tomas D. *Management By Filipino Values.* Quezon City: New Day Publishers, 1985.

_____. *Human Resources Training and Development.* Quezon City: New Day Publishers, 1980.

Angeles, Conrado P. et al. *Principles of Personnel Administration.* Quezon City: R.M. Garcia Publishing House, 1981.

Martinez, Esdras T. *Human Resources Management.* Manila: GIC Enterprises & Co., Inc., 1979.

Sison, Perfecto S. *Personnel and Human Resources Management.* Manila: Rex Book Store, 1981.

14

TRAINING PROGRAM DEVELOPMENT AND EVALUATION

THE DEVELOPMENT of a training program involves the following essential steps:

1. Analysis of training needs
2. Design and development of appropriate training program
3. Evaluation of the training program's effectiveness in meeting the needs.

I. Analysis of Training Needs

When the knowledge, skills, attitudes and habits required by the job varies from those possessed by the employee assigned to the job, there exists a training need.

The basic process then, for identifying this training need is as follows: (1) Determine what is required in the job; (2) Find out if this requirement is being met; if not, find out the reasons. If these reasons involve changes in the knowledge, skills, attitudes or habits of the employee, training will be of help.

Certain training needs are a matter of common sense. Obvious training needs occur whenever: (1) a new employee comes to work, (2) an employee is assigned to a new or different job which he does not know, (3) the methods of doing an "old" job are changed, or (4) the working relationships within the organization are substantially changed.

Other training needs which are not so obvious must be determined through careful analysis. This analysis should include institutional as well as an individual employee's problems. There may be problems in the organization, such as safety problems and discipline problems and the need to develop training programs so as to equip the concerned employees with necessary knowledge, attitudes and habits.

Clues to training needs may be found by studying:

1. *Organizational plans*
   - looking into projected changes in mission, structure, personnel, or procedures.
2. *Employee Records*
   - looking into turnover rates, absenteeism rates, sick leave notes, accident ratios, tardiness rates, grievances, composition of supervisory force
3. Management audits of departmental/group performance
4. Job requirements versus job qualifications
5. Complaints and reactions from customers/clients
6. Work flow
   - looking into production bottlenecks, fluctuations in production, backlogs, records of high costs, waste, excessive errors.
7. Communication failures
8. Morals indicators such as complaints and buckpassing

II. Tools Used in the Assessment of Training and Development Needs

A. *Interviews*

An interview reveals feelings and possible solutions to problems as well as facts. It gives maximum opportunity for expressing opinions and giving suggestions. Interviews are a must for the training officer who would keep a finger on the pulse of his company. They help understand how people feel and why. They also manifest, in a personalized way, sincere interest in what people in the organization think.

Interviews can be informal such as merienda time discussion of office problems or formal enough to permit a training officer to make notes.

B. *Questionnaires*

Written questionnaires give employees an opportunity to express their feelings anonymously, without any of the embarrassment or anxiety which can accompany the more personal techniques. Well designed, they yield data that can be processed quickly.

Any questionnaire should be pre-tested and revised as necessary for clarity, adequacy of coverage, etc. Anonymity must be safeguarded and participants must be confident that it will be.

The Employee Attitude Survey is an example of the questionnaire technique. Such surveys usually include some questions bearing directly on training, and the answers to other questions frequently produce additional clues on training needs.

The Supervisory Improvement Needs Survey Technique appeals to many because of its positive and constructive emphasis. It gets the potential trainee thinking in terms of what he wants to help him do a better job, faster or easier. Potential trainees are given a list of possible training subjects, with a brief description of content, and asked to indicate their preferences.

The Slip Survey Technique is an interesting device in which potential trainees are called together in groups, given cards or slips of paper, and asked to record, as fast as the thoughts occur to them, what they consider to be their greatest difficulties on the job—one difficulty per slip, expressed in "how to" form, i.e., "how to discipline," "how to write a report", etc. The slips are then collected, sorted and analyzed for training needs.

C. *Tests*

Tests identify specific areas of deficiency. They are also useful in selecting those potential trainees who can profit best from training. Tests of various kinds may be used in determining training needs and, once an area of need had been found, in selecting the employees to be trained. They can be especially helpful in determining whether the cause of a recognized problem is a deficiency in knowledge, or skill, or attitude.

Performance or achievement tests show what employees know or can do, and therefore help locate areas in which more information or more skill training is needed.

Aptitude tests indicate potential to learn or acquire information or skills in a particular area, and so are useful in selecting from among a group of employees those who can most profitably be trained.

Practical tests in typing and stenography can quickly establish an employee's need or lack of need for training in those skills.

Trade information tests are used to determine levels of knowledge and skill in a variety of occupations.

D. *Group Problem Analysis*

An excellent means of determining training needs is the group problem analysis, wherein supervisors, managers or executives in a given department get together to discuss their problems, and to decide what changes are needed. Some of these changes may call for training, others for management action.

This process not only identifies training needs but also builds a solid foundation of support for the training decided on. Furthermore, the process itself is training because the participants become more analytical in their study of problems.

This process may be done with or without a training officer. If he is present, he can facilitate discussion, help members classify their thinking, and advise them on what training can and cannot do.

E. *Records and Reports Analysis*

Management records and reports can also provide valuable data on training needs and excellent clues to trouble spots. It is advisable, for example, to study audit and inspection reports, personnel records (grievances, turnover, absenteeism, accident frequency and severity, tardiness, suggestions, etc.), cost and production records, etc. Though records seldom reveal causes of problems, they are clues to be followed up.

F. *Job Analysis and Performance Review*

An excellent method of determining training needs of individual is job analysis combined with performance appraisal. The process is as follows: Determine the specific duties of the job. Observe how the employee performs each of his duties. Locate significant areas which can be improved by training.

The Critical Incident Technique is a job analysis and performance evaluation device that places special emphasis on kinds of behavior that distinguish effective from ineffective performance. *First,* list only the major requirements of the job, those that make the difference between success and failure. *Second*, under each of these write brief descriptions, usually in checklist form, of observable on-the-job behavior. *Third*, let the supervisor check the forms to record his observations of each employee's behavior, adding whatever explanatory note he feels necessary.

The Appraisal Panel Method is a process of supervisory observation and evaluation, supplemented by the observations and evaluations of others who personally know the appraisee and his work.

III. Designing Training and Development Programs

The design of training and development programs involves many considerations. It includes factors that are within the control of a company and also many outside factors. Among the factors that should be considered and analysed when planning the design of training and development programs are the following:

1. *The complexity of the economy.* This includes the phenomena of increased competition, higher standard of living, etc. These factors are inputs to a well-coordinated program to maintain a company's competitive position.
2. *The changing technology.* A host of new machines are continually being introduced in Philippine companies. A company must keep abreast of the latest methods and techniques in order to maintain its position in the industry. However, when new methods or equipment are introduced, employees must be trained in their use if maximum benefits will be obtained.
3. *The nature of individual company operations.* The complexity of a company's operations has a direct bearing on its training and development programs. Bank institutions, automotive manufacturing companies, and service organizations all have varied training problems. Training and development programs have to be planned with this fact in mind.
4. *Education patterns.* The education patterns of a country have a bearing on the design of a training and development program. Owing to poor college background of some employees, many companies in the Philippines offer for example, training seminars on technical reports and business letter writing and filing and record management. Another interesting educational aspect in the Philippines is the hiring of under-graduate workers who want to finish their college studies. A training and development program helps these employees in acquiring college education.
5. *Integration with other planning.* Top management includes training plans as a vital part of overall planning for the enterprise.

6. *Relation to staffing.* Some companies have a policy that follows staff in-breeding or promotion from within. The training and development program then must see to it that positions are filled by trained subordinates.
7. *The Personnel Program.* All training and development programs must fit in with all other personnel policies, plans and programs.
8. *Effective Utilization of Training Staff and Facilities.*
9. *Choice of Programs.* The training and development programs should be integrated with other company activities and plans. Training programs should be carefully planned and closely re-lated to company needs.
10. *Selection of Trainees and Trainee Utilization.* The training program should include a built-in mechanism that ensures the proper selection of trainees. Also, the trainees should use their new knowledge as soon as possible. Thus, the program should take into consideration the circumstances that will surround the trainee's job assignment.
11. The Learning Process. One of the fundamentals of learning is the "law of effect," which states that one tends to repeat behavior which seems to bring rewards. For efficient training, then it is necessary to provide reinforcement of desired behavior.

After a training need has been determined and analyzed, the training officer must design the training which he believes will satisfy this need.

The design of a training program involves several steps:

Step 1. *Naming the Program*

In naming the program, be as specific as possible and avoid naming it in such a way as to suggest that it includes more than it does. The name should, if possible, indicate the content to be covered as well as the type and level of instruction.

Examples:

Cadet Engineers Management Development Program

Basic Supervisory Development Program

Step 2. *Stating the Program's Objectives*

Describe briefly what you expect participants to know and be able to do after the program. The objectives should be realistic and consistent with the trainee's ability, as well as with the time and facilities available.

Step 3. *Determining the Program's Specific Content*

Select from the analysis those knowing and doing units that you wish to teach. Estimate the time required. Select those units that can be included within the time limits and which will contribute the most toward the objectives.

Step 4. *Arranging Units in Teaching Order*

Arrange the units on your tentative list beginning from the least difficult. The knowing units must generally be taught prior to the related doing units.

Here are some guidelines:

1. Cover only the essentials of each subject.
2. Determine for each subject the time which a person of average intelligence would require to master it.
3. Give the initial training in fundamentals so that the trainees' ability to complete the program may be assessed.
4. Provide ample time for revision to consolidate knowledge and give tests to assess progress.
5. Link theory with practice. Follow explanation of a necessary theory by immediate practical application.

Step 5. *Selecting and Preparing Instructional Materials and Resource Speakers*

Select and prepare all necessary training aids. Instructional materials must be consistent with trainee's ability, must emphasize the key elements of the course, and must be effective in presenting information and concepts.

Decide range of operations—what tools, machines and equipment are necessary. Design exercises in order of difficulty. Later exercises should build on previous work and introduce additional tools. Decide what, how and when workshop demonstrations are to be used. Drawings should adhere to the accepted drawing conventions.

Close liaison is necessary between the training people and departmental supervision not only at the planning stages but also in the implementation and evaluation stages.

Step 6. *Planning the Lesson*

Put down on paper the things to teach and how to teach them.

IV. Evaluating Training Programs

Management is very much aware of the cost of training and development programs. Top management may ask: Do training and development programs pay off? Are they producing the intended results such as return on investment, production, and sales volume? These questions show the importance of evaluating training and development programs.

A. *The Nature of Evaluation*

Evaluation is a management function by which is carried a systematic means of assessing the extent by which training and development programs have been carried out and programmed objectives have been attained. Evaluation of training and development programs is based on feedback or information on their effects.

Evaluation creates a feedback loop, or a "self-connecting training system." It involves establishing standards, measurement of some sort, identification and analysis of shortfalls and deficiencies, selection of remedial action, and follow-up to ensure that correction has occurred.

B .*Importance of Evaluation*

In the Philippine setting, evaluation of training and development programs is of utmost importance in order to attain top management's support. Evaluation ensures that these programs contribute to organizational goals. Furthermore, evaluation helps training directors and staff because it collects the data needed to improve every aspect of the training and development system—personnel, facilities, equipment, policies, program, and procedures. In a well-controlled program weaknesses are identified and corrected by means of negative feedback and strengths and successes are amplified by means of positive feedback.

C. *Principles for Evaluating Training and Development Programs*

General:

1. Since training is aimed at change, all training can be evaluated in some way.
2. Since management cannot be expected to accept training programs based on faith alone, all training programs should be evaluated.
3. Each training program must have clearly defined objectives.
4. Pesos-and-centavos evaluation is the most impressive to top

management.

5. Results are most significant and meaningful when comparisons are ,made between:
   a. trained and untrained groups
   b. groups trained by different methods
   c. the same group before and after training
6. Evaluation should be specific in terms of a particular program, course, or activity.
7. The effects of a complex training program can be studied more effectively if each part is evaluated separately.
8. Evaluation of training is more effective if built into the program.
9. The evaluation procedure may include technical phases (statistics) which sometimes require the help of professional experts.
10. Revision of a training program must be based on the evaluation of the original program.

Specific:

1. Evaluation must be planned and consciously designed. The training staff must determine in advance what is to be evaluated, when, by what means, and by whom.
2. Evaluation must be relevant to the purposes of both training and development and the firm's programs.
3. Evaluation must be objective, employing fair and equitable standards and procedures.
4. Evaluation must be verifiable, i.e. its results can be confirmed by the same or different means.
5. Evaluation is a cooperative effort, i.e., it involves all who are a part of or are affected by the training and development program.
6. Evaluation must be a continuous and ongoing activity.
7. Evaluation must be specific, explicit and exact.
8. Evaluation must be quantitative, i.e., employing quantitative measures, as much as possible.
9. Evaluation must be feasible and administratively manageable.
10. Evaluation must be commensurate with the cost incurred.

D. Forms of Evaluation

Evaluation can take three forms which are as follows:

1. *Immediate evaluation* measures, analyzes and interprets changes in job-related knowledge, skills, and attitudes of trainees.

2. Intermediate evaluation measures, analyzes and interprets changes in on-the-job behavior of trainees.
3. Ultimate evaluation measures and analyzes changes in results achieved by the trainees when they have returned to their jobs.

E. *Levels of Evaluation*

Total evaluation of training involves these five levels:

Level I. *Reactions*

Reaction may best be defined as how well the trainees liked a particular training and development program. This means measuring the feelings of the trainee.

Why is measurement of reactions to training programs the first step in the evaluation process?

1. Trainees who enjoy a training program/course are more likely to obtain maximum benefit from it.
2. Management support to training often depends on feedback from the trainees.

Level II. *Learning*

The second level in the evaluation process involves measuring the principles, facts and techniques which were understood and absorbed by the trainees.

Level III. *Job Behavior*

The third level of the evaluation process attempts to find out whether the trainees have applied what they have learned to their respective jobs.

Level IV. *Organizational Repercussions*

The fourth level of the evaluation process measures the effects of the trainees' job-behavior changes on the functioning of the organization and/or unit in which they work.

Level V. *Ultimate Value*

Evaluation at this level attempts to relate the organizational evaluation to the ultimate criteria by which the organization judges the training's efficiency and its success or failure.

In business firms, we can label this level as the cost-efficiency level: "Are the financial benefits resulting from the training greater than the cost of training?"

F. *Methods of Evaluation*

Evaluation may be continuous or terminal. In continuous evaluation, tests are applied throughout the whole training process and are designed to measure developing performance, over the whole period of training. Terminal evaluation is assessing the effectiveness of training at the end of the program.

Objective methods of evaluation are to be preferred. However, they cannot be used unless they are scientifically sound, administratively convenient, and acceptable to management. Administrative convenience will often dictate continuous evaluation rather than terminal evaluation methods. Tests can be fitted into the program. When objective knowledge tests, tests of skills, and attitude scales cannot be used, subjective tests should be made as objectively as possible. Here are some guidelines when using subjective methods:

1. The observer or interviewer must be well-trained;
2. His subjective judgments must be based on as much factual material as he can collect; and
3. Whenever possible, his findings are compared with those obtained by another skilled and independent observer.

Training evaluation methods based on the five levels of evaluation:

A. *Reaction Level Evaluation*

Reactions are measured by a seminar/course evaluation questionnaire designed to obtain honest reactions to specific aspects of the training program. The questionnaire should be so designed that the reactions can be tabulated and quantified for evaluation.

B. *Learning Level Evaluation*

Evaluation on this level is generally done through paper and pencil tests given prior to training and after the training. This method makes use of true or false, multiple choice exams, matching items, or sentence completion tests. Scores are garnered before the training. Statistical analysis is then used to find out if there is a significant increase in the trainees' knowledge or skill, or a change in their attitudes.

Another commonly used method of evaluating learning makes use of a questionnaire or attitude/opinion survey wherein trainees appraise the learning they obtained from the training. Using scales, trainees are asked to indicate the amount of learning they had before and after the training. Data are then treated statistically to determine whether a significant change occurred in knowledge, skill, or attitude.

C. *Job Behavior Level Evaluation*

This can be done by watching and asking, or by observation and questionnaire/interview. These two techniques should be employed together whenever possible, since neither visual perception nor the spoken or written word is in itself totally reliable. The effect of each can be detected by reference to the other.

External observation may be achieved through activity sampling or through the use of observer diaries. Internal observation can be obtained by self observation by the trainee making use of self diaries.

Questionnaires or interviews are widely used as job behavior evaluation tools. Attitude change can be measured in a training program by questionnaires and attitude surveys before and after the training and by discussion with the trainees who reflect their attitudes directly to the trainer and to their supervisors.

Another source of job behavior evaluation data is records and reports of production, performance appraisal, accidents, etc.

D. *Organizational Level Evaluation*

Many organizational effects can be evaluated by techniques similar to those used at the job behavior level. Organizational evaluation is often concerned with the effect of the trainees' changes in job behavior on the attitudes and job behavior of other employees who have not been formally trained themselves.

As in the job behavior level, evaluation in the organization level may be achieved through observation or making use of questionnaire/interview.

E. *Ultimate Value Level Evaluation*

Ultimate value evaluation is usually financial and economic. The cost of training is compared with the financial gain resulting from the training—a cost-benefit analysis. This comparison can be done with training courses in which financial benefits were operationally defined in the objective-setting phase.

Using results achieved by managers, supervisors and workers is a strong basis for evaluating the effectiveness and efficiency of training and development programs. However, there are so many variables involved that fair appraisal solely on the basis of analysis of productivity indexes is difficult. Evaluation on the ultimate level is concerned with two questions:

1. How well did our training and development perform in meeting its objectives?
2. Is the result actually attributable to the training and development program?

Some of the variables to be considered in using results as the basis of evaluation are the following:

1. *Top Management.* The corporate philosophy, objectives and attitude of top management as well as their competence as leaders affects supervisors, trainers and employees at all levels and consequently affects job performance and results achieved.
2. *Trainors and supervisors.* The job performance of subordinate personnel and/or trainees is affected by motivation and morale, job satisfaction, amount and quality of supervision received, instructional environment and methods.
3. *Trainees.* The ability to learn and perform are affected by the learning potential, attitude, skills, motivation, off-the-job living conditions, problems and personal concerns of the trainees.
4. *Enterprise climate.* The job performance of trainees and, therefore, productivity indexes are affected by labor and union relations, social realities, economic constraints and national, local and enterprise rules, regulations, policies and procedures.

Below is a guide for evaluating the results of training:

1. What are the objectives? (What do we hope to accomplish?)
2. Conditions before training (What specific conditions prevail which make training necessary?)
3. Records (What records of training should we keep? What data should we collect?)
4. Conditions after training (What changes have taken place?)
5. Other factors (What factors other than training may havecontributed to the results?)
6. Results (What have we accomplished?)

Some ultimate measures of training are absenteeism rate, accident rate, customer complaints, error rate, grievance rate, machine downtime, lost time, reject rate, turnover rate, waste/spoilage rate, and work backlogs.

How To Operate Efficiently Training And Development Programs

To efficiently operate a training and development program, the first step is to have a training unit responsible for such a function. Cooperation between the training unit and the line supervisors is a must, especially in programs where a high degree of specialized technical knowledge is required. It is advisable that both the training specialists and the line people concerned work on the development and implementation of training and development programs.

It is wise to form a Human Resource Committee, with the Company's president as chairman, which formulates policy relating to training and development and periodically reviews reports on the status of overall human resources. Division heads are to be held responsible for implementing company-wide development programs. The training unit is responsible for their implementation and monitoring and for reporting on the execution of such programs. It shall also be the responsibility of the training unit to assist the supervisors by providing the following:

1. Guidelines on how company supervisors shall plan and administer their training programs.
2. Periodic check and review of the company guidelines for training and development.
3. An up-to-date list of accredited resource persons in government, the Personnel Management Association of the Philippines, and the Philippine Society for Training and Development accredited resource persons.
4. A supply of well-kept-up programmed instructor materials on induction training.
5. Arrangement of accreditation with government and other professional organizations for company's training program.
6. Guidelines for the maintenance and upkeep of training equipment such as 16 min. movie projector, overhead projector, opaque projector, slide projector, tape recorder, etc.
7. Arrangements for possible training and development agreements with foreign governments and international organizations as well as persons and organizations in the country.
8. Arrangement of technical training assistance programs for dealers, fleet-owners and business associates.
9. Preparation, periodic check and review of guidelines on how to report training and development activities to top management.

10. Preparation, check and review of guidelines on the settlement of accounts pertaining to training and development.
11. Preparation, check and review of the general procedure in implementing the company's manpower training and Development Programs.

Since training and development is a supervisory function, the supervisor will perform the following:

1. Determine the training need in his working unit.
2. Design the training program to answer this need.
3. Administer the training program.
4. Evaluate follow-up results of the training program.

However, before a training and development activity is undertaken by any working unit in the Company, Management Authorization must be sought from the company's training and development unit.

The Training Officer or unit, should act as a coordinator of a team effort, taking care to keep all the "key people" informed as the outlines of policy develop. The Training Officer must make use of all his social skills and be highly critical of his own work in the training and development.

Questions the Training Office should ask himself are:
"Is there anything I have left out?"
"Is there anyone I have left out?"
"Is there anything I could explain more simply?"
"Am I being realistic?"
"Is there anyone likely to oppose this program?"

STUDY./REVIEW QUESTIONS

1. What are the steps involved in the development of a training program?

2. Enumerate the tools used in the assessment of training and development needs.

3. Identify the factors that should be considered and analyzed when planning a training and development program in the Philippines.

4. What are the steps in designing a training and development program?

5. Enumerate the steps in evaluating a training and development program.

SUGGESTED ACTIVITIES AND ASSIGNMENT

1. Secure some tools used in the assessment of training and development needs from any organization and make a critique on them.
2. Interview a member of the Philippine Society for Training and Development and ask about activities related to the design of training programs.
3. Interview a Training Officer on how to evaluate a training and development program. Ask him to show you an evaluation of his company's training program.

REFERENCES FOR FURTHER READING

Andres, Tomas D. *Management by Filipino Values.* Quezon City: New Day Publishers, 1985.

_____. *Human Resources Management.* Quezon City: New Day Publishers, 1980.

Martinez, Esdras T. *Human Resources Management.* Manila: GIC Enterprises & Co., Inc., 1979.

PART FIVE

HUMAN RESOURCE MAINTENANCE AND CONSERVATION

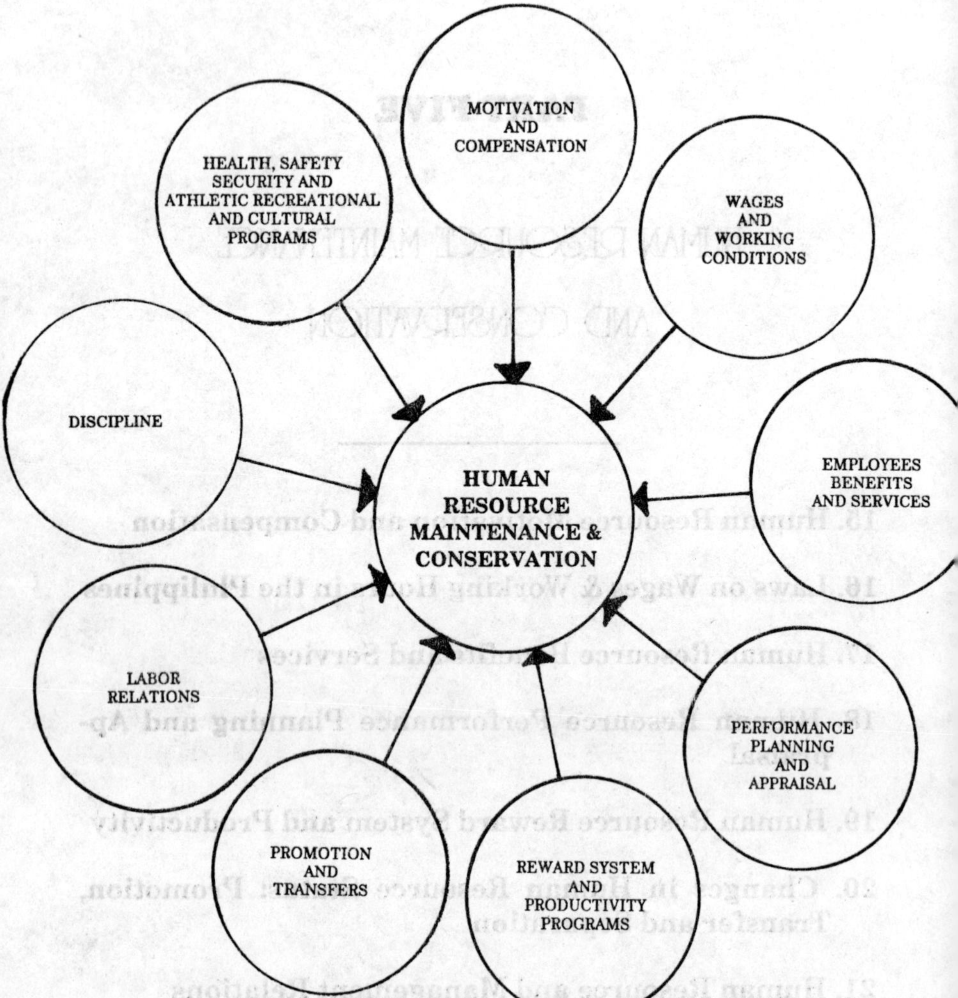

Human Resource Maintenance and Conservation

15

HUMAN RESOURCE MOTIVATION AND COMPENSATION

FOR A LONG TIME organizations in the Philippines have been trying to increase worker productivity by increasing pay, providing better working conditions and offering greater fringe b enefits. But still the industrial output is stagnant or even lags behind. Perhaps the major motivation of the employees is not monetary. It may be related to their work environment or to the way they are treated by their superiors.

The key to increased productivity lies not so much in giving employees more, but managing them better, that is, managing with concern for balancing individual needs with organizational goals. Business organizations are profit-oriented and the main concern is how to keep the employees contributing at their highest level. It is usually forgotten that employees are human beings and therefore, need to be motivated if they are to do their best. Management should consider what factors motivate or become sources of dissatisfaction.

Abraham A. Maslow states that man must meet the demands of his lower needs before those on the higher level can emerge. Maslow deduced that satisfied needs are not motivators. For example, the satisfaction of a need for food is only a motivator when one is hungry. Our needs at any time depend on what we already have. If one need is satisfied another emerges to take its place. And these needs emerge in a predictable pattern. They are basic physiological or physical needs, safety and security needs, belonging or social needs, esteem needs and self-realization needs.

The pay that an employee gets from his employer is the primary reason for his being on a job. For this reason, wage and salary administration must be a major concern of management.

It is an accepted fact that the largest number of industrial disputes involve matters concerning wages. And the losses incurred in view of these disputes, at times, can be very damaging to a firm and to some extent, to the economy of the nation.

Among Filipino employees, the matter of wage and salary increase assumes great proportions. Every time management gives any employee a salary increase, the news travels swiftly via the company grapevine and sends shock waves among the entire work force. Morale goes up or down, depending on who gets the increase. If they feel that the recipient is deserving of the raise, morale goes up.

Determining wages and salaries for different jobs has long been a problem not only of management and employees but also of the government.

The government has been taking the initiative in setting the minimum wage. The high cost of living has sparked the granting of emergency allowances and other forms of economic aid to the worker. These phenomena have disrupted salary structures of business enterprises.

Job evaluation and wage-salary administration are the answers to this critical problem of establishing an equitable relationship between jobs and wages. This involves determining the relative values or worth of jobs and paying the workers according to the level of difficulty, complexity and responsibility of the jobs they perform.

Job Evaluation

It is of great importance that the Human Resource Management Department determine with reasonable accuracy the relative worth of each job in terms of the demands that it makes on the employee who performs it. These demands and the qualifications that the employee must possess are determined through job analysis and are defined as job specifications. The relative worth of each job may be determined through the process of job evaluation.

The best way to minimize the problem of pay inequities is by job evaluation and salary classification.

Nature and Uses of Job Evaluation

Job evaluation means measuring the worth and importance of each job relative to other jobs in the organization for the purpose of determining wage and salary differentials.

The worth of a job is determined in the light of both internal relationships among positions in the organizations and external competitive conditions.

Job evaluation is the foundation of wage and salary administration. The job evaluation process is exacting. If an error occurs in the evaluation phase, it is mirrored throughout the entire compensation program. The administration of wages and salaries is relatively easy once jobs have been accurately evaluated into a viable salary structure that is keyed to competitive conditions.

The development of job evaluation dates as far as one thousand years before Christ. King Solomon made try at the evaluation of jobs. When he built a temple that took seven years to finish, he thought it well to classify his workers into three groups similar to our laborers, foremen, and artisans of today.

In the Middle Ages guilds were established. These guilds also classified their members into groups: the apprentice, journeyman and mastercraftsman.

In the Philippines, job evaluation has been used by several business firms and banking institutions.

Job evaluation concerns the job and not the person in the job. The important considerations are what the job requires, not what the man who holds the job can do.

In the administration of wages, a well-considered job evaluation program tends to make the wage level more satisfying to employees. It makes possible reasonable pay rates, simplifies solving of wage complaints, and affords a basis for regulating labor costs.

Objectives of Job Evaluation

Job evaluation seeks to determine for each job a rate range that is (a) internally consistent and (b) externally in line with general conditions in the local labor market. It specifically seeks to do the following:

1. Put group positions in their proper categories.
2. Maintain a scale for new employees, transferees and promotions.
3. Allow reasonable flexibility in coping with changes in the pay structure.
4. Facilitate personnel accounting and budgeting.
5. Ensure that payment of wages and salaries among the various structures does not go out of bounds.

Sub-Divisions of Job Evaluation

1. Job Analysis - This determines for each (a) its duties, responsibilities and working conditions and (b) its ability and knowledge requirements.
2. Job Classification - This assembles under appropriate titles individual jobs that require the same knowledge.
3. Job Grading - This groups job classifications into labor grades according to their ability and knowledge requirements.
4. Internal Job Pricing (Salary Schedules) - This determines for each salary grade, reasonable monetary differences: (a) vertically for the differences in the ability and knowledge requirements of job classifications (b) Horizontally for the differences in the performance and dependability of individuals.
5. External Job Pricing (Market Surveys) - This establishes for each salary grade monetary rate-rangers that are in line with general conditions in the local labor market.

Installing A Job Evaluation Program and a Wage and Salary System

Once the job analysis has been done—that is, gathering facts on duties and responsibilities of jobs and writing job descriptions for every job in the company—the actual evaluation takes place.

I. *Preparing the Job Evaluation Plan.*

Although numerous types of job evaluation plans are in company use, all plans revolve around two variables: (1) what is to be measured (the small job or elements of the job,) and (2) how it is to be measured (against a scale or against other jobs). There are four basic job evaluation plans:

A. *Ranking System.* This measures the small jobs against all the other jobs in the organization, one against another, until an order of magnitude is established from the lowest to the highest.

This system is particularly effective in companies with not more than 50 jobs. The method starts with a small group of key jobs that are familiar and compatible with the area and industry-going rates. Usually, committee members familiar with the jobs rank these jobs. An overall rank order is thereby established by comparing the descriptions of other jobs with those of the key jobs.

The following steps are suggested:

Step 1: Select the jobs to be ranked.

Step 2: Provide job descriptions. Evaluate jobs within their natural divisions, such as ranking factory jobs with factory jobs, and not factory jobs with clerical jobs.

Step 3: Select raters with knowledge of jobs to be ranked and the ability to give unbiased judgments and willingness to disregard current wages in rendering judgments.

Step 4: Organize for using the ranking method. Each rater independently ranks the job with which he is familiar. Then he meets the other raters to determine the proper rank order of each job.

Step 5: Develop a guide for committee members. Develop certain criteria for the common guidance of all the raters such as the need for responsibility, experience, education, skill, mental effort, physical efforts, and working conditions, etc.

Step 6: Rank the jobs in one of three principal ways (A,B & C):

A. *Using Job Description.* Analyze and compare the jobs by determining which jobs have the least and maximum skill requirements and arrange them from the lowest to the highest rank. Ranking jobs from low to high is exemplified under Table I:

Table I. **Rank Order of Jobs**

Rank	*Job Title*
1	Mechanic helper
2	Junior Mechanic
3	Senior Mechanic
4	Mechanic Supervisors
5	Chief Mechanic

To find the final rank, it is usually helpful to conduct the comparisons three consecutive times, with an interval allowance of one or two weeks. Compare the variation results of the three rankings made. Once the reasons for the variations have been established, a decision can be reached. The jobs are then placed under their respective rank orders as illustrated in Table II. The rankings are then ready for comparison with those done by other departments.

Table II. **Average of Job Rankings of Individual Rates**

Job	*1st Ranking*	*2nd Ranking*	*3rd Ranking*	*Averages*
A	1	2	1	1.3
B	2	2	1	1.6
C	3	3	3	3.0
D	4	5	4	4.3
E	4	5	5	4.6

Comparing jobs inter-departmentally is done through discussions of the general committee of raters. After the respective rankings have been appraised, the job's final rank order is then determined by majority vote or by rank averaging.

B. *Using Cards.* This method also utilizes the basic steps found in the job description method, with the only difference that in the former, the title of each job is written on a card. A set of such cards, together with a set of full job descriptions, is given to each rater who is instructed to study the descriptions thoroughly. In actual ranking, however, only the card is used.

C. *Using Paired Comparisons.* In this method, each job is paired with every other job in the series being rated. Of the two jobs paired, the rater determines which is the more difficult by using the skill requirements provided as guides. He underlines the job which he thinks requires more skills. See Figure 1.

Figure 1. **An Example of Paired Comparison Rating**

Instructions: *In each of the pairs of jobs listed below, underline the job which you believe is more difficult and should receive the higher wage. Please be sure to make a choice for each pair even though it may be hard to distinguish between the difficulty level of the two jobs.*

Information Clerk . . . . Mail Order Clerk
Mail Order Clerk . . . . Adjuster
Collection Clerk . . . . Transfer Clerk
Refund Clerk . . . . Information Clerk
Collection Clerk . . . . Mail Order Clerk

Adjuster	Collection Clerk
Information Clerk	Collection Clerk
Transfer Clerk	Adjuster
Information Clerk	Transfer Clerk
Refund Clerk	Transfer Clerk
Mail Order Clerk	Refund Clerk
Refund Clerk	Collection Clerk
Transfer Clerk	Mail Order Clerk
Adjuster	Refund Clerk
Adjuster	Information Clerk

Depending upon the number of times a job is compared by pairing it with another according to the difficulties inherent in both, the jobs under illustration will be ranked and arranged in a sequence progressing from low to high, as follows:

Job Title	Rank Order
Information Clerk	1
Transfer Clerk	2
Mail Order Clerk	3
Refund Clerk	4
Collection Clerk	5
Adjuster	6

Step 7: Integration of Rankings

For a small number of jobs, ranking may be undertaken wholly; but departmental ranking has to be used in a large number of jobs so as to limit them to a workable unit. That there may be one sequential listing of the jobs, such departmental ranking must be integrated.

The responsibility for integration may be relegated to the director of the program and his advisory committee, the over-all committee, or the original rankers. The rationale for the integration of departmental rankings is to provide the organization with a single list of job rankings for the company as a whole, and to establish horizontal and vertical equity among the various departments.

Figure 2. **Work Sheet For Comparing Departmental Ranking**

Rank Order	*Department* *Accounting*	*Purchasing*	*Production*
1	New-account Clerk Billing Clerk	Mail Clerk Shipping Clerk	Routing Clerk Coding Clerk
2	Junior Key Punch Operator Cash Clerk Junior Tabulating Machine Operator	Record Clerk Stockroom Clerk	File Clerk Junior Control Clerk Junior Draftsman
3	Verifier Operator Disbursement Clerk	Bonding Clerk Purchasing Order Clerk Receiving Clerk	Control Clerk Order Clerk
4	Key-punch Operator Junior Accounting Bookkeeping Machine Operator	Corresponding Clerk Typist	Work-sheet Typist

The horizontal alignment is checked by the committee to determine if all jobs in Rank 1 are equal in the job elements considered in the ranking process. If a job level exceeds that of the majority in the rank, this job moved into rank 2. Repeat the process from Rank 2. With a week or two of interval between studies, repeat the analysis until the jobs are complete and ready for placement into one sequential listing for the organization as a whole.

A preliminary procedure may be needed for a larger number of ranked jobs. This system compares jobs according to a final classification before they are put into a final rank order for the company as illustrated in Figure 3.

Rank all stenographic jobs under the respective departments according to the rank given them by the various departmental committees. Then the integration committee analyzes these jobs and makes the needed adjustments to a lower or higher rank.

When analysis and necessary adjustments have been made, the jobs are ready for placement so that the final rank order can be determined; and for all jobs, the final horizontal and vertical comparisons can be made.

Figure 3. **Functional Work Sheet For Comparing Job Ranking**

Functional Classification: Stenographic

Rank Order	*Accounting*	*Departments* *Purchasing*	*Production*
1			
2			
3			
4			

B. *Predetermined Grading Method.* This system establishes certain job grades, as well as a definition for each grade, against which job characteristics are matched for purpose of classification.

Determine according to their degree of importance the significantly different levels of job difficulty within each broad job grouping such as clerical, factory sales and executive.

Provide a carefully written grade-level description covering such basic elements as types of duties involved, qualifications and other requirements needed to guide judgment. Entrust to committees the key responsibilities of analyzing, and writing of job descriptions for proper classification of each job.

C. *Factor Comparison Method.* In this system invented by Eugene J. Benge, certain key jobs are rated; then the rest of the jobs are compared to these key jobs, which serve as yardsticks. The key jobs are ranked, but not against one another as complete jobs. Based on such characteristics as mental skills, physical effort, responsibility, and working conditions, separate comparisons are made. All other jobs are compared to those rankings which are converted into their money equivalents, or yardsticks.

The basic steps in developing the rating scale are as follows:

1. *Determine and develop the factors to be used in the plan.*

   Benge's factor-comparison plan includes five factors: mental effort, skill, physical effort, responsibility, and working conditions. The factors must be of basic significance for most jobs, broad and flexible for adaptation to varying situations with factor overlapping reduced to the minimum.

2. *Select and describe key jobs.* At the start some 10 to 25 key jobs are considered adequate.
   a. They should be a good cross section of all jobs in the office or plant, representing as many departments as possible.
   b. They should represent all pay levels from high to low within the scope of the plan.
   c. Their present rates of pay must be considered fair relative to other jobs within the company and in line with community rates.
   d. They must be stable, well-known jobs, the definitions of which can be clearly understood.
3. *Rank key jobs under each factor.* After the members of the rating committee fully agree on the description of each key job, each rater ranks independently the key jobs under each factor. The average ranking for each job and the ranking separately arrived at by five raters are shown in the key job Ranking Sheet for the Skill factor. The average thus obtained for each of the five factors is reflected in a summary sheet.

   If there is wide eviation in the distribution results of individual rankings, this means that the committee should meet to strengthen out differences in factor definitions or job requirements.
4. *Apportion money rates.* Apportion the current average pay rate for each key among the five factors. The basic question is: "Of the total rate for each job, how much should be regarded as being compensation for the skill required to perform the job, and how much for each of the other factors? Get the average of the submitted money equivalents by all the raters and summarize the resulting apportionment.

   Compare the original job rankings and the money ranking to provide a check. If discrepancies occur the committee should carefully discuss and consider desired changes in their job ratings under certain factors.
5. *Establish the Factor Comparison Scale and add supplementary jobs.* Drop the eliminated jobs and set up the remaining jobs in accordance with the Factor Comparison Rating Scale. To the scale should be added supplementary jobs. For these jobs there should be no disagreement on relative pay rates. On the basis of careful comparison with key jobs under each factor, the supplementary jobs are ordinarily slotted in.
6. *Evaluate the remaining jobs by the scales.* Rate the remaining jobs

on the scales by direct job-to-job comparisons under each factor. For example, between the jobs of tool-and die-maker and electrician A on the skill factor, the operating engineer job may be slotted, with consideration. Similarly determined are values for other factors, and the total value of a job thus established.

Use of Points Rather Than Monetary Values

Another practice in the factor comparison method is the use of points, instead of money, which are assigned to the values in the scale. This is to prevent the raters from being influenced by the use of money. A range of points is assigned to each of the factors. If a job, for example, is to be rated on the mental factor, the proper wage and salary level can be determined after the points are totalled. A tentative weighting of the factor relative to others is represented in the maximum points shown for each factor; but factor-comparison scales are open-ended in that the scale for any one factor can be extended upward any time the need for it arises.

Another important variation in the original Benge Method is that each scale has only a limited number of steps as choices for rating-committee members, rather than on unbroken scale of points from minimum to maximum.

D. *Point Rating Method*. Under this system, jobs are first rated and given a point total. Monetary equivalents are then assigned to the point totals. Point totals are obtained by adding the points given for each of a number of factors. Usually, 10 to 12 factors are used. To determine the points to be assigned to any one factor, the rater refers to a manual which gives the degrees and equivalent points for each factor of the same job. This manual serves as a yardstick to which all jobs are compared.

In setting up a point rating plan, observe the following:

1. Use a professionally prepared plan in its entirety, without modifications.
2. Use one or more prepared plans which may be modified.
3. Originate an entirely new plan.

Whichever of these three approaches is used:

1. Study the jobs to be evaluated and determine the factors or characteristics that can measure job worth.
2. Determine the degrees or levels needed to measure the presence of each factor in all jobs.
3. Define factors and degrees.

4. Assign weights to factors and degrees in proportion to their relative importance.

In point rating, individual jobs are measured against factors, degrees, and weights included on the basic plan. Thus, consider carefully the four basic steps:

I. *Selecting Factors*

The jobs have to be grouped according to their respective characteristics. The grouping will account for major differences in job requirements. Thus you must set up separate plans for shop, clerical, and executive jobs; additional groupings should be provided for sales, professional, and technical jobs.

To give the rater an idea of the scope of possible factors that may be included in a given plan, four headings of skills, effort, responsibility and working conditions are presented below:

A. *Skill factors* may include all abilities that an employee must bring to a given job or develop while on the job:

Accuracy	*Complexity*
Accuracy of calculation	Co-ordination
Accuracy of measurement	Co-operation
Accuracy of selection	Decisions
Accuracy of reading	Details
Accuracy of record	Education
Adaptability	Foresight
Ajustability	Ingenuity
Analysis	Initiative
Analytical ability	Innovativeness
Aptitude	Job Knowledge
Artistic ability	Job Skill
Attention to orders	Judgment
Knowing other operations	Mentality
Knowledge of equipment & tools	Motor skill
Knowledge of materials	Originality
Leadership	Personal requirements
Length of schooling	Physical Skill
Management ability	Precision
Manual dexterity	Previous training

Manual Skill
Mechanical Ability
Mental Capability

Resourcefulness
Tact and diplomacy
Training time
Versatility

B. *Effort factors* measure the energy, both mental and physical that must be expended in performing jobs.

Alertness
Application
Endurance
Exertion
Fatigue
Honesty of effort
Memory
Mental Effort

Mental stability
Monitory
Muscular Co-ordination
Physical effort
Physical pace or energy
Quickness of comprehension
Strength
Visual effort

C. *Responsibility factors* include all environmental conditions that must be endured by the job holder.

Avoidance of shutdown
Company
Confidential data
Cost of errors
Effect on subsequent operations
Equipment
Goodwill
Maintenance of pace

Material
Money
Product
Quality
Safety of others
Reports and records
Work of others

D. *Working Condition factors* include all environmental conditions that must be endured by the job holder.

Accidental hazards
Clothing spoilage
Discomfort
Environment deterrents
Eyestrain

Body contact
Current expense
Health hazard
Nervous strain
Surroundings

Determining degrees needed. The number of degrees usually differs for each factor. In determining degrees, be sure some jobs will actually fall at each degree included; the weight allotted to a factor becomes less when one or more of the top degrees of a factor are never used.

Defining Factor and Degree. Definitions of factors should be concise, objective and positive.

Weighting Factors. Certain characteristics are more important than others in measuring the difficulty and responsibility of occupations. The tool-and-die-making shop, for example, puts the greatest weight on skill factors, while a foundry shop puts the greatest weight on working conditions. Establishing factors weightings is usually based on pooled human judgment, past experience, or trial and error.

Weighting are often in the form of percentages of the total points allowed by a plan.

Assigning points to factors and degrees. Request the committee to assign a percentage to the different factors included in the plan, based upon their relative importance. The factors receiving lowest percentage are considered in the lowest degree, and these percentages then become the points.Point weights for higher degrees may then be determined.

There are three methods of allotting points to degrees: under constant progression, geometric series, and arbitrary progression.

II. *Installing the Program*

Explain and sell the Program to top management. Explain the major objectives of the program, why the organization needs such a program, the experience of other organizations, the limitations of the program and its effects on costs such as cost of installation, cost of operation and cost of maintenance.

Determine who will do the job. The program should be communicated to all employees. A committee should be appointed to evaluate jobs. A typical committee for the evaluation of management-level jobs would consist of a group of the top vice-president or senior vice-presidents. For lower-level and clerical-type jobs, the committee could consist of major department managers.

Determine how the job evaluation is to be done, which jobs are to be evaluated, how far up the organization structure the program is to be applied, what method is to be used in the evaluation process, the extent and nature of supervisory and employee participation.

Assign responsibilities for installing the program. Organize the job evaluation staff, placing it in the overall organizational structure. Then select and train the staff.

Establish the procedures and tools for job evaluation.

III. *Job Grading*

Evaluate each job according to duties, responsibilities, working conditions and job specifications. Grouping individual jobs that require the same knowledge is called job classification. This is a listing of all positions as determined by function. A job classification schedule is usually maintained by a company for the managerial, supervisory and rank and file employees. Job Grading is the process that groups job classifications into labor grades according to the importance of their basic ability and knowledge requirements.

So that different degrees of responsibilities, knowledge, and skill requirements are taken into account in compensating employees, positions are sometimes analyzed, rated, and classified into the following job grades:

Job Classification Plan and Job Grades

Job Grade I
- Administrative Services Clerk

Job Grade II
- General Clerk (Collection)
- General Clerk
- Key punch Operator
- Maintenance Men

Job Grade III
- Distributing Clerk
- Clearing Clerk (Cash)
- Foreign Exchange Clerk
- Junior Analyst
- Junior Bookkeeper
- Junior Credit Investigator
- Junior Marketing Representative
- Junior Personnel Assistant
- Junior Teller
- Librarian
- Loan Clerk
- New Accounts Clerk

Secretary
Secretaries Clerk
Senior Clerk
Senior Collection Clerk
Travelling Teller

Job Grade IV

Analyst
Assistant Trader
Bookkeeper
Communications Assistant
Credit Investigator
Foreign Exchange Assistant
Junior Credit Examiner
Loan Assistant
Marketing Representative
Personnel Assistant
Securities Custodian
Senior Clearing Clerk (Cash)]
Senior Distributing Clerk
Senior Loan Clerk
Senior New Accounts
Senior Secretary
Teller

Job Grade V

Executive Secretary
Purchasing Assistant
Senior Analyst
Senior Credit Examiner
Senior Bookkeeper
Senior Personnel Assistant
Staff Assistant (BDG - Account Manager)
Staff Assistant
System Analyst
Trader (MMD)
Trading Assistant
Trust Assistant

Job Grade VI

Supervisor - Collection (cash)
Foreign Exchange Supervisor

Head Teller
Loans Supervisor
Senior Systems Analyst
Senior Executive Secretary
Senior Trader
Supervisory Analyst
Supervisory Bookkeeper
Supervisory Credit Investigator
Supervisor, Clearing (Cash)
Supervisor, Distributing (Cash)

Job Grade VII
Bank Architect
Managing Trader
Project Coordinator
Senior Staff Assistant
Senior Supervisory Analyst
Senior Trust Assistant
Supervisory Audit Examiner

The classification of a position into its proper job grade is based on its total point ratings arrived at by applying the system applicable to the particular category of the position.

IV. *Designing Salary Structure and Pricing*

The process that determines for each salary grade reasonable monetary differences—vertically for the differences in the ability and knowledge requirements of job classifications and horizontally for the differences in the performance and dependability of individuals—is called internal Job Pricing or salary schedules/structure/scale.

The basic purpose of a salary scale is to equitably compensate employees for what they do and how well they do it. Scales are necessary to provide salary differentials between levels to compensate for the differences in the ability and knowledge requirement of various job classifications. In addition, the salary range is provided to compensate for different standards of job experience and performance.

The following is an example of a Salary Scale:

Job Grade	*Hiring Rate*	*Minimum Regular Rate*	*Maximum Regular Rate*
I	P 240	P 260	P 395
II	305	350	530
III	385	440	670
IV	460	530	805
V	540	620	945
VI	615	710	1080
VII	695	800	1215

Hiring Rate is the rate which a new employee receives for a probationary period of six months. If a regular employee is recruited from within to fill a position in a higher job grade, he may first be placed at the hiring rate subsequently adjusted to the minimum regular rate.

Minimum Regular Rate is the minimum rate at which a regular employee is paid at each job grade.

Maximum Regular Rate & Red-Circle Employees. In technical lingo, if an employee's salary is already above the maximum regular rate for a particular position, he is a "red-circle employee" or his salary is "out of line".

The determination of wages or salaries in money terms is pricing, which ultimately depends on the nature of the economy prevailing at a particular period. For a consistent rational approach, the following are the considerations in job pricing:

1. Wage Competition. The market sets prices of labor. A policy decision may be made whether to meet the market price, to pay more or less and in what ways. A policy decision may be made whether to meet the market price, to pay more or less, and in what ways.
2. Legal Requirements. The requirements of minimize wage and other laws.
3. The "cost-of-living" allowance is not viewed with equal favor by labor nor employees. In periods of inflation labor strongly demands that wages be tied in with the "cost of living". When prices of consumer goods are down, then labor will not consider this index but the employer will.
4. Productivity. The performance of a worker on a given job can be

measured and rewarded under some form of incentive pay systems.

5. "Ability to Pay". Ability to pay from the angle of labor, means greater share in the distribution of income of the company; on management's side, it involves the continuous balancing of the allocation of resources in which labor shares in wages.
6. Power of Unions. The collective bargaining and use of other legal forms of economic pressure exercises a strong influence on wage determination.
7. Non-Economic Factors. The wage may represent other non-economic factors such as seniority, family allowance, hardship pay, etc.

An accurate, objective wage-and-salary structure helps a Company to:

1. Pay employees according to job difficulty or performance.
2. Attract and retain desirable employees.
3. Avoid excessive wage and salary payments.
4. Facilitate day-to-day wage payment practices.
5. Explain pay differentials to employees.
6. Provide a sound basis for budget estimate.
7. Simplify collective bargaining.
8. Fit new jobs into the existing job and wage structure.

Most companies have separate pay structures for white collar and blue collar employees. Other companies use a single structure for all but top executives. The selection of a single or multiple structure depends upon the circumstances of each specific organization.

With regard to the internal nature of the pay structure, an organization may choose between flat rates (and a single wage line) or rate ranges (with three wage lines, an average plus upper and lower limits) and its three major types of rate ranges: (1) overlapping, (2) butt-to-butt, and (3) gap. Rate ranges are most frequently figured separately for each labor grade. Overlapping rate ranges usually permit a larger number of rate ranges and require more explanation to employees about pay differentials. A butt-to-butt range is the type where the top rate for one labor grade is exactly equal to the bottom rate for the next higher labor grade. In the gap range structure, there exists a gap between the top rate for one labor grade and the bottom rate of the next labor grade.

STUDY/REVIEW QUESTION

1. What are the steps involved in job evaluation?
2. What are the Filipino values related to human resource motivation?
3. What does a Filipino worker look for in a job?
4. Enumerate the steps in installing a Job Evaluation Program and a Wage and Salary System.
5. Describe the job pricing system in one company or organization.

SUGGESTED ACTIVITIES AND ASSIGNMENT

1. Secure from any firm the tools used in making a job evaluation and make a critique of them.
2. Interview a Compensation or Salary Officer on how his organization's Salary System operates.
3. Make a list of Filipino values which interplay in forming a Salary System in the Philippines.

REFERENCES FOR FURTHER READING

Andres, Tomas D. *Understanding Filipino Values: A Management Approach.* Quezon City: New Day Publishers, 1984.

Martinez, Esdras T. *Human Resources Management.* Manila: GIC Enterprise & Co., Inc. 1979.

Sison, Perfecto S. *Personnel and Human Resources Management.* Manila: Rex Book Store, 1981.

16

LAWS ON WAGES AND WORKING HOURS IN THE PHILIPPINES

"THE STATE shall afford protection to labor, promote full employment, ensure equal work opportunities regardless of sex, race or creed, and regulate the relations between workers and employees. The State shall assure the rights of workers to self-organization, collective bargaining, security of tenure, and just and humane conditions of work. The State may provide for compulsory arbitration," says the 1973 Constitution of the Philippines.

The laws that concern the above provisions are the Labor Code of the Philippines as amended and the other laws that are part of Labor and Social Legislation in the country, namely, laws related to the Labor Code like P.D. No. 928, as amended (on minimum wage), P.D. No. 851, as amended (on 13th month pay),and P.D. No. 525, as amended (on emergency allowance), and P.D. No. 823 as amended (on strikes and lockouts and foreign activity in the labor field) and social security laws like the Social Security Law, as amended, Revised Government Service Insurance Act and the Philippine Medical Care Act, as amended.

The Rights of Workers in the Philippines With Regard to Wages:

The International Covenant on Economic, Social and Cultural Rights speaks of the right of everyone to just and favorable conditions of work which ensure, in particular:

1. Remuneration which provides all workers, as a minimum with:
   a. Fair wages and equal remuneration for work of equal value without distinctions of any kind, women in particular being guaranteed conditions of work not inferior to those enjoyed by men, with equal pay for equal work;
   b. A decent living for themselves and their families (Art. 7).

The Philippine Labor Law provides for the following rights:

1. The right to statutory minimum wages (99) (Pres. Decree No. 928, as amended by P.D. No 1364 and 1389)
2. The right to a minimum wage duly fixed for an industry (124).
3. The right to fair and reasonable wage rates when the payment of wages is by results (101).
4. The right to an emergency allowance (P.D. No. 525), as amended.
5. The right to pay for a 13th month (P.D. No. 051), as amended.
6. The right to share in the service charge collected by hotels, restaurants and similar establishments as regards those working in these establishments.(96).
7. The right to equal remuneration for work of equal value (135).
8. The right to be paid wages in legal tender, (102) at certain regular intervals (103) and at or near the place of undertaking (104).
9. The right to be paid directly (105).
10. The right of an employee of a contractor, who is in turn performing work for another, to claim unpaid wages not only against his direct employer (the contractor) but against his indirect employer (the person for whom the contractor has performed some work) (106).
11. The right to enjoy first preference as regards unpaid wages (110).
12. In connection with an action to recover unpaid wages, the right to pay attorney's fees not to exceed ten percent of the amount of wages recovered. (111).
13. The right to dispose of wages without any limitation or interference from the employer (112).
14. The right against any deduction from wages, including deposits for loss or damage, except as duly authorized (113, 114).
15. The right against retaliatory measures that an employer may take against a worker who has filed any complaint against his employer or testified or is about to testify in such proceedings or constitute any proceedings.
16. The right against the elimination or reduction of benefits enjoyed at the time of the promulgation of the Labor Code (100).1

17. As regards a house helper, the right to an original contract for not more than two years (142), the right to a minimum wage (143), the right to an opportunity for education (146), the right to just and humane treatment (147), the right to board, lodging and medical attendance free of charge (148), the right to an indemnity for unjust termination (149), the right to leave the service (150), and the right to an employment certification (151).

The Rights of Workers in the Philippines With Regard to Rest, Working Hours and Holidays:

The International Covenant on Economic, Social and Cultural Rights speaks of "the right to just and favorable conditions of work which ensure, in particular rest, leisure and reasonable limitation of working hours and periodic holidays with pay, as well as remuneration for public holidays (Art. 7).

The Philippine Labor Law provides for the following rights:

1. Considering that the normal hours of work shall not exceed eight hours a day, (83) the right not to be required to perform overtime work except in emergency (89) and the right to overtime pay for overtime work (87).
2. The right to a meal period (85).
3. The right to night shift differential pay (86).
4. The right to a weekly rest day (91).
5. The right not to be required to work on a rest day except for emergency work (92).
6. The right to additional compensation for rest day or holiday work (91).
7. The right to holiday pay for a regular holiday as differentiated from one which is not a regular but a special holiday (94).
8. The right to a service incentive leave (95).

Minimum Wage Law

Republic Act No. 602 known as the Minimum Wage law applies to employees in private enterprises, be they in agriculture, industry or trade. Employees of religious, charitable and educational organizations are also covered by the law. The law covers all employees in the government service-national, provincial, municipal and city-or those in government-owned or controlled corporations.

This law does not apply to farm tenancy household service and employment in needlework in the houses or in any cottage industry registered with the National Cottage Industries, Development Authority. The Minimum Wage Law is applicable to all employees except homeworkers engaged in needle work by hand, workers on farm tenancy, domestic servants, retail or service establishment that regularly employ not more than five employees, and apprentices, handicapped workers, students and graduates of Nautical School.

The Objectives of this Law are:

1. To maintain workers in a state of good health, efficiency and general well-being,
2. To serve as leverage for collection wage bargaining,
3. To afford fair return of investment to the investor, owner or operator.

The minimum wages for agricultural and non-agricultural employees are periodically revised. Also the statutory minimum wages can be increased in an industry. Hence the Minimum Wage Law includes a Wage Commission.

Payment shall be made at or near the place of undertaking, except as the Minister of Labor may prescribe to ensure protection of wages (Art. 103, Implementing Rules, New Labor Code).

No employer shall pay his employees in any bar, night or day club, drinking establishment, massage clinic or dance hall, or other similar places where games are played with stakes of money or things representing money, except in the case of persons employed in said places (Sec. 4, Rule IV, Book, Implementing Rules, New Labor Code).

Payment of wages of a deceased employee shall be made to his heirs without the necessity of intestate proceedings (Sec. 6, Rule IV, Book III, Implementing Rules, New Labor Code).

Hours and Conditions of Work

Articles 82 to 90 of Title I of Book IV of the Labor Code and Rules I and I-A of Book III of the Implementing Rules and Regulations Code govern the hours of workers.

The normal hours of work of any employee shall not exceed (8) eight hours a day. Hours worked include all hours during which the employee is available to the employer. They include (a) all time during which on employee is required to be on duty or to be at a prescribed work place; and (b) all time during which an employee is permitted to work.

Waiting time spent by an employee shall be considered as hours worked if waiting is an integral part of his work or if the employee is required or engaged by the employer to wait.

Attendance at lectures, meetings, training programs and similar activities shall not be considered as working time if:

1. Attendance is outside the employee's regular working hours;
2. Attendance is voluntary; and
3. The employee does not perform any productive work during such attendance.

Meal and Rest Periods

A worker is entitled to not less than one hour time-off for regular meals, and to rest periods or coffee breaks of five to twenty minutes except as provided in the Implementing Rules and Regulations.

This meal period may be shortened under the following conditions:

1. When the work is non-manual in nature or does not involve strenuous physical exertion;
2. When the establishment regularly operates not less than sixteen hours a day;
3. When there are actual or impending emergencies or when there is urgent work to be performed in machinery, equipment or installations to avoid serious loss which the employer would suffer;
4. When the work is necessary to prevent serious loss of perishable goods.

A shorter meal period of not less than 20 minutes may be allowed, provided that this shorter meal period is credited as compensable hours worked.

Hours of Work of Hospital and Clinic Personnel

Health personnel in cities and municipalities with a population of at least one million, or in hospitals and clinics with a bed capacity of at least 100 shall hold regular office hours for 5 days a week, or a total of

40 hours a week, exclusive of time for meals. However, where the exigencies of the work require that such personnel work for 6 days or 48 hours, they shall be entitled to an additional compensation of at least 30% of their regular wage for work on the sixth day.

Hospitals and clinics, for purposes of the 40 hour-5-day work law, are defined as places devoted to the treatment of illness, disease, injury or deformity, or supplying obstetrical or other medical or nursing care.

Hospital and clinics' personnel covered by the law include all persons employed by any private or public hospital or clinic, and are not limited to resident physicians, nurses, nutritionists, dietitians, pharmacists, social workers, laboratory technicians, paramedical technicians, psychologists, midwives and attendants.

For this group of personnel, "week" shall be the work week of 168 consecutive hours, or 7 consecutive 24-hour work days beginning at the same hour and on the same calendar day each week.

Health personnel may be required to work for more than five days or 40 hours a week when the exigencies of the service so require, provided that the employee is paid additional compensation equivalent to at least 30% of his regular wage.

Night Shift Differential Pay

The Labor Code grants the right to night shift differential pay in recognition of the discomforts, disadvantages and dangers of working at night.

For night work performed on ordinary days, an employee shall be paid not less than 10% of his regular wage for each hour of night work-i.e., between 6:00 in the evening and 6:00 in the morning.

For night work performed on rest days and/or special holidays, an employee shall be paid an amount equivalent to his regular wage plus at least 30% additional amount of not less than 10% of such premium pay for each hour of work performed.

For night work performed on regular holidays, an employee shall be paid his regular wage during these days plus an additional compensation of not less than 10% of the hourly rate for each hour of work performed.

When an employee is asked to work after his work schedule, he shall be entitled to his regular wage plus at least 25%, plus an additional amount of not less than 10% of this overtime rate for each hour of work performed between 10:00 p.m. to 6:00 a.m.

Employees denied the benefit of receiving night shift differentiated pay are the following:

1. Those in the government and any of its political subdivisions, including government-owned or controlled corporations;
2. Those of retail and service establishments regularly employing not more than five workers;
3. Domestic helpers and persons in the personal service of another;
4. Managerial employees; and
5. Field personnel and other employees whose time and performance are unsupervised by the employer, including those who are engaged on a task or contract basis; those who are fully commissioned or who are paid a fixed amount for performing work irrespective of the time consumed in its performance.

Overtime

A covered employee who works beyond 8 hours on an ordinary working day shall be paid for overtime work an amount equivalent to his regular wage plus at least 25%.

A covered employee who works on his designated rest day shall be paid an additional compensation as premium pay of not less than 30% of his regular wage. If he works on such a rest day in excess of 8 hours, he shall be paid for an additional 8 hours of work plus at least 30% thereof.

An employee who works on a special holiday shall be governed by the same rule enunciated for a covered employee who works on his rest day.

An employee who works on any regular holiday shall be paid in addition at least 20% of his regular daily wage. If he works on such a holiday in excess of 8 hours, he shall receive additional compensation for the overtime work equivalent to his rate for the first 3 hours of such holiday work plus at least 30% thereof.

The regular holidays contemplated by the Labor Code are: (a) New Year's Day: (b) Maundy Thursday; (c) Good Friday; (d) April 9; (e) May 1; (f) June 12; (g) November 30; (i) December 25; (j) December 30; and (k) the day designated by law for a general election or a national referendum or plebiscite.

Employees who are uniformly paid by the month, irrespective of the number of working days therein, with a salary of not less than the statutory or minimum wage, shall be presumed to be paid for all days of the month.

A covered employee who is on leave of absence with pay shall also be entitled to receive holiday pay.

If a regular holiday falls on a Sunday, the following day (Monday) shall be considered a special holiday for purposes of the Labor Code, unless it is also a regular holiday.

Where there are two successive holidays, like Maundy Thursday and Good Friday, an employee may not be paid for both holidays if he absents himself from work on the day immediately preceding the first holiday. If he works on the first holiday, he is entitled to his holiday pay on the second holiday.

The workers who are not entitled to receive overtime pay are government employees, managerial employees as defined under Section 2, Rule I of Book III of the Implementing Rules and Regulations, domestic servants, workers who are paid by results and non-agricultural as managerial employees.

Weekly Rest Period

All employers, whether operating for profit or not, including public utilities operated by private persons, shall provide their employees with a weekly rest day as provided in the Labor Code.

As a general rule, the employer may schedule the rest day of his employees as he sees fit. The determination of a weekly rest period may be done through collective bargaining. The preference of the employee as to his weekly rest day, if based on religious grounds shall be respected by the employer. However, in case of necessity, the employer may schedule the weekly rest day of the employee's choice for only two days in a month.

The employee shall make known his preference to the employer in writing at least seven days before the desired effectivity of the initial rest day so preferred.

When the weekly rest day is given to all employees simultaneously the employer shall make known such rest period by means of a written notice posted conspicuously in the workplace at least one week before it becomes effective.

When the rest period is not granted collectively, the employer shall inform the employees of their respective schedules of weekly rest through written notices one week in advance.

An employee who works on his scheduled rest day shall be paid an additional compensation of at least 30% of his regular wage. Work performed on Sundays shall be paid an additional compensation of at least 30% of the regular wage when Sunday is the established rest day or when an employee has no regular work day and no regular rest days can be scheduled.

When special holiday work falls on the employee's scheduled rest day, he shall be entitled to an additional compensation of at least 50% of his regular wage.

Meals and /or break periods are not to be credited against the weekly rest period.

STUDY/REVIEW QUESTIONS

1. Explain the rights of workers according to the Labor Code with regard to wages.
2. Define night shift differential pay.
3. Describe the laws with regard to working hours.

SUGGESTED ACTIVITIES AND ASSIGNMENT

1. Interview a worker on the rules of his company with regard to working hours. Ask him whether those rules are being followed by both the employees and the employer.
2. Secure a time sheet from any organization and analyze its contents.

REFERENCES FOR FURTHER READING

Angeles, Conrado P. et al. *Principles of Personnel Administration.* Quezon City: R.M. Garcia Publishing House, 1981.

Bacungan, Froilan M. "The Rights of Workers in the Philippines," University of the Philippines Law Center, 1980.

Ministry of Labor and Employment. *Labor Code of the Philippines.*

Sison, Perfecto S. *Personnel and Human Resources Management.* Manila: Rex Book Store, 1981.

Study Materials used in the Workers' Institute on Labor Law-University of the Philippines Institute Staff, Quezon City, 1980.

17

HUMAN RESOURCE BENEFITS AND SERVICES

HUMAN RESOURCE benefits are compensations other than direct wages or incentive pay. They are sometimes called fringe benefits, that is, something on the edge. Human resource benefits have considerable value in promoting employee morale.

History of Human Resource Benefits

As early as the 1920's many employees believed the following:

1. Employees are entitled to more of the benefits of capitalism than was represented by their wages.
2. They should "look after" their employees because of their lesser economic and educational status.
3. They should care for employees in time of need or emergency.
4. They should make employees feel secure.

During the 1940's the unions pushed for additional fringe benefits. Increasing education and employment opportunities made the employees take the initiative in demanding more benefits.

During World War II when the U.S. Wage Stabilization Board imposed controls on wages so as to prevent a runaway inflation, companies provided special inducements such as pension and welfare programs, paid vacations, sick leave, and health and life insurance.

During the post war period, as the cost of living began to level off about 1948, it was generally accepted that employees should have better standards of health and welfare in their employment. Furthermore, the benefits granted during the war were continued because employers could not withdraw them anymore without causing labor problems.

In recent years human resource benefits have been a product of legislation and government regulations. Today employees are demanding more and more benefits.

Installing an Effective Human Resource Benefits Program

The program should yield maximum benefits to employer and employee.

In determining the optimum fringe combination, Foegen suggests the following activities:[1]

1. Assemble basic cost data of all of the fringe items.
2. Judge how much money is available to cover the cost of all fringe benefits for a given future period.
3. Assign preference values to each fringe item, using some type of weighted numerical scale which takes into account the legal requirements, employee preference, and management preference.
4. Decide on the optimum combination of the various benefits.

The steps in installing an effective human resource benefits program should be logical, objective, planned, and integrated.

Objectives of the HR Benefit Program

The goals of an HR Benefit Program should be in harmony with overall human resource management policies. The objectives of the company in giving benefits should be the following:

1. To carry out their social responsibility to their employees.
2. To maintain and enhance the effectiveness of their workforce.
3. To meet union demands and increased government regulations.
4. To maintain the worker's living standards.
5. To boost employee morale, which is a motivating factor or incentive.

Principles on HR Benefits Program

The following are guidelines for granting fringe benefits to employees:[2]

1. The program should mutually benefit management and employees. The money spent in benefits should result in increased production, higher efficiency, greater loyalty, and better morale. Two common fringe benefits—vacation leave with pay and the merienda break—are recognized as having considerable value to the employee's physical and mental health.
2. The program should enhance the operation of the business. Take the case of the sick leave benefit, if this is misunderstood by the employees as an entitlement, this can impede the operation.
3. The cost of the program should be within the capacity of the company.
4. The implementation of the benefit program must be uniform and equitable. Policies on eligibility for fringe benefits must be objectively formulated and clearly defined.
5. The benefit program should be based on measurable factors such as employee earnings or length of service. An example of a progressive method of granting benefits is granting vacation leaves based on the number of years of service.
6. There should be employee participation in the Benefit Programs. One of the prime requisites of a successful benefits program is that it receive the support of employees. Benefits such as recreation and athletic progress can be handled by employees on their own time.
7. The costs of the fringe benefits should be made known to the employees. Such costs should be communicated to employees in order that they may understand that the paycheck tells only part of the wage story. The fringe expenditures can be explained to employees as additional "earnings" or "payments". In some companies, the employees share the cost of fringe benefits. This restrains the employees from making excessive demands on management.

Types of Human Resources Benefits and Services

The five major types of benefits and services are:

A. *Financial Benefits and Services*

These are intended to provide financial assistance to the employees and their families and are concerned directly with the employee's personal finances.

1. *Productivity-Sharing Plan* - This is an output-based plan designed to appeal to the cooperative instincts of large groups. Savings resulting from a deduction in labor or production costs are divided among the employees. The kinds of productivity-sharing plans are the following:[3]

a. *Scanlon Plan*. In this plan, originated by Joe Scanlon, joint labor and management committees solicit employees' suggestions on how efficiency can be increased, production costs reduced, and waste eliminated.

It places heavy emphasis upon employee cooperation and teamwork and benefits are to be shared through steady employment, higher wages, and better working conditions.

b. *Rucher Plan*. In this plan, the financial incentive is based upon the historic relationship of the total earnings of hourly employees to the production values that they create. That is, for every one percent increase in production value that is achieved, the workers covered by the plan receive an additional bonus of one percent of their total payroll costs. This system is also known as the Share of Production Plan (S.O.P.).[4]

c. *Employee Profit-Sharing*. This is an agreement freely entered into by management and employees by which the employees receive a share, fixed in advance, of the profits. On the part of the management, there is a definite commitment to pay, over and above the fair wage, a definite percentage of company profits or declared dividends.

Employee profit-sharing instills a sense of partnership and provides group incentive and employee security.

The profits are shared either in cash or deferred payment plan wherein money is placed in a trust fund to be disbursed usually when the employee is disabled, laid off, or retired, or in a combination of cash and deferred payments.

d. *Employee Stock Ownership*. In this plan employees buy stocks which grow and flourish during prosperity and die or are discontinued during depression.

2. *Credit Union* - This is a cooperative society incorporated for promoting thrift among its members and creating a source of

credit for them at legitimate rates of interest.[5] It thus serves as a lending institution from which the employee may borrow money at a low rate of interest.

3. *Company Financial Assistance* – Some companies make loans to assist employees in the purchase of houses, cars, etc. to be repaid in regular amounts deducted from the employee's salary.
4. *Insurance Programs* – Some companies grant group life insurance. As a rule, the amount of life insured coverage for an individual employee depends on his salary level, although the trend continues toward union-negotiated, company-financed plans.

   Group medical, surgical, and dental plans are also financial services granted by companies to employees.
5. *Pension Plans* – This system makes periodic payments to workers who are retired from the company for reasons provided for in the plan.
6. *Subsidized Company Store and Cafeteria/Canteen* – This is a system wherein company-operated stores sell products at discounted prices or at cost to employees.

   Some companies also provide a cafeteria/canteen with subsidized prices.

B. *Professional Services*

Some companies have in their staff professionals who provide services to their employees at no expense. Below are some of these services:

1. Legal Accountancy Advice – Attorneys and accountants, employed in most of the larger companies can be of much help to employees. Official legal documents requiring the seal of a notary public can be duly notarized for the employee by the company lawyers. The company lawyers also provide help in drawing up a will, giving advice in contracts, and assisting employees in locating qualified lawyers to handle complicated legal cases.

   Similarly, the company accountant assists employees in computing tax returns or those who have minor problems in connection with the returns.
2. Employee Counseling Services – Some companies employ the services of professional counselors, psychiatrists or clinical psychologists to help employees with emotional disturbances.
3. Medical and Dental Benefits – Companies maintain a Dental and Medical Clinic with a permanent physician, dentist, and nurse.

4. Library and Reading Room - Some companies provide a library and reading room wherein technical and management books and scientific magazines are available for employees.
5. Employee Suggestion System - This system encourages and rewards the submission of ideas for improving operational efficiency.

   A committee evaluates these suggestions, promptly acknowledge all suggestions and reward those with acceptable suggestions in terms of both recognition and money.
6. Religious Services - Some organizations have priest/chaplains for mass celebrations on Saturdays and when religious holy days fall on working days. Holy Week retreats are also provided for employees.

C. *Recreational Services*

Companies provide employees with opportunities for the fruitful use of their leisure hours.

1. Athletic Programs - Sports programs are offered by some companies in which personnel may participate on a voluntary basis. This may be intramural or extramural sports. Out door sports are basketball, football, volleyball, golf, baseball or tennis; indoor sports are bowling, cards, etc. In addition to these intramural programs, some companies have also teams for extramural athletic contests and tournaments.
2. Social Programs - To strengthen and promote interpersonal relationships among employees, social functions are provided by some firms. They hold yearly company picnics or excursions, Christmas parties and sometimes dances. Occasionally employees' spouses or their entire families are included in these socials.
3. Special Awards - Appropriate service awards are presented to eligible employees in recognition of long and faithful service.

D. *Housing and Transportation Services*

1. Free Living Quarters - In some companies whose branch offices are located in the provinces, the company provides housing facilities.
2. Transportation Allowances - Some companies grant transportation allowances to their employees. Others offer the use of company cars or shuttle buses for use of their workers.

E. *Legally Required Benefits and Services*

1. Government Service Insurance System (GSIS) and Social Security System (SSS) Benefits

   The Social Security Act (Republic Act No. 1161) protects employees against the hazards of disability, sickness, old age and death. All employers are required by the Act to become members of the SSS from the very first day of company operations and all employees from their first day of employment. Thus, both employee and employer are required to pay a monthly contribution based on the monthly earnings of the employee.

   Social Security benefits such as salary, educational, and housing loans, disability and retirement plans, are available and follow government regulations.

   The GSIS offers the same benefits to government employees.

2. Medicare

   In addition to the SSS, the government enacted the Philippine Medical Care Act of 1969 (Republic Act 6111) which requires an equal contribution from each employee and from the company. Medical benefits can be availed of in accordance with the provisions of the law. The Medicare Act provides hospitalization expenses, surgical expenses and medical expense benefits.

3. Workmen's Compensation

   The Workmen's Compensation Law provides that an employee who becomes ill because of an accident which arose in the course of employment, or whose illness is aggravated by the nature of his employment, is entitled to compensation equivalent to a certain percent of his average daily wage. For Temporary Total Disability, the income benefit is ninety percent (90%) of the employee's Average Daily Salary Credit as determined by the System. For Permanent Total Disability, an employee shall, until his death, be paid by the System a monthly income benefit, plus 10% for each dependent child, but not exceeding five, beginning with the youngest and without substitution.[6]

4. Thirteen-month Pay

   Presidential Decree 851 provides that all employers are to pay all their employees receiving a basic salary of not more than P1,000.00 a month, regardless of the nature of employment, a thirteenth-month pay not later than Dec. 24, of every year.

5. Retirement

   Under the Labor Code, Article 297, any employee who reaches

the age of sixty-five years shall be retired, unless his employment is for a definite period beyond such age, or is, with his consent, continued by the employer.

In case of retirement, the employee shall be entitled to receive such benefits as he may have earned under this code and any collective bargaining or other agreements.

STUDY/REVIEW QUESTIONS

1. Define human resource benefits.
2. What are the different types of human resource benefits and services?
3. What are the Filipino values and Philippine customs that we should have in mind in formulating a human resource benefits and services program?

SUGGESTED ACTIVITIES AND ASSIGNMENT

1. Secure an Employees Manual/Handbook from any organization and analyze the benefits listed.
2. Make a list of Filipino values that are related to human resource benefits.
3. Interview a Personnel Manager and ask him to explain to you the different benefits given by his company to its employees.

NOTES

[1]Joseph H. Foegen, "Product Mix For Fringe Benefits," *Harvard Business Review*, Vol. 39, No. 4 (July-August 1961) pp 64-68.

[2]Perfecto S. Sison, *Personnel Management, Principles and Practices.* (Manila: Personnel Management Association of the Phil., Inc., 1973), pp. 331-333.

[3]Esdras T. Martinez, *Human Resources Management* (Manila: GIC Enterprise & Co., Inc., 1979), pp. 290-291.

[4]Frances Torbert, "Making Incentives Work", *Harvard Business* Review, Vol. 37, NO. 5 (September-October, 1959), pp. 81-92.

[5]Perfecto S. Sison, op. cit., p. 359.

[6]Employees' Compensation-Commission, "The New Employees' Compensation Program and You," Manila: MOLE Bldg. p. 7-10.

REFERENCES FOR FURTHER READING

Employees' Compensation Commission. "The New Employees' Compensation Program and You." Manila: MOLE: Bldg.

Martinez, Esdras T. *Human Resources Management.* Manila: GIC Enterprises & Co., Inc., 1979.

Sison, Perfecto S. *Personnel and Human Resources Management.* Manila: Rex Book Store, 1981.

18

HUMAN RESOURCE PERFORMANCE, PLANNING AND APPRAISAL

ALL SUPERVISORS from directors to unit heads, must make sure that what is done is that which is intended. The control process involves three steps: (1) establishing standards (2) appraisal of performance against these standards and (3) correction of deviations.

Performance Appraisal: Nature and Content

Harold Mayfield defined performance appraisal as "an attempt to think clearly about each person's performance and future prospects against the background of his total work situation."[1]

Leon C. Megginson puts it this way: "The primary value of any employee rating is to serve as a motivator of employee performance rather than to coordinate earnings with performance in an equitable manner."[2]

From this definition, we can derive the following purposes of performance appraisal:

1. To serve as a motivator of employee performance.
2. To provide reasons to support salary increases, promotions, transfers, demotions or terminations.
3. To determine needed changes in an employee's behavior, attitudes, skills, or job knowledge.
4. To serve as a basis for the coaching and counseling of the individual by the superior.

Merit rating is still used in evaluating work done in jobs that are typically paid on an hourly basis. However, such terms as "performance appraisal" and "performance evaluation" have become more popular.

Performance rating is the method by which, through observation, the worker's efficiency is appraised against a systematic performance standard. Other names used in evaluating employee performance are: efficiency rating, employee evaluation, service rating, personnel rating, and performance review.

Steps in Establishing a Performance Appraisal Program

A Performance Appraisal Program is a plan of action that guides the employees in their activities to attain their objectives.

The *first step* is to establish standards. The performance of workers in any division is geared toward meeting target dates.

Some measures to evaluate an employee's performance follow:

1. *Volume of production (quantity).* How many units did the employee turn out per day or week on the average? What amount is acceptable? What goal should be set for in the next period?
2. *Quality of Production.* How is quality measured in percentage of errors? Number of errors? What goal is the employee striving for, now and in the next period?
3. *Attendance.* How many times is an employee tardy or absent beyond what is normally allowed?
4. *Cost.* Is his cost record available? Has he contributed any cost saving ideas? Are there examples of his practising cost-consciousness?

Once goals have been set for an individual employee and he has accepted them, performance reviews can be conducted in a much less emotional climate. There can be no basis for argument when the results have been written in black and white.

When a deadline cannot be met, remedial measures are applied either by extending the target date or by adding more personnel. The objectives which are: to finish the work quantity-wise and quality-wise are the primary consideration, after which comes appraising how each employee has helped in realizing these objectives.

The daily accomplishment of the different tasks required by an operation is very important. An employee may be found to be lagging behind others. Non-improvement would then be a basis for transfer or shift in assignments.

The *second step* in appraising an employee's work is to compare it to the standards agreed upon by both the employee and supervisor. A performance appraisal indicates an employee's potentials for a better job and serves as a basis for corrective action.

The four basic steps in effective performance appraisal are the following:[3]

1. *Keep it simple.*

   The main purpose of performance appraisal should be to establish a cut off point between above-and below-average performers. It is safe for superiors to try to steer a course between the statistical insignificance of narrow ratings and the unnecessary subtle discriminations of fine lines. Overperfection of performance appraisal forms can cause more complicated systemic barriers and even necessitate a full-time staff of test administrators whose presence may deflect the company's purpose, and just as narrow scales fail to detect variations among employees' performance, subtle gradations, once applied, cannot lead to turning below-average into above-average performers.

   Another simplicity consideration is the relationship between performance appraisal and salary administration. No doubt performance evaluation is a necessary prerequisite for equitable salary disposition, but the distinction between the salaries of any two individuals are deceptively more definite than the performance deficiencies on which monetary distinctions are based. A simple evaluation system can be useful in identifying those whose salaries should be raised, but it is not useful in determining the amount of the increase.

2. *Keep it separate.*

   Performance appraisal must be kept distinct from other management systems. It is true that promotions as well as pay and raises have to be based on contribution to the business, but an appraisal is only partially reliable for making decisions concerning promotion.

   Past performance at one managerial level is only one indication of what future performance may be at a higher level. The best-performing salesman does not always make the best sales manager.

3. *Keep it contained.*

The barriers to effective performance appraisal have to be contained.

This means restricting the collection of performance appraisal data. Only two items of information about an employee need be centrally filed. The first one is his boss's appraisal of whether his performance had been above or below average for the past time. And the second is his boss's estimate of his management potential. To reduce personal bias, each boss should consult his superiors and subordinates before concluding his evaluations.

Any appraisal form used in a discussion with a subordinate should be tailored to his or her job. A quality control manager has different functions from a sales manager, and these differences should be incorporated into performance appraisal forms. In addition, this form should be the sole property of the boss and the individual being evaluated. It should never be centrally filed, and out-of-date forms should be periodically destroyed.

4. *Keep it participative.*

When planning and promotion systems are kept reasonably independent of performance appraisal, an individual's career does not hang by a single thread. However, participation in the system itself does most to emphasize the positive political and interpersonal aspects of performance appraisal.

A superior should solicit his subordinate's point of view before arriving at an appraisal of performance. He can accomplish this by asking each subordinate to appraise himself using the same form the boss uses so that each employee knows what his boss is trying to do. Honesty is rarely a problem here, although communication is. These forms however, should not be used during the appraisal interview itself. No one enjoys being rated by his superior. But most subordinates want at least a chance to present their side.

The next participative step is more difficult for it requires superiors and subordinates to listen to each other as well as to themselves. One worthwhile communication technique is to encourage a subordinate, during the first 30 minutes of interview time, to talk about how he perceives his past actions and his needs for management development. Continuous informal discussions of this sort—not waiting until formal end-of-year conferences—may in the end reap the benefit of fewer end-of-year surprises.

If, during the performance appraisal interview, superiors make a conscious effort to hear more than 25% of the words of their associates (and listen for the feelings behind them), they will gain a finer appreciation of employee work problems, and if they gain this sort of appreciation, the roles of evaluator and counselor may in the end be entirely compatible.

The main steps in a performance appraisal interview are the following:[4]

1. Review the current performance of the individual. Describe behavior which has hurt the individual in certain situations and suggest alternative, more acceptable ways of acting.
2. Agree on the particular aspects of the job where the individual can make a better contribution and improve his performance.
3. Agree on the part that the individual should play to assist the company in achieving its objectives.
4. Consider the individual's potential and suitability for promotion or advancement. Emphasize strengths on which the employee can build or which he can use more effectively.
5. Prepare a plan for the personal development or training of individual. Show desirable timing.
6. Limit plans for growth to a few important items which are possible of accomplishment within a reasonable period of time. Focus a plan on an objective; for example: "to increase effectiveness as a training coordinator" rather than "general improvement."

The following should be considered in developing a performance appraisal:

1. Selling the idea to management and employees. No appraisal will succeed unless it is fully understood.
2. The program should have the full support of the top executives as well as the line management.
3. Select the type of performance appraisal that is best suited to a particular firm.
4. Specify which employees are to be covered because the traits which may need appraising in one group may not need it in another.
5. The factor to be rated should specify the traits on which an

employee is to be rated. The factors should cover the characteristics of the employee's performance which are definitely observable, and can show the degree of success.

6. The traits must be those required by a person doing a particular job. Traits may be personal, like for example initiative, ability to learn, industry; actual work performance as shown by the employee's knowledge of the job, quantity of work done, quality of work, judgment, accuracy; or personal relations as shown by cooperation, adaptability, dependability, and attitude towards others.
7. Traits selected should be those which can be defined in unequivocal terms, observable, and capable of being rated while the employee performs his work. No two traits should overlap.
8. Supervisors should be trained for the task of appraising their subordinates' performances.
9. Employees should be informed of the Performance Appraisal Program so that they will understand the what, how, and why of it.
10. At least three people: the Human Resource Manager, the department Head concerned, and the supervisor must sit down together and discuss the performance of each employee.
11. The Human Resource Management Department must take active part in the performance appraisal program.

Common Problems in Performance Appraisal Programs:

Some supervisors are reluctant to appraise their employees. They may lack skill to handle the appraisal interviews or mistrust the validity of the appraisal instrument. It is however, the duty of the supervisors to help employees achieve both their own and the organization's objectives.

Specific problems:

1. *Difficulty in Setting Standards*—Many activities are hard to measure.
2. *Inconsistency of Rating by Different Supervisors*—Some supervisors give high ratings since it makes employees feel better; there will be fewer problems or complaints from employees, and high ratings would make them appear to be better supervisors. On the other hand, some give lower ratings thinking that high

ratings remove the incentive to improve. This problem can be minimized if the supervisor bases his appraisal as much as possible on the standards and goals mutually established by him and the employee.

3. *Failure of Form to Cover the Job*—Forms used for measuring performance must fit the job. The supervisor can suggest changes or add comments.
4. *Dislike of the Formality Involved*—Evaluation of performance is for many supervisors one of the most difficult aspects of their job. Yet it gives time for serious thought and discussion of how the employee does his work. The discussion may the latter's advancement, his pay, his personal feelings of satisfaction and his future training.
5. *Systemic Barriers*[5]—Collection obstacles in qualitative data exist when there is no simple and objective method to compare one employee with another. On the other hand, when quantitative data are collected, the rating scales are usually too narrow; 3-, 4-, or 5-point scales rather than 8-, 9-, or 10-point scales. The first cannot permit adequate discrimination. Haphazard data collection, and consequently incomplete files also present problems.

   Analysis Obstacles. No analysis of centralized data files are usually done to test the efficacy of manpower policies and practices.
6. *Behavior Barriers*[6]—Political barriers arise from superiors' fear that their peers will turn the appraisal system to their own advantage by consciously or unconsciously reporting false evaluation of their subordinates.

   Interpersonal barriers arise from the actual face-to-face encounter between subordinates and superior. Most superiors don't like "Playing God." They fear that negative appraisals, or even negative portions of otherwise favorable appraisals, will discourage rather than motivate subordinates toward better performance.
7. *The "Results" Approach Versus the "Traits" Approach*—When a superior is required to make a subjective judgment about the personality traits of his employees he is likely to run into several problems: What are really important? How should traits be evaluated? How can bias and emotion be removed from the ratings? Raters should use quantitative measures whenever possible. They should be more concerned about how well the

employees perform their job than their personalities. The object of this control is to improve behavior, skills, attitudes, job knowledge, not to reshape personalities.

When appraisal forms require evaluation of traits like cooperativeness, dependability, initiative and creativity, superiors should back up their comments with incidents.

8. *Halo Effect*—A rater may tend to give an employee the same rating on all traits or factors because of a general impression.
9. *Logical Error* is the tendency to rate an employee high or low in all characteristics as a "logical" conclusion from the high or low performance of the same employee in one trait.
10. *Central Tendency* is giving a rating of "average" on all traits for a particular employee, not daring to give extremely high or low ratings.
11. *Bias* is an influence affecting a rating because of some past incident that has no bearing on the trait for which the worker is being rated.

Types of Performance Appraisal Plans and Methods

A performance appraisal program should be designed to meet the particular requirements of a company. Different types are used for different categories of employees such as supervisors, office employees, or rank and file production workers.

Different types of performance appraisal plans follow:

A. *Traditional Types*

These are so designed that the rater can render an objective opinion of the person being rated. Examples are the following:

1. *Graphic Rating Scale*

   This scale assesses a person on quality and quantity of his work, and on other factors that vary with the job but usually include personal traits, like reliability and cooperation and specific performance items like oral and written communication.

2. *Ranking Methods*

   These are used when it is necessary to compare people. The two most effective ranking methods are alternation ranking and paired comparison ranking. Both require pooled judgment.

   a. *Alternation Ranking:* The names of the employees are listed on the left-hand side of a sheet of paper. The highest-ranked is crossed out and put at the top of the column at the right-hand side of the sheet. The ranker then selects the next highest-ranked from the remaining list, crosses out his name and enters it below the top name on the right-hand list, and so on.

b. *Paired Comparison* Ranking: Each individual in the group is compared as to his work with each of the other members of the group. Every time a person is considered superior to the other, a tally is put beside his name. The man with the most tallies is the most highly ranked, and vice-versa.

3. *Check List Method*

This involves having the rater check those statements on a list that he feels are characteristic of the employee's performance or behavior. Each trait to be considered usually has four or five descriptive statements with weighted points indicating varying degrees.

B. *Newer Types*

Following are brief discussions on the newer types of performance appraisal techniques:

1. *Essay Appraisal.* The rater is to write a paragraph or so covering an individual's strengths, weaknesses, potential and so on. The biggest drawback of this method is its variability in length and content which make it difficult to combine and compare with others.
2. *Field Review.* This is a group-judgment technique in which a small group of raters from each supervisory group goes over each employee's rating to (1) identify areas of inter-rater disagreement, (2) help the group arrive at a consensus, and (3) determine that all raters conceive the standards similarly. This technique tends to be more fair and more valid than individual ratings and develops an awareness of the varying degrees of leniency or severity exhibited by raters. However, this process is time-consuming.
3. *Forced Choice Rating.* The rater is asked to choose from among groups of statements those which best fit the individual being rated and those which least fit him. The statements are then weighed or scored. Since the rater does not know the scoring weights, bias is reduced. This technique, however, shows

distrust towards the rater and causes irritation and resistance. It is not only difficult and costly to develop forms; it also tends to be of little value.

4. *Critical Incident Appraisal.* Supervisors are asked to keep a record of each employee and record actual incidents of positive or negative behavior. Actual, incidents are discussed, thus giving the ratee an opportunity to respond or know just what those standards are.
5. *Management by Objectives.* In this method, employees are asked to set their own performance goals. This technique is popular on the managerial level but is taken lightly at lower levels.
6. *Work-Standards Approach.* The work-standards technique establishes work and staffing targets aimed at improving productivity. The employees are provided with a complete set of job duties and supervisors relate performance rating less threatening than the use of personal, more subjective standards. Its most serious drawback is comparability. People evaluated on different work-standards can not be compared for matters of promotion and salary increases.
7. *Assessment Centers.* All previous methods involve past performance. Assessment centers deal with people's future performance. Typically, individuals from different departments are brought together to spend two or three days working on individual and group assignments similar to the ones they will be handling if promoted. The pooled judgment of observers leads to an order of merit ranking for each participant. The center has been proven effective in selection as well as in giving opportunity to people of low status or low visibility in the organization to become visible, in improving morale, and in enlarging the pool of possible promotion candidates.
8. *Work Planning and Review.* Periodic meetings are held between the managers and his subordinates. During these meetings, progress on past goals is reviewed, solutions are sought for job-related problems, and new goals are established. There are frequent discussions of performance but no judgments or ratings are made. Salary-action discussions are held separately. The emphasis is on mutual goal planning and problem solving.

Rating Forms

A merit increase is a raise in salary or wage on the basis of performance or merit. It is made after an appraisal in accordance with Company policy. The movement of a regular employee's basic salary within the established salary range of his assigned position's salary level is called a merit increase. It is never tied to seniority or length of service in the company.

A certain percentage of the annual salary budget is allocated for merit increases and for promotional increases. Employees are wont to ask how objective and fair the performance rating sheets are. They want an assurance that their ratings are not left at the mercy of their managers.

While a performance appraisal rating sheet provides an "objective" assessment of the individual's performance when categories are quantified, by no means is this a guarantee that personal bias is eliminated in determining the individual's rating. We can only minimize but not totally eliminate personal bias in rating.

Mechanics of a Performance Appraisal System and Merit Increase:

1. Once a year, a company conducts a performance appraisal of its employees. The method used is a combination of the graphic rating scale, forced choice rating, the essay appraisal, and the critical incident approach.
2. The rater is briefed as to the mechanics of the appraisal. He is advised that the rating will be part of the employee's records and will affect his career in the organization. He is therefore cautioned to be extremely objective in rating the individual.
3. The criteria are given to the rater. Each factor is defined, and the rater is to choose from five statements under each factor the one that best describes the individual. The factors are given different weights according to importance such as the following:

	Weights	*Points*
a) dependability	20%	40
b) industry	20%	40
c) job performance	20%	40

d) initiative	15%	30
e) mental ability	10%	20
f) attitude	10%	20
g) personality	5%	10
TOTAL	100%	200

4. Each factor is divided into four categories and each category is further subdivided into A, B, and C, the idea being that in each category, there will still be shades of difference among the employees being rated.

   An Example follows:

Qualifications	*Rating*		
A. Dependability: (Reliability and Punctuality)	A	20% B	40% C
1. Needs constant watching. Habitually tardy.	[ ] 10 pts.	[ ] 7.5 pts.	[ ] 5 pts.
2. Fairly reliable but needs some watching and a great deal of direction.	[ ] 20 pts.	[ ] 15.5 pts.	[ ] 15 pts.
3. Can be relied upon but needs some direction. Generally punctual	[ ] 30 pts.	[ ] 27.5 pts.	[ ] 25 pts.
4. Above average sense of responsibility. Hard and conscientious workers.	[ ] 40 pts	[ ] 37.7 pts.	[ ] 35 pts.

5. After accomplishing the evaluation sheet, the rater submits it to the Unit Head, who will in turn interview the ratee. The ratee will be praised for his good points, and criticized on his bad points. He is advised to do better next time. If he does not accept the rate, he indicates his points of disagreement. The Unit Head thereafter returns the sheet to the Human Resource Management Unit, which will determine the overall current performance. If the ratee agrees to the evaluation made, he acknowledges the evaluation sheet with his conformity.

In appraising over-all current performance the following ratings are used:

A — Exceptional: Rarely equalled.
B — Well above Average: Clearly exceeds normal expectations.
C — Completely Satisfactory: Meets normal expectations.
D — Barely Satisfactory: Plenty of room for improvement.
E — Substandard: Below normal expectations.

Over-all Appraisal of Current Performance: [ ]

6. Merit rating is tied up with salary adjustments in accordance with some schedule.

Rating	*Amount of Budgeted Increase*
A.	100%
B.	75%
C.	50%
D any amount below	50% as recommended by supervisors
E. terminate employment	

7. Since some supervisors, are by nature over-generous while some are overly strict, officers are forced to distribute their ratings according to some standards. Below is an example of each standard:

A. not more than	25%	of the employees in the division/department/branch.
B. not more than	25%	
C. the rest		
D. the rest		
E. the rest		

Performance Planning to Improve Employees' Performances

One of the findings of General Electric's Behavioral Resources Service was that superior results were observed when the manager and the employees together set goals to be achieved rather than merely discussed needed improvements. Goal setting, not criticism, should be used to improve performance.

Performance planning is one of the most difficult and critical duties the supervisor has to perform. The employees' development, progression, pay raises, and job performance are directly affected by the quality of the performance planning process a supervisor conducts.

Performance planning and performance appraisal are two separate activities.

Employee Performance

Planning Appraisal

If performance planning is done right, the following ought to occur:

1. Employees will know what the Company is trying to accomplish.
2. Employees will know what specific contributions they ought to be making.
3. Employees will know how to do a better job.
4. Employees may be more deeply committed to their jobs via their participation in defining the job.

Steps in Performance Planning:

1. *Set the proper climate.* There should be mutual respect and openness between the supervisor and the subordinate. The supervisor seeks mutual understanding, not necessarily complete agreement.
2. *Proper timing.* The performance planning meeting should be fitted to the Company's work cycle. Often a semi-annual or quarterly schedule is adopted. A formal session should be held at least once a year.

   A group meeting will also do as long as all the people in the unit know what to expect.
3. *There should be understanding of accountabilities.* There are three questions which clear up the accountability issues:
   - What are the person's major responsibilities?
   - Which are most important?
   - In what way can the person make the greatest contribution to the Company's earnings?

   These accountabilities or responsibilities should be written down and should serve as a guide.
4. *Set Objectives.* Involve the employees in defining these specific

objectives. Make each objective a real challenge which requires extra efforts from the employees.

5. *Insure adequate resources.* Make sure that events outside the contract of the person have been taken into account.
6. *Record critical incidents.* Note and file incidents when an employee does particularly well (or poorly) in his job.

Briefly these can be summarized into three basic steps:

Step 1. Communicate what a unit should accomplish in the coming period. Clarify the purpose and procedure for the individual performance planning sessions you will conduct with them.

Step 2. Meet with individuals to review accountabilities and set objectives. Do this in a climate of respect, openness and mutuality.

Step 3. Review progress toward objectives frequently on an informal basis. Make changes in the performance plan as needed.

STUDY/REVIEW QUESTIONS

1. What is a Performance Appraisal?
2. Identify and explain the steps in performance planning.
3. What are the different types of Performance Appraisal Plans and Methods?
4. How do you conduct a good performance interview?

SUGGESTED ACTIVITIES AND ASSIGNMENT

1. Make a list of Filipino values that interplay in a Performance Appraisal Program.
2. Secure a Performance Appraisal Program from any organization and criticize it.
3. Interview an employee about his experience the first time he had a performance appraisal interview.

NOTES

[1]Mayfield, Harold, "In Defense of Performance Appraisal" Reprints from *Harvard Business Review,* Performance Appraisal Series, 1972, p. 27.

[2]Megginson, Leon C. *Personnel: A Behavioral Approach to Management.* Revised Edition; 1972, Illinois: Richard I. Irwin, Inc.

[3]Patz, Alan L. "Performance Appraisal: Useful But Still Resisted," *Harvard Business Review,* June 1975.

[4]Martinez, Edras T. *Human Resources Management.* Manila: EIC Enterprises & Co. Inc., 1979, pp. 162-163.

[5]Patz, op. cit.

[6]Ibid.

REFERENCES FOR FURTHER READING

Andres, Tomas D. *Understanding Filipino Values: A Management Approach.* Quezon City: New Day Publishers, 1984.

Martinez, Esdras T. *Human Resources Management.* Manila: EIC Enterprises & Co., Inc., 1979.

Megginson, Leon C. *Personnel: A Behavioral Approach to Management.* Illinois: Richard I.Irwin, Inc., 1972.

19

HUMAN RESOURCE REWARD SYSTEM AND PRODUCTIVITY

THE REWARD SYSTEM is a key subsystem of human resource management. The total reward system consists of both intrinsic aspects (supplied by the work itself) and extrinsic aspects (supplied by the organization). Extrinsic rewards have both financial and non-financial elements.

The intrinsic reward system consists of those elements of the work itself which provide a sense of achievement, responsibility, challenge, control and participation. It includes financial reward.

The term productivity refers to the relationship between output (quantity and quality of goods and services produced) and input (quantity of labor, capital, land energy and resources used in the production of goods and services) during a given period. When productivity results in price reduction, all benefit from it. When wages are raised, only the workers are benefited. When no increase in wages is given and there is no reduction in prices, all the benefits of productivity accrue to capital in the form of larger profits. The goal should be a balanced relationship between prices, wages and profits.

Although the national level of living and real wages has risen with increased productivity in specific industries there is no correlation between productivity and changes in wages and non-wage benefits.

Management and The Key to Productivity

Management is the key to productivity, which has the following categories:

1. Employee productivity - measured as output per employee per manhour
2. Machine productivity - measured as output per machine per hour.
3. Asset/resource productivity - measured as output per peso input.

The category contributing most highly to total productivity is the employee productivity since machine and capital factors could not otherwise be utilized effectively. Thus, the first strategy for productivity in business is to concentrate on human resources.

There can be no productivity without logic. Furthermore, there is a need for the psycho-logic of productivity. Productivity is also a matter of the spirit and the heart. If we have good logic bit not good psycho-logic, we cannot achieve productivity in business because of the following reasons:

1. It lacks the spirit on which the management system is built.
2. People do not like to feel like "cogs in a machine."
3. People want to be involved mind, heart and hand in productivity.

There are two main factors which determine how a person will perform on the job:

1. his motivation, and
2. his ability

An employee's motivation and ability are determined by many complex factors. Employee motivation is influenced by individual needs and the organization atmosphere. Individual needs are determined by:

1. Cultural Background
2. Economic Condition
3. Personal Situation
4. Reference Group
5. Level of Aspiration

The organization atmosphere concerns the formal organization and the informal organization. The formal organization is determined by:

organization structure
working conditions
management climate

communication
personnel practices
leadership

while the informal organization is determined by:

group dynamics
cohesiveness
peer standards

Along with motivation, ability in performing a job greatly affects productivity. Ability is in turn determined by skills, which are brought about by previous education, training and experience and aptitude.

The Need for a Responsive Reward System

It is important to determine the role which compensation and benefits are expected to play in the total reward system. Furthermore, it is important to determine appropriate balance between financial and non-financial rewards.

A modern form of reward system gives each individual a number of options as to his or her total compensation package. The employee is told how many compensation cost units have been granted to him and is allowed to use them to select from among the options offered.

Wage and Salary Administration, to be responsive, should have the following objectives:

1. To establish fair and equitable compensation in order to attract capable employees to the company and to retain them once they are in.
2. To control costs and to maintain the company in a reasonable competitive position.
3. To utilize wages and salaries as incentives for employees to utilize their ability and exert their best effort.
4. To maintain good employee relations.
5. To comply with the requirements of minimum wage laws and regulations.

Top management, through the Human Resource Management Department must formulate a sound wage policy. Wage policies should be carefully developed in connection with the interests of the owners or stockholders, employees, consumers, community and the government with its Labor Code, Court Decisions and other statutes. The policy should provide for salary raises.

Wage policies must be flexible enough to meet economic contingencies such as inflation. In the Philippines, from 100.00 index point in 1972, inflation has risen to index point 260.00 as of September, 1979.[1] These figures indicate that as of September, 1979, the peso purchasing power has gone down to 0.3846. In the early part of 1978 the government in implementing the five-year development plan: 1978-82 drew two lines to check inflation rate. The first line is the seven (7) percent guidepost; while the second is the ten (10) percent benchmark. If the rate of inflation does not go beyond seven (7) percent, inflation is under control. But if the rate of inflation exceeds the guide post and threatens to go beyond the natural benchmark, then it will be necessary for government to use both monetary and measures to hold down inflation at seven (7) percent level. Inflation rate beyond the benchmark of ten (10) percent is considered runaway. This is what the Philippines experienced in 1973 and 1974 when it ranged from sixteen (16) to thirty four (34) percent due to the oil embargo.

When the workingman's pay is fast being reduced to a low real value since 1974, the government saw fit to periodically increase the money wage by direct intervention, making use however of tripartism as a means of aiming at decisions as to what form these increases shall take-increase in basic minimum pay or increase in supplementary increase through mandatory allowance or a 13th month pay. During the last five years, the two forms were used. 1974, 1978 and 1979 saw increases in supplementary income, while 1976 and 1978 saw increases in basic pay. The basic pay plus the supplements is what we call "effective minimum wage".

In computing the real wage, it is very important that a realistic peso deflator be used. This deflator known as the "Consumer Price Index" (CPI) should be a most representative cost-of-living indicator/deflator for minimum wage workers. The "Consumer Price Index" for Low Income Agricultural and Non-agricultural Households in the Philippines was brought about by the Wage Commission in its continuacy search for a most representative cost of living indicator and approved by the Statistical Advisory Board of NEDA. This new series reflects changes in the cost of a "fixed basket" of goods and services customarily purchased by low waged and salaried households free from the influence of expenditure patterns of any other income groups. The Wage Commission's CPI use a "market basket" of 295 items for non-agricultural workers and 228 for agricultural workers while the Central Bank's CPI for the income index use 456 items in the "market basket." Through the

CPI, correct measurement of real income is assured.

The Wage Commission analyzes the movement of prices and wages and determines the level of income in real terms and indicates how low the peso purchasing process has sunk by ascertaining the impact of the OPEC OIL price increase on domestic out products and subsequently on the prices of consumer goods. Knowing this, the CPI, as deflator, is computed and the money wage is reduced to its real terms. Knowing the real value, one comes to know how much was lost to the worker's purchasing power. The formula used to determine how much the increase in the minimum wage or in the supplementary income should be is: "To restore the purchasing power of the money wage to its 1972 level (in real terms)".

Wage Indexation is the "automatic quarterly cost-of-living adjustments." It is commonly used to describe the process whereby wages are regularly adjusted to movements of a price index. The objectives of wage indexation are usually in terms of its equity property, that is, its ability to maintain real incomes. Lastly, advocates of wage indexation added price stability as another goal.

Wage Indexation is an institutional way of increasing wages in sectors where unions lack power or there are no unions existing. The components of Wage Indexation are Wage level, regularity of Wage adjustments and price index. As to Wage Level, indexation can be applied to the total wage, that is, full indexation or only to a portion of it, the minimum wage act by laws, or it can be partial indexation. As to regularity of wage adjustments, the more frequent wages are adjusted, the better real wages are protected. As to price index, this should be as comprehensible as possible, that weighting correspond to the consumer's consumption pattern and the base year chosen should be such as to highlight the effects of price increases.

Adopting the wage indexation system as a component of the government's wage policy will institutionalize the process of adjusting the national minimum wages in the agricultural and non-agricultural sector to the price increases to maintain their real value. If industry wages should be standardized, the five factors in wage determination should never be overlooked. These are namely: workers' needs, capacity to pay, wages elsewhere in the economy, the peculiarities with the industry and the imperative of social and economic development.

Productivity and Pay

A combination of regular changes in productivity with uniform changes in pay rates, assuming a stable price level, would yield three alternatives, namely:[2]

1. Productivity gain exactly equal to the change in wage rates. The result will be unchanging unit labor cost and the full gains of productivity obtained by workers.
2. Productivity is more than the rise in hourly earnings. In this case a large part of the productivity gains will be available for price reduction, increasing profits, or meeting costs of government, so as to extend further gains to labor in the form of non-wage benefits or shorter hours.
3. Productivity is less than rises in the wage rates. This situation will increase labor cost per unit.

Wage and Salary administration involves planning, developing, and controlling all phases of employee compensation.

Problems arise when workers desire to earn more money and management wants to operate at greater profit. As a rule, employers want to pay wages as low as possible, in order to earn more profit while workers constantly agitate for higher wages and for shorter hours of work.

Types of Compensation

Salary usually applies to the pay of such personnel as white-collar employees, or persons in positions of responsibility and authority in the firm.

The compensation for manual labor-skilled or unskilled-is called wages. Wages are measured by the hour, day, or week.

A raise in the salary or wage of an employee on the basis of performance merits is called a merit increase while an hourly or daily rate of pay, usually a single rate for an occupation or trade, set up by an agreement reached through collective bargaining, is called a union rate. The general wage raise affecting all the employees within a plant, company, or industry, usually as a result of collective bargaining, is called an across-the-board increase. Such an increase may be granted in the form of a percentage of the current pay or a specified amount in centavos or pesos per hour, per day, or per month. The actual number of pesos an employee receives is called money wage while the amount of goods and services he can buy with his money wage is called real wage.

Payment on the basis of time (by the hour, day, week, month, or year)is often referred to as base pay for a given job, while pay for all or a large group of employees is called supplementary (fringe benefits) pay. Payment on the basis of output and given to different people on the same job as an incentive for increase in production is called incentive pay.

Wage Incentive Plan

A wage incentive plan is a method of paying workers in direct relation to their production above a predetermined minimum requirement.

To attract and retain qualified personnel in the organization is the main purpose for establishing base pay, whereas to motivate these personnel to a higher level of performance is the purpose of the Wage Incentive Plan.

There are three types of incentive plans:

1. The Piece Rate System -In this system, a person employed in piece work is paid proportionate to the quantity of the work he finishes. Such a plan is very popular in many industries because it is easy to apply. It has the advantage of having direct relation between what a worker produces and what he earns.
2. Group Incentive -Sometimes a group works as a team. The total production of the group is measured and each member of the team is given an equal share.
3. Wage Salary Plus Bonus -The bonus plan consists of two elements; namely: (1) a standard or minimum requirement and (2) a bonus or premium. The pre-determined output during a given period of time is established as the minimum requirement or the standard. The worker or the laborer is paid a bonus if his output exceeds the minimum requirement.

Job Enrichment

To introduce satisfying experiences such as feelings of achievement, recognition, responsibility and personal growth, jobs may be restructured so that workers find incentives that result in greater overall efficiency.

There are five concepts in redesigning the existing job content:

1. Completion of a natural unit of work rather than performance routinely of a piece-meal work component.
2. Development of client identification and accountability for a specified piece of work.
3. Vertical and horizontal job considerations by pulling into the current job new responsibilities of a higher order and more challenging quality which make the worker feel a sense of growth and learning.
4. Efficient feedback system about the performance of the worker on both current and additional tasks to serve as sources of recognition and control.
5. Task advancement which includes establishment of career paths for advancement through promotion to higher job levels and/or establishing wider proficiency levels.

Supervisors and employees must understand well the concept and practice of job enrichment. The supervisors' participation is a crucial factor. Team participation is also important in the work rearrangements which have to be made.

Creating More Meaningful Work

Monotonous mechanical labor finally results in a drop in efficiency. Companies can create more meaningful work by introducing a job-rotation program that changes work assignments if not the jobs themselves. Another way is to permit increased employee-participation and job involvement, aligning individual and company goals or to focus on actual changes in the work itself giving employees opportunities for achievement and recognition.

More informal approaches give employees more control over their jobs, involving them in the problems of the business.

Principles of Manpower Productivity

When employees are highly productive, highly trained and in turn, highly paid, there may be no need to hire more people.

The following principles on manpower productivity may achieve this objective:

1. Analyze job contents and procedures, and other variables so as to

firm up a minimum work force.

2. Establish definite standards for performance evaluation to really justify additional staff. If vacancies arise, closely evaluate whether replacements are necessary, positions can be abolished, or jobs can be absorbed by others.
3. Attract and retain competent employees regardless of the source of their recruitment. Hire the man who is best qualified for a job.
4. Involve the employees' minds and hearts for peak performance. Give them total responsibility for high performance of their specified contribution.
5. Set high standards of performance. Place each employee where his strengths will be of maximum use. Require high levels of competence and performance.
6. Hire potential officers. Do not simply hire people who can do the job at hand, but hire potential officers.
7. Make opportunity for advancement company-wide. Promote employees from any unit to higher positions as long as they are the best qualified.
8. Promote not only the well-qualified candidate but also one who is a potential candidate for the next higher position.
9. Manpower Development is the responsibility of everyone. Employees' training must be programmed and closely supervised by officers. Everyone in the organization must be training-and-development oriented.
10. Develop freedom of discussion between employee and superior as to work assignments, promotion opportunities, compensation, training, complaints, etc.
11. Set up appropriate economic incentives and rewards so as to encourage higher performance and discourage poor performance.
12. Create human competence. Productivity requires rapid growth of talents and opportunities to employ them.

STUDY/REVIEW QUESTIONS

1. What is the meaning of productivity?
2. How does a human resource reward system increase productivity?
3. What two main factors determine how a person will perform on the job?

4. Explain what a job enrichment program is.
5. What are the principles of manpower productivity?

SUGGESTED ACTIVITIES AND ASSIGNMENT

1. Make a list of Filipino values that can be of great help in fomenting productivity among employees.
2. Secure a Productivity Program or Scheme from any organization and criticize it.
3. Interview a Human Resource Manager on the relationship of productivity to a reward system.

NOTES

[1]Rachel E. Fidelino, "Pay and Productivity: Critical Variables", Paper read at the 16th National Conference of the Personnel Management Association of the Philippines, November 29, 1979, PICC, Manila.

[2]Ibid, p.6.

REFERENCES FOR FURTHER READING

Andres, Tomas D. *Management By Filipino Values.* Quezon City: New Day Publishers, 1985.

____. *Understanding Filipino Values: A Management Approach.* Quezon City: New Day Publishers, 1984.

____. *Organizational Development For Productivity In The Philippine Setting.* Quezon City: New Day Publishers, 1983.

Martinez, Esdras T. *Human Resources Management.* Manila: EIC Enterprises & Co., Inc., 1979.

Sison, Perfecto S. *Personnel and Human Resources Management.* Manila: Rex Book Store, 1981.

20

CHANGES IN HUMAN RESOURCE STATUS: PROMOTION, TRANSFER AND SEPARATION

CHANGES are bound to happen within an organization with respect to its structure, functions, and work load. These changes affect the number and types of jobs that are to be staffed within the organization. Similarly changes occur within the human resource of an organization, in terms of qualifications, capacities, attitudes and behavior. All these changes necessitate changes in the placement of the human resource by means of transfers, promotions, separations, and sometimes even layoffs. This movement is a function of placement, defined as the assignment of the right man to the right job.

Job requirements continually change to meet the operational needs of certain departments and management must be able to meet the required changes in the qualifications of employees to make full use of the employees' talents, provide chances for employees' advancement and growth, bolster employee morale, and upgrade employee relations.

Changes in human resource status should be compatible with organizational objectives and the welfare of its human resource.

Transfer

The transfer of an employee encourages versatility and flexibility. Many Filipino employees improve their qualifications by taking evening courses hoping to be considered for promotion or transfer to a job which will give them greater satisfaction. Transfers are made to meet organizational needs. The primary purpose of a transfer is to increase effectiveness in attaining objectives. It should be the aim, therefore, of any organization to transfer employees as soon as their capacities increase and opportunities warrant.

Control of Transfers

The organization must make definite plans like:

1. Who should be authorized and be responsible in deciding on transfers;
2. Who would be approached in cases of employees requesting transfers;
3. Who should be empowered to recommend such transfers;
4. What criteria will determine when to effect a transfer.

The *Lagaring Hapon* system of Japanese business somewhat approximates the Filipino *Compadre System*, if properly directed and oriented. Most large Japanese companies have an informal network of senior middle management people who act as sponsors to the young men who enter the company's employ directly from the university.

During the first ten years of their career in the company, these young men move in the shadow of their sponsors, who may have as many as a hundred "godchildren" at any one time.

The sponsor is rarely a young man's direct superior or a member of top management but a highly respected member of the middle management group. If the young man is stuck under an incompetent manager, it is the sponsor who pulls the strings to effect transfer to another manager without anyone in the company knowing about it. If the young man needs to be disciplined the sponsor administers the discipline in private. By the time the young man is thirty years old, the sponsor knows much about him and so does top management.

The Filipino "Compadre System," if properly oriented and controlled, like the Japanese "Lagari System," can be very beneficial in human resource management.

The transfer of "problem employees" must also be carefully handled. It is typical in Filipino personnel management to transfer "problem employees" from one department to another. Too often such action does not remove the cause of the problem but merely passes the problem on to some other manager or superior. Correcting such conditions involves proper counseling with employees and proper training. If improvement in an employee's behavior cannot be achieved by such means, it may be preferable to discharge him rather than to transfer him from job to job. Postponing discharge action through such transfer can only make an eventual discharge more difficult.

An employee who is constantly seeking to change jobs may not need a transfer as much as he needs psychological help. If many transfer requests originate within a particular department, however, the fault may lie with the superior or with the conditions within the unit rather than with the employees.

Kinds of Transfers

There are two kinds of transfers:

1. *Temporary* - When an employee is transferred temporarily to another job created by vacation or sick leaves, he has an opportunity to show his versatility and expand his knowledge and ability.
2. *Permanent* - While the transferee has the opportunity, he must prove his worth by consistent development of his skills in coping with the present trends, particularly in matters of leadership.

Types of transfers may be grouped into:[1]

1. *Production transfer.* This is intended to avoid layoffs on the job while workers are being hired for a similar type of work elsewhere.
2. *Replacement transfer.* The intention is similar to that of production transfer. However, the employee with a long service record is transferred to a similar job in another department where he replaces another with a shorter service record.
3. *Versatility transfer*. This is intended to train workers to handle a variety of jobs in preparation for production or replacement transfers or for small companies.
4. *Shift transfer.* When shift assignments do not rotate, transfers are made from a less favorable shift to a more favorable shift.
5. *Remedial transfer*. This is intended to correct faulty selection or placement of an employee.

Reasons for Transfers

Reasons for an employee's transfer may be the following:

1. The organization finds itself with a surplus of men in one group or department and a shortage in another.
2. To put the employee's talents and training to a more effective use.
3. To encourage versatility and flexibility among employees.
4. To train employees for advancement or promotion.
5. To meet the demands of business expansion.
6. To correct erroneous placement.
7. To meet personnel requirements of a certain unit during peak hours, days, or seasons.
8. To effect retrenchment when business is down.
9. To absorb excess personnel during slack periods, and
10 To protect the health and safety of the employee, as in the case of old age, etc.

Promotion

Promotion is the advancement of an employee to a better job involving greater responsibility, greater prestige, greater skills, higher pay and better hours or better working conditions.

Organizations need a systematic method of screening and promoting employees.

Purposes of Promotions

The reasons for promotions are the following:

1. To maintain employee loyalty to the organization.
2. To keep good and competent employees.
3. To reward proven ability, skills and integrity.
4. To boost employee morale;
5. To encourage employees to render the best service they are capable of;
6. To reduce labor turnover.

Promotion within the ranks should be done whenever possible. In case there are no candidates for a vacancy in the same unit, a search for any candidate within the company should be made.

Bases for Promotion

Job analysis provides information on the skill, experience, training, responsibility, and environmental factors involved in each job. Comparing such information for various jobs shows which jobs have similar requirements. Then, on each job specification, the other jobs from and to which changes can logically be made are listed.

If it happens that a particular person filling a job has the qualifications to enter another line of progression, this should be permitted. This is a matter of personal qualifications and does not destroy the validity of natural job relationships.

When job relationships have been fully explored, it is wise to construct a promotion chart. To determine job requirements, use the job description and job specification.

Performance and ability, or potential, are the two principal criteria for determining promotions. Performance refers to the individual's productivity in his present position. Potential or ability refers to how well the individual will perform when placed in a new position of authority and responsibility.

A traditional basis for promotion was the "seniority rule." Today, organizations give greater weight to performance and ability, than to the seniority factor. Progressive managements prefer to promote the employee for his performance and ability rather than for his length of service. Seniority is only given weight as a basis when other factors are equal.

Types of Promotions

There are two types of promotions:[2]

1. *Vertical Promotion.* This is promoting from one rank to the next in the same department. If a company is organized into a few major departments, this plan of promotion has fewer disadvantages than if it is subdivided into numerous specialized units. In the latter case, it limits both the experience and the opportunity of an employee because he has only a limited contact with the business as a whole.
2. *Horizontal Promotion.* Under this plan an employee may be transferred from a position in one department to a position of higher rank or of the same rank in another department. Horizontal promotion is most easily followed in a company that has a number of units performing similar activities.

Promotion Policies

Promotion is done to increase the overall efficiency of the organization and to aid in the personal development and interests of the employees.

A good policy should contain:

1. A statement of management's intention that higher paid and better jobs will be filled by promotion from within whenever possible, rather than by hiring from outside the organization.
2. Encouragement for superiors to permit capable employees to leave the unit if better opportunities are available elsewhere. If a good employee is held back, he is not likely to remain satisfied. An open job-bidding system encourages this internal mobility.
3. Progression-ladders of promotion established within the organization. Job analysis can be used to develop a chart showing basic job requirements (in competence, experience, formal education, etc.) and how each job leads to another. Employees need to know what is expected in higher-rated jobs in order to prepare themselves for advancement.
4. Line responsibility for making promotions should be established with the advice and assistance of the Human Resource Department in a staff capacity. The supervisor should propose promotions, which should then be subject to approval by his immediate superior. This serves as a check on the fairness of promotion and ensures that the policy will be consistently administered.

Provision for employee or union challenge of a particular promotion should be included in the promotion policy and the union agreement. Ordinarily a management or a Human Resource Manager who always adhered to a sound promotion policy has little to fear.

Two procedures that are important for the success of a promotion policy are:

1. Posting a notice of openings for promotions, so that interested employees may apply within a specified period, usually several days or a week. If possible, the news should be posted and the candidates selected before the job actually becomes vacant. If the job is temporarily filled by an employee who is subsequently advanced to the job permanently, the other applicants are likely to feel that the posting procedure is a farce.
2. Provision for training as a means of preparation for promotion. Special on-the-job training schools, night classes or vocational

courses as well as special retraining programs should be available. The changing job requirements in an age of science and technology require extensive retraining of employees if they are to qualify for better jobs.

Separation

Separation from employment can happen in three ways:

1. By resignation. When the employee himself quits.
2. By lay-off. When the employee's employment is terminated by the employer through no fault of the worker without prejudice to the employee.
3. By discharge. When the termination of employment is initiated by the employer for cause. To pinpoint the cause of a resignation, an exit interview is held. This interview gives the company vital information on its policies regarding employee relations and wages and salaries, and on conflict of personalities.

Article 272 of the New Labor Code provides that an employer may terminate the services of an employee when:

1. The closing of the establishment is necessitated, or when the employer has to reduce his work force by more than one-half owing to serious business reverses, unless the closing is done so as to circumvent the provisions of the Code.
2. There is serious misconduct or willful disobedience of orders in connection with the work.
3. There is gross and habitual neglect of duties.
4. Fraud or betrayal of trust.
5. A crime or offense has been committed against his employer or any immediate member of his family or representative.
6. Other analogous situations occur.

When an employee suffers from a disease and his continued employment is prohibited by law or is harmful to his health or to the health of his co-employees, the employer shall not terminate the employment unless a competent public health authority certifies that the disease cannot be cured within six months even with proper medical treatment. If the disease or ailment can be cured within this period, the employer shall ask the employee to take a leave. The employer shall restore the employee to his former position immediately upon his regaining normal health.[3]

In unionized firms, the discharge procedure is spelled out in the collective bargaining agreement. The limits to dismissal of employees are: unfair labor practice, breach of contract of employment or collective bargaining agreement and when discharge is a violation of a specific provision of law.

Lay Offs

Almost every organization, at one time or another, is faced with the necessity of laying off employees for lack of work. Some lay offs are temporary and are expected by employees because of the nature of the job. When a change in operations or a decline in business necessitates permanent lay offs, however, the problem is more difficult.

In both types of lay offs, but especially in the latter when long-service employees will be affected, there is need for a definite lay off policy. The cold written notice in the pay envelope, "Your services are no longer required" or the casual words from the boss, "I guess we don't need you any more after tomorrow," will not suffice. Such methods are destructive of employee morale, not only for those dismissed but for those who remain.

Union seniority rules guarantee that long-service workers will not be the first to be laid off if operations decline.

Formulating a sound policy is not easy because of various possible alternatives and the conflicting demands of seniority and efficiency. These apply with almost equal force to unionized and non-unionized firms. One major problem of top management is: Will hours of work be reduced before any employee or certain groups are laid off?

What shall determine who will be laid off first? Seniority is often accepted as the sole factor. Efficiency is protected by (1) careful selection when new employees are hired, (2) weeding out clearly incompetent employees, (3) promotion on the basis of ability, (4) consideration of skill and ability, (5) Considering the residence and family status. Exceptional employees may be retained regardless of seniority, for they are the ablest employees.

How should seniority be determined? This involves two points. (1) seniority in the unit-occupation, department or entire company and (2) interruptions in length of service that might abrogate seniority rights. Both points require negotiation with the union in unionized firms.

It would be advisable to have the following policies regarding lay offs:

1. Advance commitment regarding laying off will cushion the shock of lay off. Under the straight seniority policy the last employee laid off is the first one recalled.
2. Permanent lay offs should be planned as far in advance as possible. At least one week's advance notice of lay off should be given and a longer notice to long-service employees.
3. Management should consider the possibility of compensation for permanent displacements caused by technological change, shutting down of less efficient plants, etc. The amount of compensation should vary with the employee's earnings and length of service.
4. Management should make an effort to place laid-off employees with other firms in the community. It can work with agencies in the labor market that are seeking to place workers in new jobs.
5. Management should train workers to do several jobs so that they can be transferred rather than laid off.

STUDY/REVIEW QUESTIONS

1. What is a transfer? How is it differentiated from promotion, separation and lay off?

2. How should separation and lay off be done properly in the Philippine setting?

3. How can promotion be used as a human resource conservation tool?

SUGGESTED ACTIVITIES AND ASSIGNMENTS

1. Make a list of Filipino values that should be considered in implementing promotion.

2. Make a list of Filipino values that should be considered in implementing lay offs.

3. Secure policies on transfer, promotion and lay off from any organization and criticize them.

NOTES

[1]Paul Pigors and Charles A. Myers, *Personnel Administration.* Sixth Edition (New York: McGraw-Hill Book Co., Inc., 1973), pp. 428-430.

[2]William R. Spriegel, *Principles of Business Organization.* Third Edition, (New York: John Wiley & Sons, Inc., 1955), pp. 239-240.

[3]Section 8, Book VI, *New Labor Code Rules. Labor Code of the Philippines* (Manila: Government Printing Office, 1975), pp. 114-115.

REFERENCES FOR FURTHER READING

Angeles, Conrado P. et al. *Principles of Personnel Administration.* Quezon City: R.M. Garcia Publishing House, 1981.

Martinez, Esdras T. *Human Resources Management.* Manila: EIC Enterprises & Co., Inc., 1978.

Sison, Perfecto S. *Personnel and Human Resources Management.* Manila: Rex Book Store, 1981.

Yoder, Dale et al. *Personnel Management and Industrial* Relations. Englewood Cliffs, New Jersey: Prentice-Hall, Inc., 1982.

21

HUMAN RESOURCE AND MANAGEMENT RELATIONS

LABOR is an important factor of production which is made up of human beings who, treated unfairly by management, may become resentful. Hence, production suffers. But modern management has proven that human resource can be impelled to do their best by proper management and leadership.

In order to promote ideal labor-management relations, management must realize that labor has basic needs and wants. Certain management attitudes, policies and practices cause friction between labor and management. Foremost is the desire of management to maximize profits to the neglect of the worker's welfare. It is liable to look at labor as a production cost instead of as a part of company resources.

Another source of employee-management disputes is the latter's indifferent and arbitrary attitude. Management tends to be too impersonal and to make arbitrary decisions on matters involving human resources, overlooking their needs and thus antagonizing them.

Common employee grievances are also due to ineffective supervision and the practices of discrimination and favoritism. Too, often, these two factors lead to the formation of labor unions.

On the other hand, certain practices and acts of labor are irritants to management. The most common are the defiant attitude toward management of some labor union leaders. Small issues are blown up. Labor and management often fail to understand each other's problem. This communication gap is due to lack of education and training in the low levels of the labor force.

This problem results in strikes and harm to both labor and management. Labor and management must be considered as a single wheel that makes a business roll.

Laborers who roll the machinery of management must be given due respect, fair treatment, just salaries and benefits. On the other hand, labor must understand the problems and predicaments of management. In most cases, laborers feel that they are being denied fair wages, unaware that management cannot really pay what is demanded owing to the present economic situation.

Labor Relations

Labor relations are the relationship between employees or labor unions on one hand and management on the other. These relationships are governed by (1) the labor standard law, (2) social legislation, and (3) the labor relations law. These laws and regulations are now embodied in the Labor Code of the Philippines as amended. The law on labor relations includes applicable court decisions and the regulations by government agencies affecting employee-employer relations.

Labor Relations in the Philippine Setting

Filipino workers today are enjoying rights and benefits never before experienced in the Philippines. Under the regime of Martial Law, the tripartisan concept (government, worker and employer) was adopted, paving the way for working man to seek for himself and his family a living worthy of his dignity.

In pre-Spanish times slavery was practised in the Philippines. Up to 1930 farm laborers were burdened with debt and were compelled to till the land of their masters who plunged them into more debt. The Commonwealth Era provided for the protection of labor and promoted the workers' rights to self-organization and to collective bargaining respecting terms and conditions of employment. Act No.103 created the Court of Industrial Relations.

On June 17, 1953, Republic Act No. 875 or the Industrial Peace Act was passed by Congress. It transferred the power of the government to secure the proper conditions of employment and to settle disputes, to the workers and employers themselves through collective bargaining, including the right to resort to economic sanctions, or strikes on the part of labor, and lock-outs, on the other hand, for the employers.

This Act, referred to as the Magna Carta of Labor, has given workers the right (1) to organize, (2) to form, join, or assist a labor organization of their own choosing, and (3) to engage in collective bargaining and mutual aid or protection.

Article 212 of the New Labor Code provides a National Labor Relations Commission, under the supervision of the Secretary of Labor, and composed of a chairman and two members representing the public, two members representing the workers and two members representing the employers. Article 210 comprises the following aims:

1. To promote free collective bargaining, including voluntary arbitration, as a mode of settling labor disputes;
2. To promote free trade unionism as an agent of democracy, social justice, and development;
3. To restructure the labor movement in order to eradicate inter-union and intra-union conflicts;
4. To promote adequate administrative machinery for the quick settlement of labor disputes;
5. To enlighten workers concerning their rights and obligations as union members and as employees; and
6. To ensure stable and just industrial peace.

Article 243 of the New Labor Code provides that all persons employed in enterprises operating for profit have the right to form, join, or assist labor organizations for purposes of collective bargaining.

With the establishment of Martial Law in the Philippines, labor was granted its rightful place in the struggle toward social and economic development. The Labor Code of the Philippines was established through Presidential Decree No. 442. Consequently, the present tripartite National Labor Relations Commission was created. Also under Martial Law, Presidential Decree 823 allowed strikes in non-vital industries in certain cases when negotiations remained unsolved.

The more important labor laws fall under three classifications, namely: Labor Standards Laws, Social Security Laws and Labor Relations Laws.

Labor Standards Laws/Conditions of Work

These laws can be invoked by employees who fall under their coverage, thereby making it necessary for them to have an appreciable knowledge of these laws.

A - Law on Employment
A - Law on the Employment of Women and Minors
A - Law on the Employment of Househelpers
B - Law on Weekly Rest Periods
B - Law on Service Incentive Leave; Maternity Leave; Sick Leave
B - Law on Holiday Pay
C - Law on Wages
C - Law on Cost of Living Allowances
C - Law on 13th-Month Pay
C - Medical and Dental Service Law
C - Law on Occupational Health and Safety
C - Law on Employee Discipline and Law on Dismissals

Social Security Laws

A knowledge of the benefits, application and coverage of these laws is necessary. The following are the most important laws that promote the health, well-being and safety of individuals:

1. Employees' Compensation and State Insurance Fund
2. Social Security Law
3. Revised Government Service Insurance Act, 1977
4. Philippine Medical Care Act of 1969
5. Land Reform Law
6. Social Amelioration Fund

Labor Relations Laws

The following are the more important labor relations laws:

1. Law on Labor Organizations
2. Law on Collective Bargaining
3. Law on Strikes and Lockouts and other Concerted Activities
4. Law on Labor Disputes and their Settlement

Labor Unions

A Labor Union is an association of workers organized to secure the most favorable conditions of employment such as wages and hours of work. The character and power of a union depends on the personality of its leaders, the problems of the organization, the circumstances under which the union was organized and the attitude of management towards the union leaders.

There are two general types of labor unions-the industrial and the craft. The *industrial union* includes all workers in a particular firm or plant regardless of occupation. The *craft union* cuts across many companies and industries. Its members belong to one craft or to a closely related group of occupations.

How a Union Is Organized and Registered

Sec. 4 of the Labor Code Requirements for registration of local unions - The application shall be signed by at least 50% of the employees in the bargaining unit which the applicant union seeks to represent, and shall be accompanied by the following:

(a) Fifty pesos (P50.00) registration fee;

(b) The names of the officers, their addresses, the principal address of the labor organization, the minutes of the organizational meetings and a list of the workers who participated in such meetings;

(c) The names of all the members in the bargaining unit it seeks to represent;

(d) If the applicant union has been in existence for one or more years, a copy of its annual financial reports;

(e) Four copies of the constitution and by-laws of the applicant union, minutes of its adoption or ratification, and the list of the members who participated in it; and

(f) A sworn statement by the applicant union to the effect that there is no recognized or certified collective bargaining unit concerned.

The application for registration and all the accompanying documents shall be verified under oath by the Secretary and attested to by the President.

The Regional Office shall decide upon the application within thirty (30) days upon receipt.

Sec. 5. Requirements regarding constitution and by-laws in local industry unions and sub-industry unions. They should:

(a) Conform with Article 233 of the Code;

(b) Provide a definite procedure for settling internal disputes;

(c) Provide for an education and research fund; and

(d) Provide for a three (3) year term for the officers. Upon the effectivity of the Code, all incumbent officers of a legitimate labor organization shall be allowed to complete their terms. Thereafter, the election of union officers shall be held once every three (3) years.

Sec. 6. Denial of registration of local unions. The Regional Office may deny an application on any of the following grounds:

(a) Non-compliance with the requirements enumerated in section 4 hereof;

(b) Non-compliance with the requirements enumerated in section 5 hereof, and

(c) Engaging in the "cabo" system or other illegal practices.

The decision of the Regional Office denying the application for registration shall be in writing, stating in clear terms the reasons therefor.

The Functions of a Union

The chief objective of a union is to secure a labor contract from the employer which defines the rights and duties of both management and the workers. Unions in developed countries provide a broad range of personal benefits for employees and their families, such as vacation retreats and various recreation facilities for their members, health clinics, legal aid, college scholarships for members' children, free eye glasses, prepaid dental plans, cut-rate drugs, psychiatric care, dance lessons, and courses in arts.

Rights and Conditions of Membership in a Union

The Labor Code provides that all persons employed in commercial, industrial and agricultural enterprises, including religious, medical or educational institutions operating for profit, have the right to form, join or assist labor organizations for purposes of collective bargaining. Persons not eligible to join are security guards and other personnel employed for the protection and security of the personnel, property, and premises of the employer (Article 244), government employees, including employees of government-owned and/or controlled corporations (Book V, Rule II, New Labor Code), managerial officials (Article 245), and employees of religious, charitable, medical, and educational institutions not operating for profit, provided the latter do not have existing collective agreements or recognized unions at the time of the effectivity of the Code or have voluntarily waived their exemption (Article 243).

Members of a labor organization are entitled to full reports from their officers concerning all financial transactions; they elect their officers by secret ballot at intervals of not more than three years; they determine by secret ballot any question affecting the entire membership unless such secret balloting is impractical, in which case the board of directors of the organization may make the decision on behalf of the general membership.

Article 241 also provides that no excessive initiation fees shall be required; no labor organization shall knowingly admit as member or continue in membership anyone who engages in a subversive activity; no one who has been convicted of moral turpitude shall be eligible for election as an officer or for appointment to any position in the union; no member of a labor organization shall collect any fees, or other contributions in its behalf or make any disbursement of its money or funds unless he is duly authorized. The funds of the organization shall not be used for any purpose other than those provided in the constitution and by-laws or expressly authorized by written resolution adopted by the majority of the members at a general meeting called for the purpose; the officers shall not be paid any compensation other than the salaries and expenses provided for in its by-laws, or in a written resolution by a majority of all the members at a general membership meeting duly called for the purpose.

The same article of the Labor Code states that the treasurer of any labor organization and every officer thereof who is responsible for the accounts of the organization shall render a correct report of all moneys, bonds, securities and other properties of the organization entrusted to his custody or under his control. The rendering of the account shall be made:

1. At least once a year within thirty (30) days after the close of its fiscal year;
2. At such other times as may be required by a resolution of the majority of the members of the organization; and
3. Upon vacating office.

The account shall be duly audited and verified by affidavit and a copy thereof shall be furnished the Minister of Labor and Employment.

Article 241 also provides that the book of accounts and other records of the financial activities of any labor organization shall be open to inspection by any officer or member thereof during office hours.

Union Recognition and Security

Until a union is recognized by management as a bargaining agent for the employees, it cannot negotiate conditions of employment. The term union security refers to the right of a union to continued existence in a particular company. Traditionally employers oppose labor unions and because of this, many unions have attempted to negotiate union security clauses into their labor contracts. Complete union security is obtained when an employer agrees neither to hire anyone who is not a member of the recognized union nor to retain on his payrolls anyone who ceases to be a member of the contracting union. Generally the first thing a labor union tries to secure from management is its recognition as the exclusive bargaining representative of all the employees in the company, plant, or trade. Its second aim is to recruit and retain members.

The form of security that is granted to a union is determined by the types of shop that it is permitted to maintain. They are listed in the order of the least important to the most important from the viewpoint of the union:

Open shop exists where no union is recognized as the bargaining agent for the company's employees.

Bargaining for members only. This type of shop merely acknowledges the presence of a union and its rights to bargain for those employees who are members.

Exclusive-bargaining shop exists when an employer is required to bargain exclusively with the union over conditions of employment within that unit of the company that it represents.

Maintenance-of-membership shop exists when employees who are union members after a given cut off date are required to retain their membership in a union or suffer the loss of their jobs. Employees hired after this date are usually required to join the union.

Union shop is an agreement between a firm and a labor union whereby the former agrees that its employees or the employees in the bargaining unit may be required, after a certain period, to join the union and remain members in good standing in order to retain their jobs in the company. In this kind of agreement, a non-union member may at the start be eligible for employment but is obliged to join the union after a certain period in order to retain his employment.

Closed shop is an arrangement between an organization and a labor union whereby the employees covered by the bargaining unit must be members of the union in good standing during the life of the agreement between the company and the union. An employer agrees to hire only members of the contracting labor union who are of good standing.

Additional security or Check-Off is an arrangement under which the employer deducts union dues and offer assessments from the wages of union members and transmits the sum to the union. Republic Act No. 602 (Minimum Wage Law) allows check-off provided that the employer has recognized it or has been authorized in writing by the individual employees concerned (Sec. 10 (b), Republic Act. No. 602).

Collective Bargaining

Collective bargaining is a process in which a legitimate labor organization and the employer meet to negotiate a contract or agreement which specifies the nature of the employer-employee union relationship concerning wages, hours of work, and grievance procedure. According to the Labor Code, "the labor organization designated or selected by the majority of the employees in an appropriate collective bargaining unit shall be the exclusive representative of the employees in such unit for the purpose of collective bargaining. However, an individual employee or group of employees shall have the right any time to present grievances to their employer."

Procedure Governing Representing Issues

The Labor Code states: "When a question concerning the representation of employees is submitted to it, the Bureau shall decide the controversy and certify in writing the name of the labor organization that has been designated as the appropriate bargaining agent. In such cases, the Bureau shall provide for a speedy and appropriate hearing and if there is any reasonable doubt as to who the employees have chosen as their representative for the purpose of collective bargaining, the Bureau shall order a secret ballot election to be conducted by the Bureau to ascertain who is the freely chosen representative of the employees.

Procedure in Collective Bargaining (Article 250, New Labor Code)

A. When a party desires to negotiate an agreement, it shall serve a written notice upon the other with a statement of its proposals. The other party shall make a reply thereto not later than ten (10) days from receipt of such notice;

B. Should differences arise on the basis of such notice and reply, either party may request a conference which shall begin not later than ten (10) days from the date of request;

C. If the dispute is not settled, the Bureau shall intervene upon request of either or both parties to participate fully and promptly in the conciliation meetings the Bureau may call;

D. During the conciliation proceedings in the Bureau, the parties are prohibited from doing any act which may disrupt or impede the early settlement of the disputes;

E. The Bureau shall exert all efforts to settle disputes amicably and encourage the parties to submit their case to a voluntary arbitrator; and

F. If no amicable settlement is reached after exhausting all possibilities of conciliation, the Bureau shall certify the dispute to a Labor Arbiter for compulsory arbitration. The Labor Arbiter shall decide the case within forty-five (45) days from the first hearing."

How Management Prepares for Collective Bargaining

Collective bargaining negotiation is a delicate and highly technical process in labor-management relations. It is a primary concern not only of the human resource/personnel and industrial relations manager but especially of top management. The top manager, more than anybody else, should therefore understand the methods of collective bargaining. There are three stages in the preparation of management for collective bargaining:

First Stage: Collect data relevant to the issues which will come up: wage levels, seniority, etc. It will be wise to solicit suggestions and these data from the human resource/personnel or industrial managers and from plant managers or supervisors.

Second Stage: Select the members of the management negotiating committee before final preparations begin.

Third Stage: Make the final preparation by drafting specific proposals for changes in contract language, determining the general size of the economic benefits that can be offered during the negotiations and the final limits acceptable as the last resort. Prepare other documents needed.

Provisions of a Collective Bargaining Agreement

The Labor Code provides that a collective bargaining agreement should "ensure mutual observance of the terms of the agreement and establish a machinery for the adjustment of grievances."

The regulations promulgated by the Minister of Labor and Employment to implement the Code provide that a collective agreement should also have as provisions, among others, the following:

"Provisions for the promotion of family planning in the bargaining unit; and provisions for labor-management cooperation schemes for increasing productivity, sharing of the benefits resulting therefrom, workers' education, reduction of monotony at work and recreational activities and job enrichment."

Rules and Regulations implementing the Code provide: "Unless circumstances require otherwise, the life of the collective agreement shall be at least three years."

Protection of the Rights to Self-Organization and Collective Bargaining

To protect the rights of workers to self-organization and collective bargaining, the Labor Code provides that it shall be an unfair labor practice for an employer or a labor union to restrain or coerce employees in the exercise of their rights to self-organization or collective bargaining.

Law on Strikes

Section I of Presidential Decree No. 823 reads:

The State encourages trade unionism and free collective bargaining within the framework of compulsory and voluntary arbitration. Therefore all forms of strikes, picketing and lookouts are strictly prohibited in vital industries, such as transportation and communication, lubricating oil, essential commodities for export, and in banking as well as hospitals and schools and colleges.

However, in other cases, any legitimate labor union may strike and any employer may lock out but only on grounds of unresolved economic issues in collective bargaining, in which case the union or the employer shall file a notice with the Bureau of Labor Relations at least 30 days before the intended strike or lockout. Should the dispute remain unsettled thereafter, the union may go on strike and the employer may lock out unless the National Labor Relations Commission, in the intent of national security and public safety, automatically enjoins the strike or lockout.

The NLRC shall decide the dispute within 30 working days, which decision shall be final unless appealed to the Minister of Labor and Employment.

If not certified to the NLRC, the union may strike and the employer may lockout. At any time, however, the president or his representative may, in the public interest certify the dispute to the NLRC for compulsory arbitration, immediately after which the employees shall return to work and the employer shall resume operations and readmit all employees pending resolution of the dispute.

Facts on Collective Bargaining in the Philippines

The Yearbook of Labor Statistics in 1975 prepared by the Labor Statistics and Information Service of the Ministry of Labor and Employment reveals among other things that:

1. The number of unions whose registration permits were cancelled is disturbing since, more often than not, inactivity appears to be the reason. According to the Bureau of Labor Relations, the common grounds for cancelling permits are: non-submission of annual financial reports or of an up-dated list of members, or of officers or of amendments to their Constitution and by-laws, if there were any.
2. The number of unions applying for registration from 1964-1975 shows that the organization of workers has been persistent but there were no dramatic attempts at accelerating these efforts.
3. Except for very few exceptions, collective bargaining in the Philippines takes place at the enterprise level. While collective agreements are entered into by a union and a single employer, the same federation is the bargaining representative of employees working for different employers engaged in the same industry. In a situation of this kind, more often than not, the federation involved has the same set of demands as it bargains with the different employers. Important tripartite conferences have been convened by the Minister of Labor and Employment. A good

example is the National Tripartite Conference on Wages, Income and Employment Policies for National Development held from 25 to 27 of April, 1976. This conference was the specific basis for Presidential Decree No. 928 which provided new minimum wage rates effective May 1, 1976. Tripartism in labor relations is a State policy in the Philippines. The State encourages the representation of workers and employers in policy-making bodies of the government.

Labour Arbitration

The Labor Code, in enumerating the kinds of disputes that may arise between the employer and his workers, includes "unresolved questions in collective bargaining" or "deadlocks in collective bargaining." The Bureau of Labor Relations shall have fifteen (15) working days to act on all labor cases, subject to extension by agreement of the parties, after which the Bureau shall refer the cases to the appropriate Labor Arbiters.

If dispute concerns provisions of a collective bargaining agreement, the Labor Code provides for a grievance procedure and then arbitration by an arbitrator or panel of arbitrators selected by the parties themselves or else by the Bureau of Labor Relations.

If a dispute concerns the renewal or conclusion of a collective agreement, the Bureau of Labor Relations will help bring about a voluntary settlement. If not, the dispute is certified for compulsory arbitration, through the administrative machinery set up by the Labor Code for the settlement of labor disputes.

Contract Negotiation

Contract negotiation is the process by which employers and employees deliberate, argue, and haggle with one another in order to agree on wages, hours of work, and other conditions of employment. Eventually a labor-management contract is made. Human beings are not physical goods. Social, political, physiological and emotional as well as economic and technological issues are involved. In addition, once a labor-management contract is signed, both parties must agree to bargain in good faith in the future. Because dealings cannot arbitrarily be broken off, the union and management must learn to live with one another whether they like it or not.

All employer and employees agreements tend to progress through the following stages: (1) pre-negotiation; (2) selection of union and management representatives; (3) formation of a negotiation strategy; (4) implementation or negotiation tactics; and (5) the final labor-management contract or agreement. Saving face and putting on a show are as much part of the negotiation process as are hard facts and figures. The formation of a labor-management contract cannot be properly understood unless analyzed from both a reality (economic) and a reality (political) perspective.

Contract Administration

Contract negotiation and contract administration together constitute labor relations-collective bargaining. Administering a labor-management agreement means carrying out all the subject matter in the negotiated contract.

Management-Labor Union Relations

Management has several courses of action relating to labor unions. One is to fight the union. This is not advisable because outright discrimination against union members is unlawful. A second alternative would be to have an armed truce, exerting effort to contain the union and preserve managerial rights. This occurs when the interests of the company and those of the union are in conflict and a power struggle exists over union security and management rights. A third alternative is for management to work harmoniously with the union, that is, to help the union become responsible by taking the initiative in seeking to establish friendly relations based on fair dealings and understanding of each other's problems and goals. An ideal relationship exists when both union and management accept a common responsibility in matters affecting both the company and the employees, such as increased productivity, better quality control and cost production.

Here are some guidelines for management in relating with the union:

1. Remember that the employees are not the enemy.
2. Encourage honest recognition of the union.
3. Recognize that union and company objectives can be harmonized.
4. Establish and communicate the company's labor relations policy.
5. Write labor contracts that are clear and that protect management's right to manage.
6. Avoid the "happiness syndrome" of peace at any price.

STUDY/REVIEW QUESTIONS

1. What are labor relations?

2. Explain the Philippine laws that regulate labor relations in the Philippines.

3. What is a Labor Union? How can a Labor Union be a positive factor for the good of the entire business organization?

SUGGESTED ACTIVITIES AND ASSIGNMENT

1. Make a list of Filipino values that should be taken into consideration in dealing with Labor Unions.

2. Make a list of Filipino values that should be taken into consideration in collective bargaining.

3. Secure a copy of the Collective Bargaining Agreement of any organization and discuss it.

4. Interview both a union president and a legal labor counsel for an organization about the desirability of unionism in the Philippines. What are the similarities and dissimilarities in their opinions?

REFERENCES FOR FURTHER READING

Andres, Tomas D. *Management By Filipino Values.* Quezon City: New Day Publishers, 1985.

Chruden, Herbert J. and Sherman, Arthur W. Jr. *Personnel Management.* Chicago: South Western Publishing Company, 1968.

Ministry of Labor and Employment. *Labor Code of the Philippines.*

Sison, Perfecto S. *Personnel and Human Resource Management.* Manila: Rex Book Store, 1981.

22

HUMAN RESOURCE DISCIPLINE, COMPLAINTS AND GRIEVANCES

HUMAN RESOURCE DISCIPLINE means doing the right thing at the right time at the right place with the right intention in the right manner. It does not mean strict and technical observance of rigid rules and regulations. It means cooperative working and b ehaving in a normal and orderly way. In this sense the best discipline is self-discipline. Human resource managers make people understand what is required of them so that they can be counted on to do their job effectively and with good cheer.

Coming to work on time, following the supervisor's instructions, avoiding fighting and drinking, punching the time clock-all these are accepted by the majority of employees as reasonable and necessary conditions of work. In some organizations, new employees need orientation seminars. Even before starting to work, mature people know that following instructions and abiding by fair rules of conduct are necessary. Most employees can be counted upon to exercise a considerable degree of discipline. They will respond to positive leadership and need not be threatened or punished. Whenever effective teamwork exists, group discipline can supplement self discipline.

Nevertheless, business and industrial corporations in the Philippines are beset with such problems as tardiness, absenteeism, dishonesty and insubordination. These problems require effective management and constructive discipline.

Three Types of Discipline

A. *Preventive Discipline*

Preventive discipline is based on criticism and reminder-gentle, freely given, constructive. Employees know there is no stigma attached because all are subject to it.

In preventive discipline, management, through its supervisors, explains what went wrong or might be going wrong; uses an informal, helpful approach, and lets the subordinate follow through by himself.

B. *Positive Discipline*

This is a more formal and is handled behind closed doors. Its purpose is to correct and to control. Positive discipline offers a second chance. "What you are doing is not acceptable but things can be all right again if you make certain changes." The supervisor has to gain agreement from the subordinate on the procedures and he has to monitor them.

C. *Punitive Discipline*

Punitive discipline is a last resort. It is sometimes called "corrective" or "progressive" discipline because it calls for increasingly severe penalties each time an employee is disciplined. Except for very serious wrongdoings such as stealing or falsification of official documents, an employee is rarely discharged for a first offense. Before a worker is discharged, evidence should show that the supervisor made an effort to rehabilitate the rule violator.

Ordinarily, the sequence or stages of punitive discipline are as follows:

1. Verbal Warning
2. Written Warning
3. Disciplinary Suspension
4. Dismissal

Verbal Warning. When a man fails to maintain standards, or has broken a rule, a clear verbal warning is in order. The supervisor should concentrate on helping the subordinate figure out ways to prevent his troubles from recurring.

Written Warning. This is the first formal stage of punitive discipline.

Psychologically, it is not different from verbal warning, but it is made part of the employee's record and can be presented as evidence if more serious penalties follow or if the case is under arbitration.

Disciplinary Suspension. This is a temporary lay off due to repeated violation of a rule or policy of the organization. The length of suspension depends on the gravity of the offense.

Dismissal. This is used less and less commonly considering the impact it has on the employee and the cost it may incur for training a new employee.

Principles of Discipline

The foundation of human resource discipline is good instruction, training and education. Management must always be ready to help its employees understand that if things are not done according to specified norms of behavior, some form of penalty will be imposed. Employees must be instructed in the rules and the penalties attached in case of violation. Let them know that management has the authority to administer penalties. A good human resource disciplinarian knows the psychological needs of his people. Everything is done to win employee loyalty, thus decreasing the number of disciplinary problems. Management must keep in mind the educational function of discipline. Consistent discipline helps to set limits, that is, to inform employees what they can and cannot do; inconsistent discipline leads to confusion and uncertainty. When some rules are permitted to go unenforced, employees may either decide to ignore all rules or become confused about what is really required of them.

Discipline should be neither greater nor less than expected. If the degree of discipline comes as a surprise, the company may have failed to give adequate warning; if it is less than expected, the company will have difficulty in gaining acceptance of a more serious penalty in the future.

Guidelines for Effective Disciplining

Rules must be emphasized and not personal desires. Make the rules reasonable. Disciplinary rules are intended to foster at all times the high morale that makes for self-discipline in every employee and group discipline within every work team.

Publicize the rules in language understandable to all concerned. Ignorance of rules is a good excuse if the employer fails to publicize them. Announcing the rules to all employees can be done through handbooks, letters, memos, union contracts, and bulletin board notices. When publicizing rules, it is wise to announce the penalty for violation—a warning slip, suspension or discharge. The exact authority for each step in discipline must be clearly defined.

The discipline should not rob the employees of their dignity. Whenever and wherever necessary, the reasons for each rule should be explained.

The rules should establish the proper procedure for investigating the circumstances of each case before taking disciplinary actions. In most instances, especially in a dismissal case, the manager must show clearly that his employee was guilty of the alleged crime or violation. When guilt has been established, disciplinary measures should be promptly and consistently applied.

Responsibility for Discipline

Discipline is everybody's responsibility in organizational life. However, the immediate superior is responsible for maintaining discipline among the people under him. The following are especially responsible for maintaining discipline:

1. *The supervisor* - The supervisor is the company officer closest to the workers. He must understand the principles, rules and regulations necessary to good conduct. He must know his people as individuals and treat them fairly and impartially. He trains his subordinates and knows that because of individual difference, discipline cannot be a routine matter. In disciplining, he knows that the burden of proof is his.
2. *The Human Resource/Personnel Department* - The Human Resource/Personnel Department trains supervisors and managers in matters related to disciplinary action. It familiarizes them with the legal aspects of disciplinary action.
3. *Labor Union* - The Labor Union can be a very potent arm in implementing discipline. In the spirit of good relations, it is advisable to give union officers advance notice of the corrective action contemplated for an employee who is covered by a labor agreement.
4. *Top Management* - Top management must give due support to

the human resource disciplinary system. It must lead and set the example.

5. *The Workers* - The workers can discipline one another by reminding them of the rules to be followed in order to achieve the organizational objectives.

Disciplinary Processes

When breach of discipline occurs, the employee concerned must be alerted. This will establish the basis for the investigation and possible disciplinary action.

In handling disciplinary situations, gather as many objective and concrete facts as possible. Check the erring employee's previous record of offenses and accomplishments. Give the employee concerned the opportunity to fully state his side of the story. Hold interviews privately so as to avoid embarrassment on the part of employees who can provide you with factual information. At the same time assure them that all their statements will be treated confidentially. Simultaneously, tactfully warn them that their words will be relied upon as true statements and that any falsehood will bring them some unfavorable consequences. Hold interviews as soon after the offense as possible. Exert every possible effort to verify every statement given. Find out what has been done with similar cases within the department, and what has been done with similar cases in other departments.

Disciplinary Interview - Be sure that you are in the right mood before you conduct a disciplinary interview. In the disciplinary interview, counseling is given to employees who need to improve or realign their behavior. Professional guidance is given to the individual by utilizing psychological methods especially in gathering case history data, and testing interests and aptitudes.

Here are some guidelines for holding disciplinary interviews:

1. Treat each employee as an individual different from the others.
2. Begin the interview with a question or a request for information, not an accusation. Ask the who, what, where, when, why, and how in a friendly manner.
3. Ask the employee to give his position regarding the problem.
4. Listen sympathetically to the employee's reason. Keep calm. Be careful not to show anger. Don't threaten or argue.
5. Let the employee give his explanation and defense on the evidence you have and the evaluations you have made.

6. Criticize the wrong-doing, not the wrong-doer. Do not scold. Maintain your high respect for the employee.
7. Focus the employee's attention on the correction of the mistake. Make allowance for an honest mistake.
8. Encourage the employee to give possible solutions to correct his wrong-doing.
9. Offer your sincere help in doing this.
10. Agree on specific corrective action and follow-up.

After weighing all facts gathered before and after the disciplinary interview, do the following in imposing discipline:

1. Find out what has been done in similar cases in your department and in other departments.
2. Do not let personalities affect your decision.
3. See to it that the discipline fits the violation and will prevent a recurrence.
4. See to it that the disciplinary measure will maintain morale and encourage the employee's initiative.
5. See to it that the measure creates a desire in the employee to do what is right.
6. Check your measure with your immediate superior and the Human Resource Department.
7. If the employee has been previously disciplined for the same type of misconduct, study hard the measure to be imposed.

To administer the corrective measure properly do the following:

1. If there are several violations of the same nature, consider whether the offenders should be suspended or reprimanded individually or collectively.
2. Explain to the employee concerned why the action is necessary.
3. Be firm in your decision but be understanding.
4. Assure the employee that you will not hold a grudge against him in the future.
5. Elicit a favorable reaction from the employee concerned. Reassure him that you know his good qualities as well as the bad.
6. Express your faith and confidence in the employee.
7. Report promptly the disciplinary action to the Human Resource/Personnel Department. Fill out a Personnel Folder Memo covering the decision and/or action taken.

After administering discipline, make the necessary follow-up:

1. Learn whether the measure had the desired effect on the employee.
2. Do everything possible to overcome any resentment.
3. See to it that the employee is convinced that the action was for his best interest.
4. Compliment the employee on his good work.
5. Notice whether the disciplinary measure had the desired effect on other employees of the company.

Reprimand

A reprimand serves as a warning to the employee. It is a severe formal reproof; a censure, especially by one in authority. A reprimand can be either oral or written.

Since the very purpose of discipline is to build a man and not to destroy him the following principles will be effective:

1. Reprimand in private, never in front of others.
2. Be sure the reprimand is deserved.
3. Present the facts calmly. Avoid sarcastic words, anger or abuse. But be firm and explain clearly.
4. Know your employee and suit the reprimand to his individuality. Consider his previous penalties, latest infraction, and sense of responsibility. Fit the reprimand to the individual and his offense.
5. Reprimand promptly.
6. Use tact and be constructive.
7. When the employee has admitted his error, the reprimand is over.
8. Encourage him to do better and let him know the incident is closed. Do not nag. Show confidence in him.
9. Record the reprimand and inform the Human Resource/Personnel Department.
10. Later, follow up with a casual and friendly contact at his workplace.

Suspension

Suspension is temporary removal from the service. Preventive suspension is done when the employee's continued service poses a threat to his co-employees or his employer or to company property.

Admonition

Admonition is a friendly reproof or counseling against a fault, error or oversight. It expresses authoritative advice. A single admonition may be sufficient.

Dismissal

There are times when an employee's work is no poor or his behavior so unacceptable that dismissal from the company is a must.

If you must discharge or recommend for dismissal an employee, be guided by the following:

1. Know whether the employee has been adequately trained for the work.
2. Know whether he realizes the seriousness of his situation or whether he has been given promotions and other indicators of adequate service.
3. Know whether your decision to discharge him or to recommend his dismissal is rational.
4. Discuss the matter with other officers, your superior and the Human Resource/Personnel Department.
5. Plan for someone to take over the employee's job.
6. Prepare the other employees so that their reactions will not be unfavorable.
7. Keep in mind the importance of public and employee relations, as well as the feelings of the discharged employee. Make the experience as painless as possible.
8. Discharge should be resorted to when the employee's record shows clearly that no warnings and other disciplinary actions have impressed the employee with the error of his ways, or when an offense is of so serious a nature that it cannot be ignored.

Human Resource Complaints and Grievances

A complaint is an expression of protest or resentment. A grievance is dissatisfaction with a company's practices or its executives. A grievance is formally presented to a management representative or to a union official.

Grievances are dangerous because of the damage they do to productivity. Efforts should be made to ascertain if there are smoldering areas of unrest. Managers have to be concerned with all forms of discontent regardless of their opinion of its validity.

Causes of Complaints and Grievances

Complaints and grievances are rooted in individual differences. The way in which employees interpret company policies and practices may differ from what management intends.

Some complaints and grievances concern wages or hours of employment, working conditions, inequitable work distribution, promises not kept, "juggling" piece rates, failure to promote from within or lack of human interest on the part of management. Most grievances arise from failure of the employees to derive satisfaction from their jobs, from a threat to their security on the job, from failure of the supervisors to understand them, or from an employee's maladjustment.

Principles of Handling Employees' Complaints and Grievances

Attending to employees' complaints and grievances calls for proper understanding. Bigger problems can be avoided by nipping dissatisfaction in the bud.

A. *The Supervisor* has the responsibility to discover and settle complaints and grievances. He should be alert to correct unsatisfactory conditions before grievance develops. Complaints should be entertained and welcomed. If supervisors are hostile towards employees who complain the latter will not voice their gripes, their feelings accumulate, and their morale is lowered.

Fearing that the supervisor will take drastic action against them, they take their grievances to the union.

When an employee approaches a supervisor because he has a complaint or grievance, the superior must feel honored. It is a sign of his good leadership. Moreover, it affords him the chance to show that particular employee and to others that he can be trusted to remedy the situation. The supervisor must remember that he is the "management" as far as his men are concerned, and for every success in satisfying their desires, he earns something for the employees, for the management and for his leadership. In handling employees' complaints, the supervisor must be:

1. A good listener.

2. Able to elicit the employee's full and complete story.
3. A judge of the evidence the employee presents.
4. Fair to the employee.
5. Able to deduce what benefits the employee is trying to gain.
6. Able to tell his side of the story.
7. Able to show how the employee will benefit.
8. Able to show disadvantages of hazards to the worker.
9. Frank in telling what he cannot do-and what he can do.
10. Able to follow-up on subsequent events.
11. Able to say "no" in the right way if "no" is the right answer.
12. Able to avoid snap judgment.

B. *Management.* Management should welcome employee grievances so that they can be settled promptly before they spread to other departments. This attitude gives management a chance to improve employer-employee relations. Management should know the root cause of the complaint, what is actually bothering the employee. Management should encourage employees to first take their grievances to their supervisors.

Management should consider the following:

1. During the interview regarding the employees' complaints management should gain the employees' confidence.
2. It should avoid implying that subordinates are ignorant.
3. It should display a sincere interest in the problems of employees and willingness to help.
4. Every grievance should be considered important no matter how insignificant it seems.
5. In grievance interviews people should be taken for what they are-their strengths and weaknesses.
6. Grievance handling involves a number of people dealing with problems that go through a number of stages and may extend from days to months.

C. *Human Resource/Personnel Manager.* The Human Resource/ Personnel Manager must train and develop both supervisors and managers in handling effectively grievances of their employees. He must make the supervisors aware of the four kinds of grievances:

1. Real grievances: Here the cause is obvious; grievance is legitimate; facts are clearly presented; and the worker can be reasoned with.
2. Imaginary grievances: These exist only in the mind of the worker;

the worker feels he is being picked on—"my supervisor doesn't like me," are usually the result of rumors, half-truths and gossip.

3. Silent grievances: The employee keeps his gripes to himself says nothing, is resentful, discontented.
4. Expressed grievances: The employee complains openly, talks about it; tells supervisors what is "on his mind—gets it off his chest.

The sources of grievances must be taught to the supervisors. There are three types of sources:

1. Inside the Company: Poor working conditions; unjust criticism; unfairly denied promotion or pay increase; favoritism in job assignments.
2. Outside the Company: Political and economic propaganda which gives employees distorted views; employee is convinced by friends, who don't know the facts that he is being unfairly treated.
3. Within the Employee: Personal problems; employee is highly emotional, easily offended; employee is very nervous.

The following guidelines will aid the supervisor in preventing grievances from becoming major problems:

1. Constantly observe employee at his work: Is his work satisfactory? If not, what is wrong? Does he want to work? Has his output or quality of work dropped?
2. Know the employee as an individual: What is his attitude? Does something seem to be bothering him? How does he get along with his fellow workers? Does he have personal difficulties?
3. Recognize danger signals: Signs of bad disposition, change in work habits, change in punctuality, decreased production, low morale of department, rumors and gossip.
4. Know the union officers: Are they emotionally stable and reasonable? Are they courteous? What is their general attitude toward company policies? Are they fair and honest? Do they present all the facts? Do they tell you how to run your department?

Steps in Handling Grievances

Suppose an employee is dissatisfied. He talks with his fellow employees who agree within. Finally he expresses his dissatisfaction in the form of a complaint to the supervisor.

There are three steps in hearing a grievance:

1. Listen to the employee's story. Let him get the complaint "off his chest."
2. Calm him down by being friendly. Build up his self-confidence and make him feel satisfied and cooperative.
3. When he reaches reasoning level, do something about the grievance.

The handling of grievances requires the following steps:

1. Define, the nature of the grievance as clearly and as fully as possible.
2. Gather all the facts that explain when, how, where, to whom, and why the grievance occurred.
3. Establish tentative solutions.
4. Gather additional information so as to ascertain the best possible solution.
5. Apply the solution.
6. Follow up on the case to see that it has been handled satisfactorily and the trouble eliminated.

Organizationally, grievance handling is shared by first-line supervisors, staff and middle management executives, top management, and a labor union representative.

Grievance Procedure

This is the process whereby the employer, the employee and the union analyze and discuss a complaint hoping to establish effective machinery for its solution. More specifically, the purposes of grievance procedure are:

1. To protect the workers' democratic rights on the job—
   a. Management exercises full power and control over workers' tenure when there is no union; therefore, no appeal could be made on management system of discipline.
   b. Aggrieved workers may appeal through grievance procedure

provided in the collective bargaining agreement.

2. To establish a system whereby the contract is checked and fully enforced.
3. Provide proper channels in processing complaints or grievances.
4. Provide worker with collective support of the union in seeking justice or redress for his grievance.
5. To improve the efficiency of the company—
   a. Grievance procedure uncovers sources of friction before they spread and impair production.
   b. Contented workers have higher outputs than unhappy ones.
   c. Grievance machinery enables top executives of a company to check on the effectiveness of their supervisors.
6. To promote harmonious relations between labor and management—
   a. Grievance procedure, by requiring both parties to work together in settling small disputes, gives them valuable experience for future contract negotiations.
   b. Grievance procedure fosters mature collective bargaining.

Steps in Grievance Procedure

The steps in grievance procedure provide a method of appeal to higher authority. The number of steps depends on size of the company, the number of levels of supervision, size and structure of the union whether local or national.

Step 1: Worker brings grievance to steward and together they take grievance to Shop Foreman. Time limit: 2 days or as agreed upon.

Step 2: If no settlement or adjustment is achieved, the shop steward consults department steward and/or union grievance committee and bring the case to Plant Superintendent or Local Manager of the Company.

Step 3: If no settlement in step 2 is obtained, then the case is brought to Local Union President and/or Representative of National Federation, and the case is taken up with the General Manager of the Company or its Labor Relations Manager.

Step 4: If no settlement in Step 3 is obtained, then the case is submitted to arbitration for final disposition.

Labor Arbitration: Voluntary, Compulsory, Conciliation and Mediation

Arbitration is a means of settling a dispute between a firm and a union by a third party previously selected and agreed upon by them. In voluntary arbitration both parties agree in advance to abide by the decision of the arbiter.

Voluntary arbitration awards or decisions shall be final, unappealable and executory. However, voluntary arbitration awards or decisions on money claims involving an amount exceeding P100,000 or 40% of the paid up capital of the respondent employer, whichever is lower, may be appealed to the National Labor Relations Commission but only on the following grounds:

1. Abuse of discretion; and
2. Gross incompetence. (Art. 263 of Labor Code)

Voluntary Arbitration

The State encourages voluntary arbitration on all labor-management disputes. Any case filed with the Labor Relations Division, Labor Arbiters and compulsory arbitrators may be referred for voluntary arbitration at any time before submission of the case for decision. It is a part of the collective bargaining process and, in fact, its terminal point. It is a settlement of disputes without recourse to a court of law. However, the decision rendered by the arbitrator has the force and effect of law.

The Arbitrator

The arbitrator is a person fully authorized to judge or decide a certain case. Voluntary arbitrators have exclusive and original jurisdiction to settle and decide all disputes, grievances, or matters arising from the implementation of a collective bargaining agreement, after going through the grievance procedure.

Steps in Voluntary Arbitration

Once the parties have come to an agreement to settle their dispute by voluntary arbitration and have selected the arbitrator, and the date, time and place of hearing have been set, the order of proceedings will be as follows:

1. Oath of arbitrator to hear and decide the case impartially and to render justice to the parties. This is considered waived if not re-

quested by the parties.

2. Definition of the issue or submission agreement. The primary purpose of the submission agreement is to define the issue.
3. Stipulation of facts. The parties write down the facts mutually admitted by them.
4. Agreement on order or presentation. The arbitrator can suggest the order of presentation. Usually, the union has the burden of "going forward" because it has raised the grievance. In discharge and discipline cases, the employer has the burden of initiating the presentation.
5. A brief introductory statement by each side. It includes a definition of the issue, the statement of mutually agreed facts, the pertinent clauses of the Collective Bargaining Agreement, and a brief enumeration of the arguments.
6. Presentation of case by the initiating party. Witnesses may testify on direct examination subject to cross-examination. Strict technicalities are frowned upon and arbitrators will tend to err in favor of liberality, care, and prudence.
7. Presentation of case by opposing party. He may also present witnesses.
8. Summation. Parties may orally summarize the evidence they have presented in support of their respective contentions, citing pertinent contractual provisions as well as pertinent laws, and leading cases, if any.
9. Post-hearing briefs or memorandums. The parties must submit a written summation.

Once the decision is given, the interested party files a motion for execution before the labor arbiter in the regional office of the Department of Labor.

Compulsory Arbitration

In compulsory Arbitration the person designated to decide cases is not selected and appointed by the parties themselves.

The Commission or any Labor Arbiter selects other government officials or qualified private citizens to act as compulsory arbitrators. He fixes the fees for such compulsory arbitrators, taking into account the nature of the case, the time consumed in hearing the case, the professional standing of the arbitrators, the financial capacity of the parties, and the fees provided in the Rules of Court.

Conciliation

Cases on money claims, unfair labor practices and deadlocks in collective negotiations are filed with the Regional Office.

If an employer-employee relationship still exists, the Regional Director shall handle the case in accordance with Article 127 of the Labor Code and Rule X, Book III of the Rules.

If the relationship no longer exists, the Director shall appoint a "Conciliator" who shall, within five days, call the parties to a meeting. The Conciliator shall have fifteen days in which to effect amicable settlement.

If no settlement is reached the Regional Director shall certify the case to a Labor Arbiter immediately.

Mediation

Mediation means friendly intervention in the disputes of parties with their consent. Disputes brought to the Regional Offices are tried through mediation hoping to make both parties sèttle their differences amicably without conciliation or arbitration.

Mediation is a less formal method of settling industrial disputes. The conciliator, who is not a party to the dispute, may promote negotiations between the disputants that to lead either to amicable settlement or an agreement to submit the controversy to arbitration.

A mediator bears messages between the parties, and also makes his own proposals for acceptance by the disputants.

STUDY/REVIEW QUESTIONS

1. What is the proper way of disciplining a Filipino employee?
2. Who are responsible for maintaining discipline in an organization?
3. When and how should a reprimand be given to a Filipino employee?
4. How effective is suspension in the Philippine setting in disciplining a Filipino employee?
5. What are the common causes of complaints and grievances of Filipino employees?
6. How should labor arbitration be done in the Philippine setting?

SUGGESTED ACTIVITIES AND ASSIGNMENT

1. Make a list of Filipino values related to discipline.
2. Make a list of Filipino values related to labor arbitration.
3. Secure a copy of a company's Code of Discipline and criticize it.

REFERENCES FOR FURTHER READING

Andres, Tomas D. *Management By Filipino Values.* Quezon City: New Day Publishers, 1985.

Angeles, Conrado P. et al. *Principles of Personnel Administration.* Quezon City: R.M. Garcia Publishing House, 1981.

Sison, Perfecto S. *Personnel and Human Resources Management.* Manila: Rex Book Store, 1981.

23

HUMAN RESOURCE HEALTH AND SAFETY

EMPLOYERS in the Philippines need to reduce work injuries and advance the health of their people for two reasons: First is the humanitarian concern for their human resources. They should genuinely seek to prevent human suffering and maintain a safe, healthy environment. Second is the concern of the Government to protect employees, which is expressed in the Labor Code as well as Presidential Decree Number 442 as amended in Book IV on Health, Safety and Social Welfare Benefits. The Presidential Decree includes Medical, Dental and Occupational Safety.

Safety Program

The safety of personnel whether in an office, in the shop, or in field activities, is the definite responsibility of management.

A good company safety program consists of the following elements:

1. *Support by Top Management.* Top management must lend a safety program its active support and give more than just lip service. Foremen and supervisors should be the first to know about the program. If management actually supports the safety program through commendation, reprimands, promotion, transfer and the like, lower management will respond.
2. *Appointment of a Safety Officer*. Someone must be made responsible for installing and maintaining a safety program.
3. *Engineering a safe plant and safe operation.* Human engineering

refers to developing tools, materials, equipment and workplaces in such a way that they can be effectively operated by a human being. The first objective of human engineering is to improve performance. The second objective is to enhance the individual's physical and mental condition through making his work more comfortable and less fatiguing and hazardous.

4. *Educating all employees to act safely.* The employee must be educated to act, think and work safely. Here are ways in which this education can take place:
   a. Part of the induction of new employees can be devoted to the safety policies of the company. Warning should be given concerning danger points of job operations.
   b. Emphasis on safety points during training sessions, particularly in on-the-job training.
   c. Special efforts made by the first level supervisors.
   d. Establishment of an Employee Safety Committee.
   e. Holding of special employee safety meetings.
   f. Warnings printed in the company periodical.
   g. Charts, posters, and displays emphasizing the need to act safely.
5. *Accident Analysis.* An accident should be studied in all of its aspects: the man and the job, tools and equipment involved, particular acts, the department in which it happened, manner in which the employee was injured.

A group of safety engineers concluded that:[1]

1. Industrial injuries result only from accidents;
2. Accidents are caused directly only by:
   a. The unsafe acts of persons or
   b. Exposure to unsafe mechanical conditions;
3. Unsafe actions and conditions are caused only by faults of persons, and
4. Faults of persons are created by environment or acquired by inheritance.

According to this group of safety engineers, an injury is invariably caused by an accident which in turn, is always the result of the factor that immediately precedes it. A diagrammatical analysis of this sequence is as follows:

1. The injury is caused by the action of a preceding factor.
2. The unsafe act and mechanical hazard constitute the central

factor in the accident sequence.
3. The removal of the central factor makes the action of preceding factors ineffective.

Here are some guidelines for accident prevention:
1. Publicize and enforce all safety regulations within the organization.
2. Include Accident Prevention Instructions as a part of job instruction.
3. Keep all safety devices in proper condition.
4. Watch constantly to detect unsafe practices.
5. Keep safety posters, bulletins, and instructions posted and up-to-date.
6. Never ignore a violation of safety instructions.

A good Accident Prevention Program results in the following: saving of life and limb, insurance-premium reduction, continuity of service, increase in production, decreased labor turn-over, and improved labor-management relations.

The Safety Committee

To maintain first-rate safety performance, the full cooperation of everyone is needed. The safety committee is one means of obtaining this cooperation.

This is a group of employees appointed to aid and advise management on matters of worker safety. The committee may be composed of a top manager and two or three supervisors and workers. The chairman should be a supervisor chosen for qualities of leadership, interest in safety, and ability to get results. It is practical to appoint an engineer, supervisor or master mechanic to the committee with full authority to correct unsafe conditions.

The committee should hold regular monthly meetings and make monthly inspections of selected areas. The safety committee keeps management informed as to the condition of buildings, grounds, and equipment, and as to requirements for increased safety. The definite functions of the Safety Committee are:[2]

1. To aid the employer in all matters pertaining to the safety and health of his employees
2. To aid management in initiating a sound safety program and in

supervising and directing all safety activities

3. To study and plan safety promotional and educational projects
4. To recommend and help in handling suggestions aimed at eliminating hazards, and unsafe work practices.

Bureau of Labor Safety Order No. 7 requires all establishments to organize a Safety Committee within 30 days after their first day of operation.

Health Program

The nature of the health programs and the types of services provided to employees vary according to the size, location and special needs of the organization. The typical functions of a Health Program are: recognizing and controlling health hazards, providing medical assistance, and training personnel.

One of the main objectives of company health programs is to educate personnel on the principles of good physical and mental health. The success of the program depends upon stimulating interest among employees. This may be done through posters and films and talks and interviews with employees. A good Health Program consists of the following:

A. *Physical Health:*

1. Pre-placement physical examination.
2. Periodic physical examination for all key personnel.
3. Voluntary periodic physical examination for all personnel.
4. A well-equipped and staffed medical dispensary.
5. Availability of competent medical consultants.
6. Systematic attention devoted to health hazards.
7. Periodic and systematic inspections of provisions for proper sanitation.

B. *Mental Health:*

1. Availability of psychiatric counselling
2. Cooperation of outside psychiatric specialists and institutions
3. Education of company personnel concerning the nature and importance of the mental health program.
4. Development and maintenance of a proper human relations program.

Athletic, Sports and Physical Fitness Program

The efficiency of a company's human resource depends on their health and physical fitness. The physically fit individual moves more efficiently; hence he has a greater capacity for productive work. This is the rationale for an Athletic, Sports and Physical Fitness Program.

Philosophy. An athletic, sports and physical fitness program creates attitudes which will promote corporate growth and stability. The program molds better people on whose shoulders will fall corporate responsibility.

Such a program should enable as many employees as possible to train and compete. The program should never aim to produce a few super athletes. Medals and trophies can warp the basic philosophy.

An athletic, sports and physical fitness program can develop and nurture the mental, emotional, spiritual and psychological qualities needed for change and progress. Qualities and attitudes such as honesty, integrity, self-discipline and team spirit will be developed. Business is essentially competition. Such a program can help form the proper attitudes toward competition and fellow competitors. The true rewards of a sports and physical fitness program lie in developing immeasurable human qualities, for it is in this way that the employee becomes more energetic and productive.

Objectives. Sports and physical exercise develop man's mind, body and soul. No one area should be left behind.

This program aims to make employees adept in a variety of sports for all seasons of the year, to which they can turn for enjoyment, body maintenance and regeneration.

It aims to develop good health habits and to impart reasonable skills in leadership, and followership translatable in the actual work atmosphere. The program aims to develop the emotional stability needed to meet the strain of business imperatives. It aims to develop good sportmanship, self-discipline and the idea of fair play.

Physical Fitness. Physical fitness is the capacity to do one's daily tasks without undue fatigue and still have ample energy to enjoy leisure and meet emergencies. With regard to his physical fitness, a person should either maintain it or improve it. Any activity related to physical fitness maintenance or improvement must be governed by personal needs, objectives and inclinations.

Physical fitness requires:

1. Muscular strength - the capacity to exert a single maximal force, as in lifting up a typewriter, spare tire, or a grocery bag.
2. Muscular endurance - the capacity to persist in a localized muscular effort, such as standing up for a long time while waiting for a bus, or typing a voluminous company report.
3. General endurance - also known as cardiovascular or circulo-respiratory (CR) endurance. This is the capacity to postpone fatigue and persist in a given strenuous task involving total body movement. Jogging, swimming, disco dancing, or a hard game of pelota or basketball requires this endurance.
4. Flexibility - the capacity to move through such normal motions as bending, twisting and reaching. Lack of adequate flexibility has often caused low back pains, as well as muscle and joint injury.

In addition to these physical fitness components are traits ascribed to motor fitness:

1. Muscular power - the capacity too move forcefully and explosively, as in executing a serve in tennis or pelota, or in passing and shooting a basketball.
2. Speed - the ability to perform rapid movements as in running after a bus or in a "fastbreak" for the winning goal.
3. Agility - the ability to move suddenly and quickly.
4. Coordination - the ability to integrate different types of movement into a smooth, accurate, rhythmic and effective whole.
5. Balance - the ability to maintain one's equilibrium.
6. Reaction time - the time an individual needs to respond to a specific stimulus, like jamming the breaks of his car to avoid crashing into jaywalkers.

Principles of Physical Fitness Training. **Physical fitness programs are designed to improve an individual's muscular strength and resistance to fatigue, and, hence, his work output and efficiency. Physical fitness training is governed by certain principles:**

1. Overload Principle - Improvement in physical fitness is achieved by continuously subjecting the body to an increasing exercise load.
2. Specificity Principle - One gets what he trains for. For example, jogging enhances general endurance and the leg muscles. In order to improve all aspects of physical fitness, one must include

in his training program exercises to develop the body all around.

3. Time for Exercise - The time depends upon the inclination and timetable of the individual.
4. Exercise Time Patterns - Distributed practice sessions are better than one massed session.
5. Principle of Motivation - Motivation should be present in every physical fitness activity.

Physical Security Program

The degree and type of physical security required for an organization depend upon its size, its mission, vulnerability of equipment, geographic location, the economic and political situation of the area, the proximity of external support, and the capabilities of a threatening outside force.

Security consciousness must be acquired. The minimum requirements of an effective security program include the following:

1. Direction and guidance at major command level, and active support by the management.
2. Mandatory indoctrination of all personnel at the time of employment.
3. An advanced and continuous program to selected audiences foster a high degree of security consciousness.
4. The distribution to managers and supervisors of kits consisting of posters, placards, and suggestions pertaining to physical security.

The goal of security education is to explain the reason for security measures and to secure cooperation. It must be continually reiterated that a locked gate or file cabinet is merely an element in the overall security plan. Management should attempt to instill in all personnel willingness to learn and comply with all security regulations, to prevent infractions and violations, and to report violations or breaches of the security system promptly to the proper authority.

All newly assigned personnel must be given security indoctrination. This should include a discussion of those hazards common to all personnel, with emphasis on the danger of loose talk and operational carelessness. It should define in detail general security measures, such as the pass system, private vehicle control, and package inspection.

Plans and training personnel, technicians, and craftsmen require a higher degree of instruction. Supervisors and executives require still broader understanding of their security responsibilities. Separate instruction programs for each group will fit its security interest.

Legal Aspects of Safety and Health Programs

Government policies and laws on industrial health and safety follow:

1. The National Pollution Control Commission has issued standards with which industries are to comply if they are to operate. Industries that emit excessive pollutants are to stop operation.
2. Presidential Decree No. 274 ordered the immediate implementation of the Pasig River Development Program to protect the health of residents as well as employees in offices and plants located in its vicinity.
3. Presidential Decree No. 522 - This decree prescribed sanitation requirements for establishments and facilities for the protection and convenience of the traveling public as well as those employed in these establishments.
4. Section 2 (a) Rule I, Book IV, Rules and Regulations Implementing the Labor Code of the Philippines - This Rule requires that employees be given adequate, immediate and necessary medical and dental attention in case of injury or sudden illness suffered during employment irrespective of whether or not such injury is work-connected.
5. Section 3, Section 5, Rule I, Book IV of the Labor Code of the Philippines - This Rule requires employers to keep in their workplaces first aid medicines, equipment, and facilities and enter into a written contract with the nearest hospital in case of emergency.
6. The general occupational health and safety standard, Section 2, Rule II, Book IV - This standard prescribes that every employer covered by Rule II shall keep his workplace free from hazards that are likely to cause physical harm to the workers or damage to property.
7. Labor Code of the Philippines, Presidential Decree No. 442 as Amended:

Art. 155. Every employer should furnish his employees in any locality with free medical and dental attendance and (a) the services of a full-time registered nurse when the number of employees exceeds fifty (50) but is not more than two hundred, except when the employer does not maintain hazardous work places, in which case the services of a graduate first-aider shall be provided for the protection of the workers, where no registered nurse is available; (b) the services of a full-time registered nurse, a part-time physician and dentist, and an emergency clinic, when the number of employees exceeds two hundred but is not more than three hundred; and (c) the services of a full-time physician, dentist and full-time registered nurse as well as a dental clinic, and an infirmary or emergency hospital with one bed for every one hundred employees when the number of employees exceeds three hundred.

Art. 157 - A comprehensive health program for the employees should be developed and implemented by the physician engaged by an employer.

Section 7, Rule II - A sufficient number of supervisors and technical personnel should be trained in occupational safety and health.

STUDY/REVIEW QUESTIONS

1. Explain the different elements of a Safety Program.
2. What are the components of a Health Program in the Philippine setting?
3. Why is an Athletic, Sports and Physical Fitness Program important for the development of human resources?
4. What are the minimum requirements of an effective security program?

SUGGESTED ACTIVITIES AND ASSIGNMENT

1. Secure a copy of the Safety Program of a company and analyze it.
2. Interview the company doctor and/or nurse of any organization on its health program.
3. List the Filipino values that are related to an effective security program.

NOTES

[1]Regional Manpower Development Office Region IV, "Basic Supervisory Development Course Industrial Safety and Accident Prevention", Module GS-14/RT, pp. 57-59.

[2]Bureau of Labor Standard Safety Order No. 7, Integrated Safety Systems, Inc. *Industrial Safety Training Manual,* 1764 Taft Avenue, Pasay City, pp. 6-7.

REFERENCES FOR FURTHER READING

Sison, Perfecto S. *Personnel and Human Resources Management.* Manila: Rex Book Store, 1981.

Martinez, Esdras T. *Human Resources Management.* Manila: EIC Enterprises & Co., Inc., 1979.

Chruden, Herbert J. et al. *Personnel Management.* Chicago: South & Western Publishing Company, 1968.

PART SIX

HUMAN RESOURCE INFORMATION RECORDS, ACCOUNTING AND MEASUREMENT

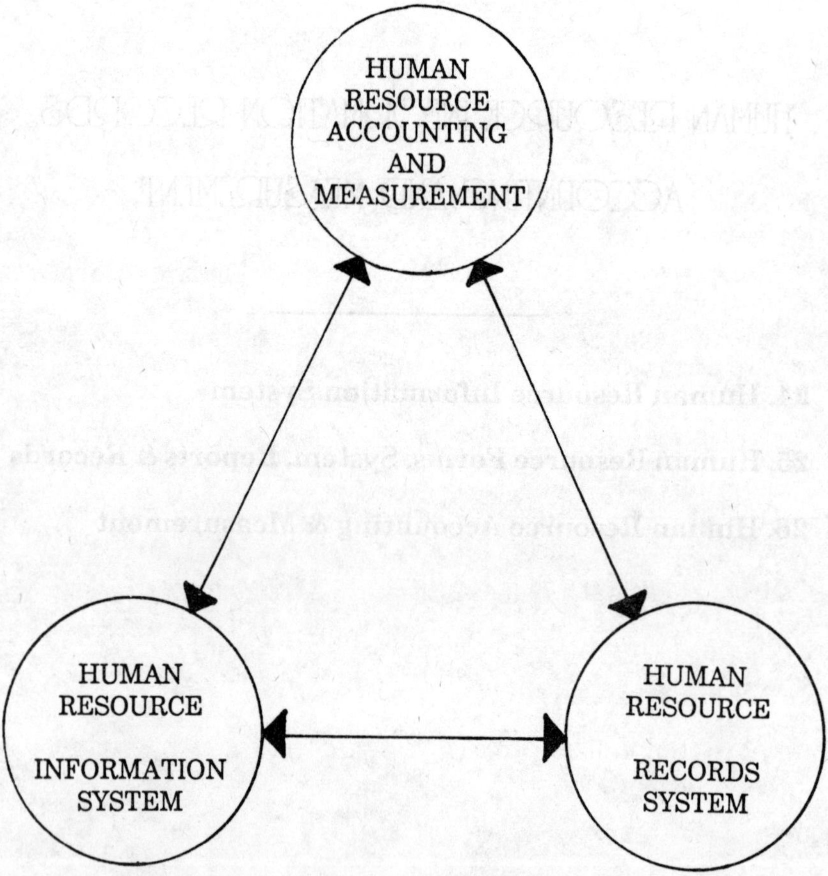

Human Resource Information, Records, Accounting and Measurement

24

HUMAN RESOURCE INFORMATION SYSTEM

AN INFORMATIVE SYSTEM is a logical, valid and reliable grouping of interpreted data which is useful for management decision making.

A Human Resource Information System involves data and guidelines for more effective management of human resources.

Human Resource Accounting aims to have both a balance sheet statement and an income and expense statement on human resources while Human Resources Bookkeeping, identifies the information that must be kept or should be kept and aims to collect and have available for retrieval such information on a cost/efficiency basis.

Characteristics of a Human Resource Information System

A Human Resource Information System has the following basic characteristics:

1. It effectively integrates component parts of information sub-systems. It thus produces a total information system consisting of integrated reports, letters, memoranda and electronic data processing.
2. The system is linked to electronic data processing facilities for ease of access, updating, and analysis.
3. The information is gathered, analyzed and presented in the form desired by decision makers in the organization.
4. As a corollary, the information is presented in the user's language, not the gatherer's.

5. The information is timely and cost-effective; that is, managers can still use it to effect a decision, and the benefits derived from using the information outweigh the cost of gathering, analyzing, and reporting.
6. The information is accurate, that is, reliable and valid.
7. Only those portions of information are presented to individual managers which relate to the scope of their job and its decision requirements.

Objectives of a Human Resource Information System

The basic purpose of this is to provide management with the information needed for human resource decisions such as decisions in acquiring, utilizing, maintaining and accounting for the resources of the organization.

Formerly, records were kept on personnel giving such data as previous employment experience, medical history, marital status, etc. This information was useful for employment decisions, but since it was not often updated, it had little use for managerial decisions some years after the initial date of employment. Managers had no timely, reliable, valid information to help maximize human resource effectiveness in the organization.

The Human Resource Informative System aims to reflect accurately an organization's human resource capability. Its information must be fully integrated into the management decision structure of the organization.

Components of a Human Resource Informative System

Only information units which enhance effective human resource decisions should be components of the Information System.

Data that predict future human resources performance greatly assist human resource decisions. Some companies' Human Resource Information Systems identify key variables that they think will affect future performance and focus on these.

Some components of an information system which are useful to managers in the four areas of human resource decisions are the following:

A. *Selection*

Typically, initial job selection decisions are based on such criteria as past educational achievement, past work experience, employer, and academic references, tests, and performance during an interview. Other data which are usually obtained are age, sex, race, marital status, and number of dependents.

To improve the human resource information needed in selection, the steps are the following:

1. Identify those factors which characterize effective job performance in each job class, in as explicit terms as possible. These ought to be stated terms perhaps along the lines suggested by a system of management's objectives.
2. Determine whether a job candidate can achieve these outputs by measuring, as directly as possible, whether he has and is likely to exercise the kinds of skills and knowledge needed by the job.
3. Examine each criterion in the present job selection process to determine if it gives valid prediction for the job class and, if so, if it is being objectively measured.

B. *Utilizing*

The initial information at the time of hiring should be supplemented with additional information. To determine, therefore, whether an individual will be effective in a new job to which he is to be promoted or transferred, the information needed is the individual's aspiration level and interests, career plans, and also job performance appraisal.

C. *Maintenance*

Health and life insurance accruals, pension accruals, standard salary progressions (as opposed to incremental financial rewards provided for outstanding performance such as a bonus), absence rates, tardiness rates, grievance rates, and disciplinary actions, are examples of human resource information concerned with the maintenance decisions.

The other data that reflect human resource maintenance activities are routine training to maintain present skills, changes in demographic information such as current address, marital status and number of dependents.

Human resource maintenance decisions are routinary.

D. *Human Resource Accounting*

A full accounting of the value of human resources for an organization is the final aim of a Human Resource Information System. It is important to measure the key dimensions of an organization at different time periods, say, at one age (T1) and now (T2). A suggested key dimension is the increase in a company's profit which can be directly attributable to increase in human production. If profits increased from P2,000,000 to P2,100,000 in one year and if 50% of this improvement came about through more productivity of workers then we can say that the value of the human resource increased by P50,000. Thus, if costs turnover, absenteeism, tardiness or waste fall by P50,000 in a given year, it can be deduced that the value of human resources increased by P50,000 in a year.

Balancing annual decreases and increases in the value of human resources tells the total human resource worth. This can be done by relating human resource performance, for example, to profit improvement. Looking at the market replacement value of the organization's human resources is another way of assessing the value of human resources. This is done by putting a peso value on such costs as recruiting, selection and placement, training, and cooperative working relationships and salaries needed to attract the employees.

Implementing a Human Resource Information System

A comprehensive Human Resource Information System is implemented in the following manner:

First, it is important to pinpoint responsibilities for gathering data. Generally the human resource data are provided by the employee, the Human Resource Management Department and Line Management. The HRM Department should provide the forms to be used and explain how information is to be analyzed and reported.

Second, the HRM Department compiles, synthesizes and summarizes the data. Then the Department analyzes these data and presents them in the user's language.

Third, the human resource information system should conform to the organization's management information system (MIS), avoiding duplication of its other components.

Fourth, the human resource information system should conform to the electronic data processing system (EDP). It should develop particular data items for identification purposes and utilize people in personnel who are trained in using computers. Relevant information which may already have been gathered and stored by computer may be used. Then, the analyzed data should be provided to the line managers.

Fifth, determine the forms which can be used for gathering and reporting data. Identify the output formats of the system such as HR Status Report, actual performance Report, etc. Furthermore, identify the input documents which will come from the different units. It shall be the unit's responsibility to include all needed data. All input data shall be kept in a historical file which may be retrieved when needed. Identify also the process involved in the system. The two (2) principle distinguishing processes are Status Report Generation and Performance Analysis Report Generation.

Sixth, identify the receivers of the information and the time it is to be given them. Generally the receivers of the information are the following: line managers to make utilization decisions; the Human Resource Management Department to recommend action to line managers; government agencies for monitoring purposes, other employers for personnel survey; and the employee himself to ensure accuracy and to have an opportunity to contest items in the file. The primary users of the information will be the HRM Department and line managers, who need it in a timely fashion to make appropriate reward, promotion and evaluation decisions. How often the information is needed will be told usually by the line managers, whether weekly, monthly, quarterly, or annually.

Implementation Strategy

The following are basic preconditions to guide the implementors of the system:

A. *Functional Strategy*

The Human Resource Management Department has to establish the policy that the Information System is the responsibility of the general and executive management. This means that top management must not only support the system but also spearhead the entire effort.

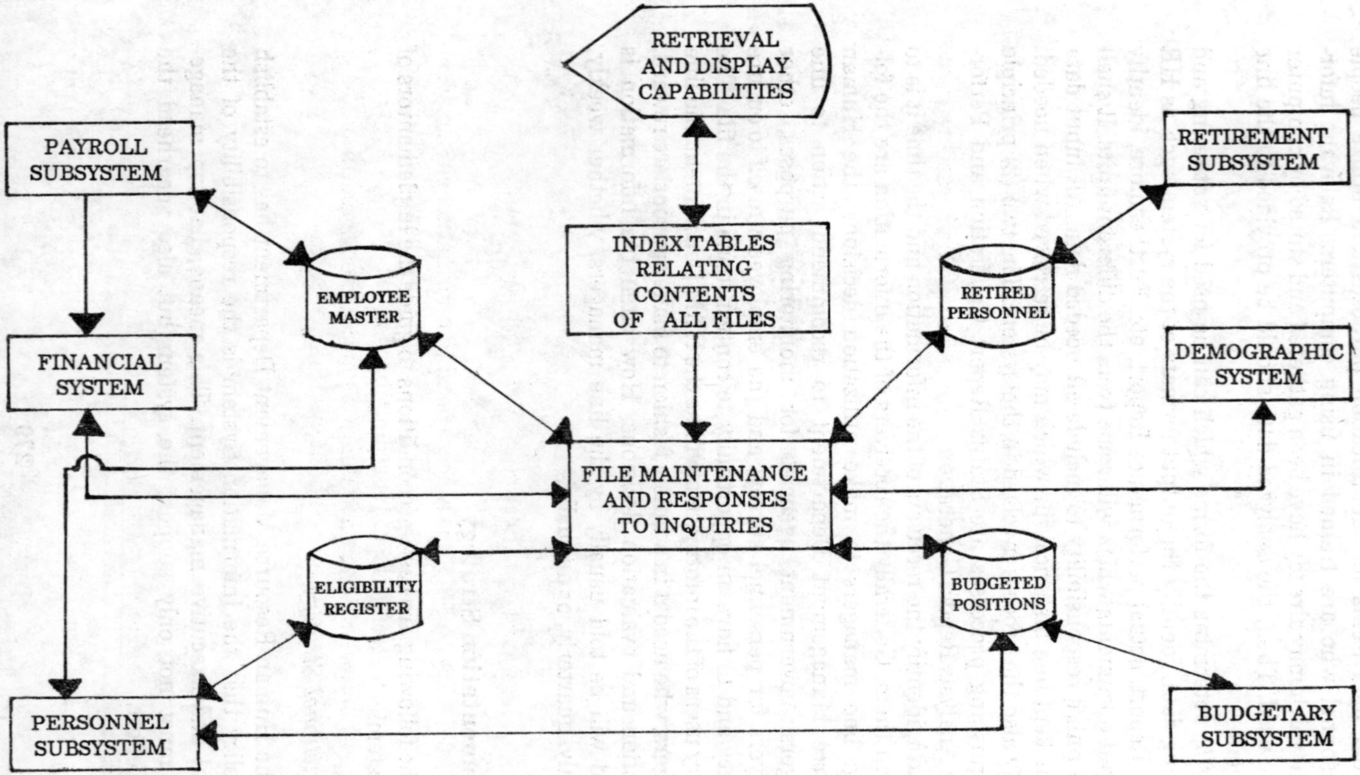

Employee Information System

B. *Training*

To ensure complete understanding and acceptance of the proposed system, line managers and staff concerned must be trained and briefed on the information-gathering procedure.

C. *Testing and Acceptance*

The testing of the system presupposes:

1. Formal approval of the proposed system by top management;
2. Formally assigning the system's functions and responsibilities to the Human Resource Management Department.
3. A conscious effort by employees and line managers to participate in the system; and
4. Availability of a computer program to process/generate needed reports.

STUDY/REVIEW QUESTIONS

1. What is a human resource information system?
2. What are the uses of a human resource information system?
3. What is the most important objective of a human resource information system?

SUGGESTED ACTIVITIES AND ASSIGNMENT

1. Make a list of Filipino values related to information on people.
2. Interview the personnel manager of a company that has a Human Resource Information System regarding its uses.
3. Find out what data on human resources are stored in a computerized Management Information System.

REFERENCES FOR FURTHER READING

Andres, Tomas D. *Management By Filipino Values.* Quezon City: New Day Publishers, 1985.

Anthony, William P. "Get to Know Your Employees: The Human Resource Information System", PMAP 15th National Conference, Nov. 22-24, 1978, Baguio City.

Pigors, Paul et. al. *Personnel Administration.* Tokyo: McGraw-Hill Kogakusha, LTD., 1973.

Sison, Perfecto S. *Personnel and Human Resources Management.* Manila: Rex Book Store, 1981.

25

HUMAN RESOURCE FORMS, SYSTEMS, REPORTS, AND RECORDS

IT IS ESSENTIAL that human resource executives have sufficient records that supply information as and when required and that this information be up to date.

Requirements for Good Record Forms Design

A good record form design has five basic characteristics: ease of entry, ease of use, reduction of errors and economy in paper and printing.

For ease of entry, it must allow sufficient writing space for data, proper spacing of writing lines for hand and machine entry, correct arrangement and sequence of data, and correctly placed instructions for filling out the form.

The design of a form must consider two classes of people: (1) those who place the data on the form and (2) those who draw information from it.

The factors affecting the use of the form are: visibility, readability so as to prevent eye fatigue, intelligent and clearly stated captions, orderly arrangement of the information, sufficient writing space without waste of paper, and identity of design among related forms.

The factors which help to reduce clerical errors are: requiring complete data, and avoiding unnecessary data, clear segregation of related vertical columns, ease and accuracy in following a reading line across the page, clear association of filled-in data with the proper printed caption, and generally well-designed forms.

Economy in paper and printing can be achieved by combining different forms doing the same thing, eliminating variation in multiple-part forms, selecting proper printing processes, and also correct paper sizes and weights.

Information System Design

There are three phases of the design of an information system: (1) specification of the output of the system (2) development of efficient means of processing the data, and (3) programming, or the development of interactions, for the operation of the system.

The type of output, the quantity of output, the frequency of output and the accuracy of output are the requirements of the information system. A systems analyst must be assigned to determine what data files must be maintained, what inputs are required and the best methods for processing the data efficiently and effectively. If the detailed instruction for ongoing operation of the system is a computer system, this will include developing flow charts and block diagrams, testing, and all activities subsequent to the actual running of the system in the computer; if it is a manual or mechanical system, this includes developing detailed procedures and instructions.

The total design must reflect both the input-output chain of each subsystem and the interrelationships among different subsystems. The output of one subsystem may be the input of one or more other subsystems, or it may be the final output requested by management.

There is a need for a master systems plan. Management at each level and for each unit must specify goals and types of information needed for planning and control. Each operating system or subsystem is guided by information and in turn, produces other information. Data must be increasingly multi-purpose and compatible serving as many needs as possible and expressed in the same units of measurement time scale and in machine language whenever possible.

Human Resource and Managerial Reports

Information is communicated upward and downward to the organization through reports. Reports establish basic objectives for a unit;

control reports evaluate progress in relation to the planning reports.

Reports prepared at the lowest levels of management are numerous and contain considerable detail; as information in these reports is transmitted upward, details are eliminated, resulting in concise, integrated reports. The data are summarized. The primary interest of middle and top management is exceptions to standards, budgets and predetermined plans, while details in order to take corrective action are the interest of first-line management.

Purpose, timing, and style are the three basic qualifications of human resource reports. The purpose is usually planning or control, timing is periodic or special, style is formal or informal.

The factors considered in a planning report are: appraisal of the standing of the firm within the industry, identifying opportunities for improvement, estimating the effect upon the firm of adopting various alternatives, identifying trends in the firm's operations and making comparisons with industry trends and with competitor trends.

Planning reports emphasize historical data; control reports emphasize performance measurements such as human resource, productivity work load (man-hour efficiency), quality, and cost or expense.

For example, to determine a company's average monthly office expenses for the last three years in order to establish a general standard, the general human resource administrative and office expense must include the following:

A. Personnel
   1. Salaries and Wages
   2. Overtime
   3. Employee Benefits
B. Office Furniture and Equipment
   1. Depreciation
   2. Rentals
   3. Repairs and Maintenance
C. Space
   1. Rent and Depreciation of Building
   2. Repairs and Maintenance
   3. Improvement
   4. Taxes and Insurance
D. Staff Transportation
   1. Depreciation
   2. Fuel Expenses
   3. Repair and Maintenance

E. Office Supplies and Miscellaneous Expenses
1. Stationery and Supplies
2. Communication
_ PLDT
_ Telegrams
_ Stamps
_ Messengerial
3. Reproduction

Areas of human resource planning reports are profiles of the work force, census projections, new positions, successive projections, labor demands and supply projections, staffing costs, organizational models, human resource development requirements, compensation levels, payroll cost projection, labor relations, management technology and environmental conditions. Areas of human resource control reports are basic personnel data, personnel strength, salary administration, manpower planning and control, labor turnover statistics, appraisal scheduling and control, personnel status, and vacancies.

Human Resource Forms, Reports and Records Management Program

I. *Identity Forms, Reports and Records*

Forms, reports and records processed and handled by each department should have a form number assigned to each one. Forms, reports, and records are basic work units around which office procedures resolve.

Examples of human resource forms:

A. Recruitment and Selection Forms:
1. Notification of Vacancy/Manpower Requisition Forms
2. Employment forms
a. Application forms
b. Interview forms
c. Engagement forms
d. Employment contract

B. Personnel Records
1. Personnel records card
2. Identification cards
3. Attendance forms
a. Time and Wage Sheets

b. Clocking Systems
c. Time and Attendance Records
d. Absence Records
e. Leave Records

4. Status Change/Personnel Action Forms
5. Insurance Records
6. Medical and Dental Records/Physical Examination Records
7. Accident Investigation Reports

C. Other Personnel Forms
1. Job Analysis Forms
2. Job Description Forms
3. Merit Rating Forms
4. Personnel Inventory
5. Appraisal Forms
6. Training Records
7. Termination Forms
   a. Clearance Forms
   b. Exit Interview
   c. Quit Claim Forms
8. Ministry of Labor Report Form

201 File contains the employment records of employees kept by the employer in or about the premises of the workplace. The record contents are usually the following:

1. Pre-employment data
   a. Contract
   b. Provident
   c. Medical
   d. Birth Certificate
2. Transcript
3. Picture (passport-size)
4. Rate Changes
5. Highly Confidential memos

202 File contains employees' records that usually include the following documents:

1. Performance
2. Memos
3. Transfers
4. Annual Medical Check-up
5. SSS Membership record

6. Marriage Contract/or Change of Status
7. Change of Address or Residence

II. *Numerical Control and Functional Index Files*

The Numerical Control File is an ordinary work file containing samples of each form arranged in form number sequence by department. The file, in addition to samples of the form, has a copy of the specifications for production of the form, a copy of the latest revision, and letters or names having to do with the changes in the designing of the form. It also includes information on who uses the form, the approximate annual usage for each user, when it was revised, and any other information directly pertinent to the form.

To construct a numerical control file, do the following:

1. Collect three samples of each form from the using department.
2. Prepare a listing of form titles by numerical sequence for those numbered, arbitrarily assigning members for those unnumbered. The Form Number Record form will be used for the listing and the departmental code will be used in prefixing the assigned number.
3. Separate one copy from the other two sample forms.
4. Enter usage data on the face of the form and return the other two copies to the department folder.
5. File numerically.
6. When all forms in the first department have been filed, take second department forms which are identifiable and file with first department.

For forms not yet encountered:

7. Repeat steps No. 3, No. 4, and No. 5.

For forms already encountered.

8. Lay aside all three copies until newly encountered forms have been handled.
9. Remove form from file, enter annual usage on face, restore form to file and destroy additional samples of form.
10 Repeat above until all forms have been filed in the numerical control file.

The Functional Index File is one where all forms, irrespective of the department using them, are classified: first by subject, second by operation or condition and third and lastly-by function.

To build a Functional Index File the steps are as follows:

1. Pick up single samples of forms from Department File Folder.
2. Sort the extracted form by subject.
3. Sub-sort by operation/condition and later by function.

Example:	Subject	-	Employment
	Operation	-	Extension of
	Condition	-	Status of
	Function	-	To notify

4. Eliminate duplication from Index.
5. Assign code number to each Functional Index File.
6. Stamp Functional Index Form samples for identification.
7. Cross Index Numerical File folder to the Functional Index.

Form Number Assignment Code

Office/Department
Forms Common Company-Wide

Code No.	*Manufacturing*
1	Office of the General Manager
2	Manufacturing, Planning and Control
3	Quality Control
	Marketing
4	Office of Marketing Manager
5	Marketing Services
6	Dealer Operation
	Human Resources
7	Office of HR Manager
8	HR Procurement
9	HR Maintenance
10	HR Enhancement and Development
	Finance
11	Office of Finance Manager
12	Credit and Collections Department
13	General Accounting

III. *Controlling the Creation of New Forms*

To control the creation of new forms when there are existing forms designed for the same function, all new forms or revisions of existing forms, except normally stocked stationery items, must be accompanied by a "Forms Data Sheet and Requisition Form" (See page 291).

If there is a form existing for the same purpose as one of the newly designed forms, the old form may be used. But if found to be new and necessary, the form will be re-designed to suit basic standards.

IV. *Describing the Functions of a Department and the Tasks of an Individual*

There are three elements that should be present in functional description:

1	2	3
INPUT	ACTION	OUTPUT
Production	Process	Production
Raw Materials		Finished Goods
Office		Office
Paper		Reports
Requests received		
Studies Initiated		

Distinction must be made between:

a. Function - major system of activities

b. Task - subsystem of function forming or treating-assembly

c. Operations - subsystem of operations process steps.

In the Functions List Forms (See page 294) all the activities or functions presently being performed in the department are to be written down. In case of a very big department with several sections the Functions List will be broken down by sections.

In the Task List Form (See page 295) detailed record of each type of work performed by each worker and the average number of hours spent on it per week are entered. This is to find out what each worker in the Department or Section contributes to each activity and what tasks he performs in making that contribution. The second form on page 296 is an elaboration of that on page 295

The Task Data Sheet (See page 297) is used when there is great difficulty in determining the employee's specific tasks, the quantity of output and the hours spent weekly on a specific task.

FORMS Data Sheet & Requisition Form	This form, completely filled out, must accompany all requests for new forms or revisions of existing forms. Do not use this for normal stationary stocked items.

TO: Administrative Service Dept. FOR CONTROL UNIT			FROM: (Requesting Dept.)	Date
Quantity	Unit	Form Number	FORM TITLE (Descriptive & Brief):	

OTHER USING DEPARTMENTS

PURPOSE & BENEFITS	Is it sent outside? [ ] YES [ ] NO
EFFECT ON EXISTING PROCEDURES	Are envelopes used? [ ] YES [ ] NO
DATA TO BE ENTERED FROM	DATA TO BE CARRIED TO
AFFECTED FORMS TO BE REDESIGNED	WHAT FORMS [ ] Replaces [ ] Obsolete
DISPOSITION OF OBSOLETE STOCK [ ] Destroy [ ] Use before new stock	OTHER DISPOSITIONS
FILLED IN BY elite Pica/ Exec. [ ] pencil [ ] pen [ ] typewriter [ ] typewriter	OTHER MACHINE
TO BE USED [ ] Inside Office [ ] Outside Office	TO BE REPRODUCED BY OTHER PROCESS [ ] Mimeograph
TO BE PREPARED OTHERS [ ] Daily [ ] Weekly [ ] Monthly	NUMBER OF COPIES

WILL NEW EQUIPMENT BE NEEDED?

[ ] Yes [ ] No [ ] Filling Equipment [ ] OTHERS (Specify)

COPY	COPY FURNISHED TO (Using Dept)	RETENTION PERIOD Months-Years	HANDLING FREQUENCY Daily, Monthly, etc.	MANNER OF FILLING Fasteners/ Binders
1 2 3				

[ ] Yes [ ] No

[ ] Sheets [ ] Sets [ ] Pads [ ] Books

THIS FORM IS [ ] [ ] Temporary (For how long)	PADDED OR BOOK BOUND [ ] Yes [ ] No	DUE DATE

APPROVED BY	DATE	APPROVED BY	DATE

V. *Transcribing Functions and Tasks Description onto a Work Distribution Chart*

To show all the person does grouped under the proper major function of the department, use a Work Distribution Chart. The major activities in the Functions List and the specific tasks in the Task List are merged. The analyst accomplishes the Distribution Chart.

The procedure in accomplishing the Form is as follows:

Box 1 - Organizational Unit.

- Indicate if the content is the present or proposed system by checking the small box.
- Analyst's name and signature below.
- Department Head's signature who, after reviewing the work distribution chart in final form signs to express agreement on the charted distribution of existing work system.
- Date when Work Distribution Chart is completed and approved by Department Head.

Columns 1, 2 & 3 - Analyst determines what activities each tasks supports - completes the "posted to activity" column of the Task List and enters in the Work, Distribution Column under Columns 1, 2,3 and on the same line as the activity description that a task support, the Task Description and Number.

Columns 4 & 5 - Hours spent by each individual in each assigned task is posted in Columns 4 and 5.

- Total number of hours per week worked by all employees is found by adding the number of hours recorded for every employee or tasks listed against the activities; all totals is entered in column 6.

VI. *Comparing Input - Output of Function and Task Descriptions with Forms, Reports and Record Listing*

This comparison is done to determine whether forms, reports and records as listed in the Form Number Record and Receiving Reports Listing forms are mentioned in the Work Distribution Chart or Forms, Reports and Records cited in the Work Distribution Chart are not included in the two listings.

The following steps are accomplished:

1. List all forms, reports, and records enumerated in the Work Distribution Chart.
2. Correlate the list extracted with the two listings of forms, reports and records.

3. Take note of the discrepancy or discrepancies.
4. Include in or eliminate from the Work Distribution Chart the discrepancy upon verification from Department Heads.
5. Finalize Work Distribution Chart and have it signed by the Operating Manager for his agreement that it truly describes present activities or his approval if he concurs with the proposed improved work distribution.

VII. *Functions and Task Analysis of Work Distribution Chart*

Determine the benefits of each function or task. If there are no benefits, recommend immediate elimination of functions/tasks in Form. Determine the cost of the Functions/Tasks. Determine if the benefits are greater than their cost. If cost of function/task is greater than benefits; proceed to Flow Process Chart Analysis.

In case of duplication between two departments, discuss with those involved by which department/individual the function should be performed, considering which department can more effectively discharge the function at issue, and the relationship of that function to the other functions of each department/individual. Results of findings are discussed with the operating manager of each and a "conforme" signature is requested from each in Form on page 299.

In re-distributing functions/tasks that are too thinly or heavily distributed, the procedures are as follow:

1. Pinpoint functions of the Department/individual which are most remotedly related to the other functions.
2. Explore to which department/individual the function should more rightfully belong.
3. Confer with the Department Head from which the function is being deleted and the Department Head to which the function is being transferred for their "conforme" signature on Form on page 299.

VIII. *Flow Process Chart Analysis*

A Flow Process Chart is a detailed record of a sequence of events which gives a bird's-eye view of the job and provides a picture of the job separate from its background and surroundings. This will establish whether "options" are necessary or could be eliminated, whether transportation could be eliminated or the distance from point of origin to point of destination or transportation could be reduced, whether inspection could be eliminated, whether storage is done properly and

FUNCTIONS LIST FOR WORK DISTRIBUITION CHART	Division	Department	Section	[ ] Present [ ] Proposed System

Functions Number Col. 1	F U N C T I ON Col. 2	Work Unit Col. 3	Input Identified Col. 4	Output Identified Col. 5	Quantity Col. 6

Supervisor	Prepared by	Date Completed
		Date Approved
Department: Head's Name	Analyst's Name	

TASK LIST FOR WORK DISTRIBUTION CHART	NAME	POSITION	SECTION		DEPARTMENT		DIVISION	
TASK NO.	TASK DESCRIPTION	SPECIFY WORK UNIT	QUANTITY PER					MAN-HOUR CONSUMED PER
			DAY	WEEK	DAY	QTR	YEAR	
REMARKS		SUPERVISOR	REVIEWED BY					DATE

TASK LIST FOR WORK DISTRIBUTION CHART	Analyst's Name	Position
Date Completed	Department	Section

Task Number	DESCRIPTIONS	Quantity	Posted to Utility Number	Hours Per Week
		TOTAL		

SUPERVISOR	REVIEWED BY	DATE APPROVED

TASK DATA SHEET FOR WORK DISTRIBUTION CHART	DEPARTMENT/SECTION	DATE
NAME	POSITION	SUPERVISOR

TIME	TASK NO.	INTERRUPTION		QTY (NO.)	TASK NO.	DESCRIPTION	TOTAL TIME	TOTAL UNITS	UNIT TIME
		PHONE	OTHERS						
:00					1				
:15									
:30					2				
:45									
:00					3				
:15									
:30					4				
:45									
:00					5				
:15									
:30					6				
:45									
etc									
:30					A				
:45					B				
:00					C				
:15					D				
:30					E				
etc.						TOTAL			

WORK DISTRIBUTION CHART		ORGANIZATION UNIT		PRESENT		PREPARED BY		APPROVED BY		DATE	
ACTIVITY		NAME POSITION TASK		NAME POSITION TASK		NAME POSITION TASK		NAME POSITION TASK		NAME POSITION TASK	

SUBJECT: FUNCTIONS/TASKS RECOMMENDATIONS SHEET FOR

DELETION   COMBINATION   RE-ASSIGNMENT

RECOMMENDATION

DELETE	COMBINE . . . WITH			TRANSFER . . . AS		
#	#	#	OF	#	#	OF
#	#	#	OF	#	#	OF
#	#	#	OF	#	#	OF
#	#	#	OF	#	#	OF
#	#	#	OF	#	#	OF

RECOMMENDED BY		APPROVED BY	
DEPARTMENT COORDINATOR	GENERAL COORDINATOR	DEPARTMENT MANAGER	DEPARTMENT MANAGER

FUNCTIONS AND TASKS LISTING

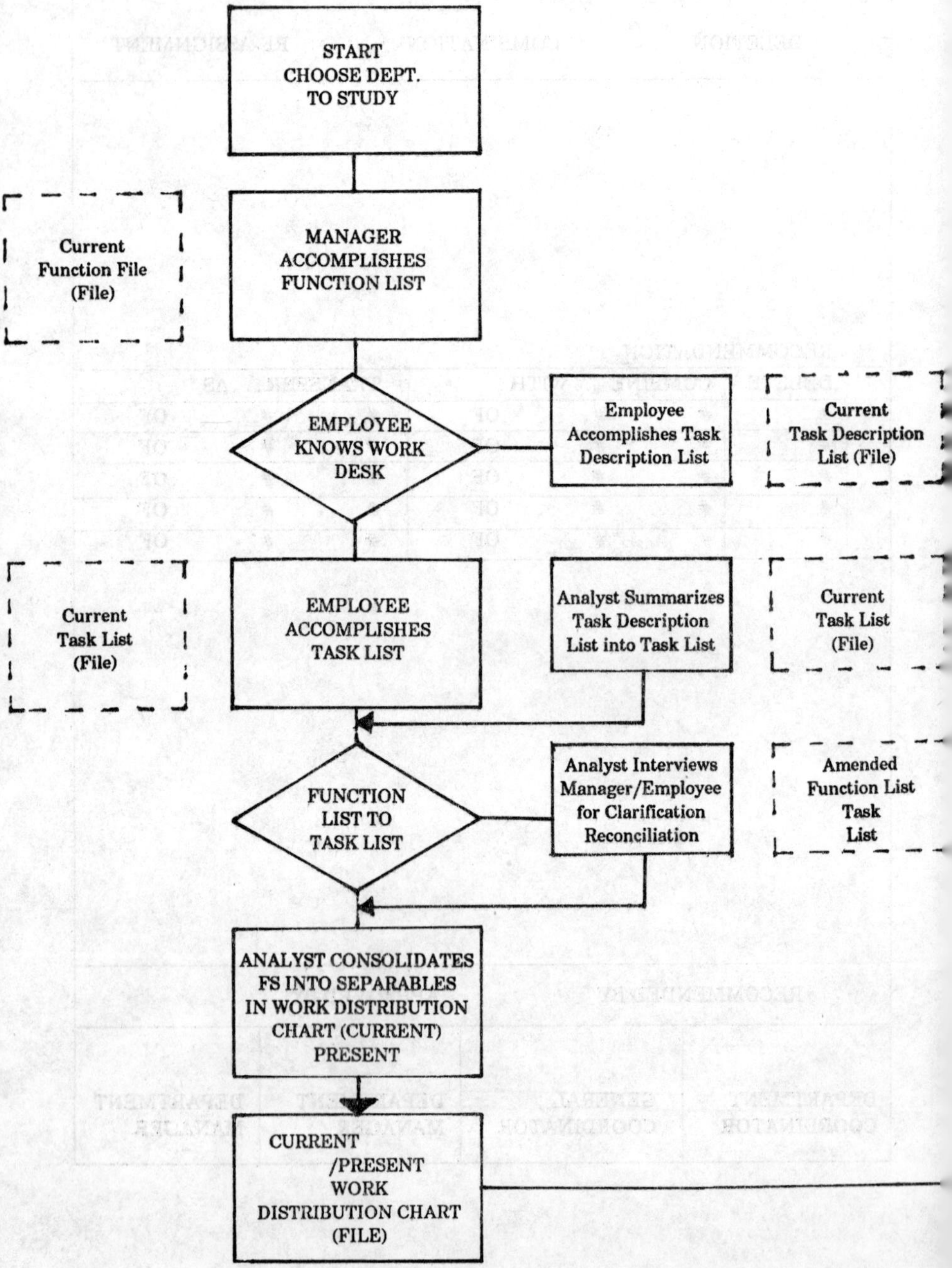

FUNCTIONS & TASKS SIMPLIFICATION

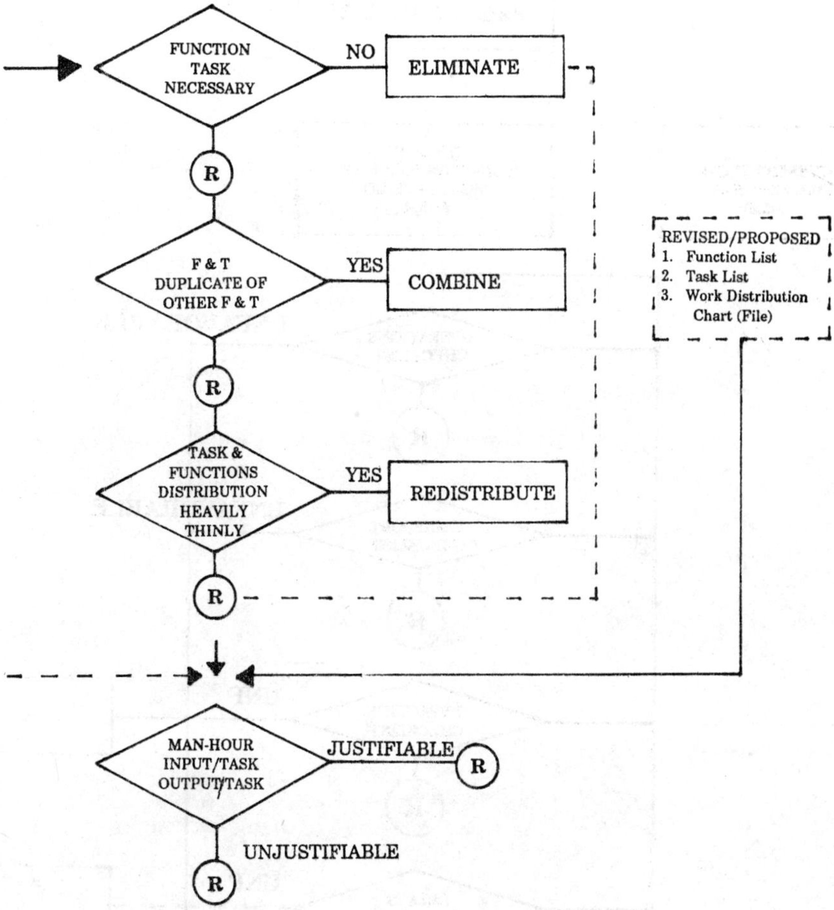

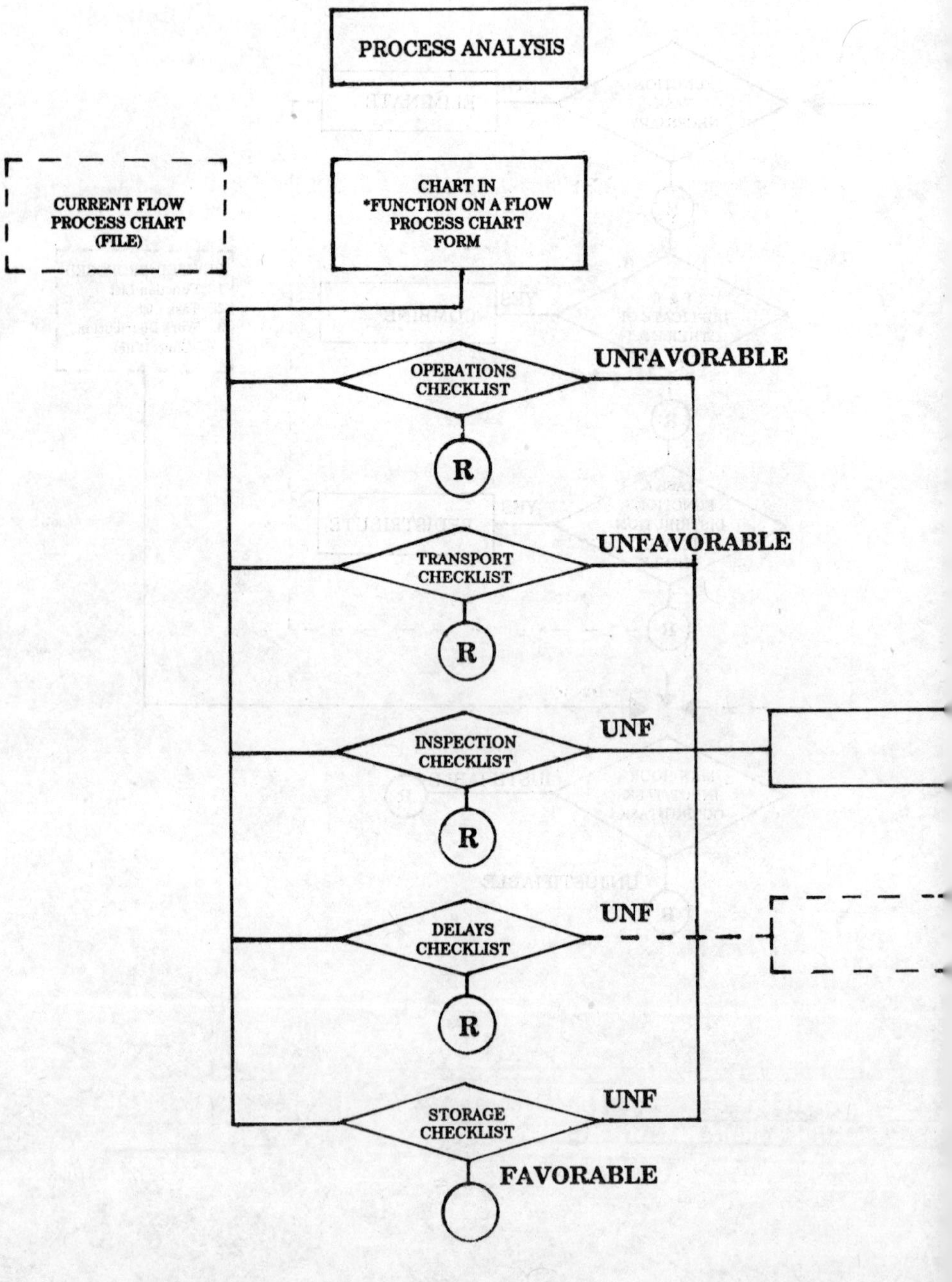
PROCESS ANALYSIS
CURRENT FLOW
PROCESS CHART
(FILE)
CHART IN
*FUNCTION ON A FLOW
PROCESS CHART
FORM
OPERATIONS
CHECKLIST
UNFAVORABLE
R
TRANSPORT
CHECKLIST
UNFAVORABLE
R
INSPECTION
CHECKLIST
UNF
R
DELAYS
CHECKLIST
UNF
R
STORAGE
CHECKLIST
UNF
FAVORABLE

whether delays could be minimized if not eliminated.

The following are the steps in making a Flow Process Chart:

1. Indicate the Flow Process Chart Number.
2. Fill up the Organizational Unit form.
3. Choose the subject to be chartered-either a person or paper form.
4. Choose a starting and ending point and jot them down in the appropriate boxes.
5. Write a brief description of each detail by using action verbs. Number the steps sequentially.
6. Classify the steps. Every step of the job can be classified as one of the five elements of work-operation, transportation, inspection, delay and storage.
7. Apply the symbols. Draw a line connecting parts of the graphic picture of the process.
8. Enter distance and time.
9. Summarize the results of the flow process chart and fill in the data on the corresponding columns at top left hand corner of the form.
10. Sign under "Charted By" and indicate date of completion.
11. Analyze the Flow Process Chart using the following principles and checklist:

A. *Operations:* The three parts of an operation are: prepare, do, and put away. Only the *do* part advances the work to completion. If the *do* part can't be eliminated, the *prepare* and *put away* should be studied.

Ask:

1. What is done in this operation?
2. Why is it done at all?
3. In what other way could this result be accomplished?
4. Where is this operation done? Why there?
5. Where else could it be done?
6. At what other time could it be done?
7. Who does it? Why this person? Who else could?
8. How is it done? Why this way?
9. In what other way could it be done?

Find Out:

1. Is the operation made necessary because of an improper performance of a previous operation?
2. Can the operation be made safer?

4. Would changes in materials, design, finishes, tolerances make this operation easier, cheaper, while still fulfilling its purpose?
5. Is the machine or equipment of the correct capacity, type, and precision for the type of work being performed on it?
6. Are the machine operations being carried on in the most efficient manner?
7. Are the correct speeds and feeds being used?
8. Could the tools, jigs, and fixtures be improved?
9. Can the principles of motion economy be applied?
10. Would an operation analysis of this operation be justified? Why? Why not?
11. Should a worker in this classification be doing work on this skill level?
12. Can this transcribing (copying)be avoided?
13. Can this form be redesigned to facilitate putting information on it? Taking information from it? Checking of information on it?
14. Can the printed information simplified and made less subject to misinterpretation?
15. Could reports, memoranda, or letters be shortened to reduce dictating, typing, or reading time?

B. *Transportation:*

Ask:
1. What is being done in this transportation?
2. Why is it done at all?
3. In what other way could this result be accomplished?
4. Where is this transportation going? Why?
5. When is this transportation done? Why?
6. At what other time could it be done?
7. Who does it? Why this person? Who else could?
8. How is it done? Why this way?
9. In what other way could it be done?

C. *Find Out:*

1. Is the work being delivered close to the point of use in the next operation? Is handling kept to a minimum?
2. Can an operation be performed during transportation?
3. Is the most effective type of equipment being used for transporting this type of work?
4. Is the handling equipment being kept busy? Is there enough

material handling equipment? Is it the right type?
5. Should this transport be planned and scheduled in advance?
6. Can the rearrangement of the sequence of operations (or of work stations, or of desks) reduce the backtracking and the amount of travel?
7. Is the batch of material that is being transported the most economical size?
8. Can gravity be used?
9. If a helper is needed to handle heavy parts at a work station, can a mechanical means of handling be substituted?

D. *Inspections*

Ask:
1. What is done is this inspection?
2. Why is it done at all?
3. In what other way could this result be accomplished?
4. Where is this inspection done? Why there?
5. Where else could it be done?
6. When is this inspection done? Why?
7. At what other time could it be done?
8. Who does it? Why this person? Who else could?
9. How is it done? Why this way?
10. In what other way could it be done?

Find Out:
1. Can weighing on bulk measurement or the use of compartmental racks be substituted for counting?
2. Can a later operation or assembly act as an inspection?
3. Are tolerances closer than necessary? Is the quality requirement higher than justified by the uses of the finished product?
4. Is this inspection equipment the best for this kind of inspection?
5. Can statistical quality control be used to reduce the cost of inspecting?
6. Does this inspection prevent errors? Is it set up to uncover and report defective work so that corrective action can be taken promptly?
7. Are the check and control points in the procedure justified or would taking a calculated risk be cheaper in the long run?
8. Are there too many controls? Would delegating authority and responsibility further down the line decrease the need for some of the controls?

9. What are the inspection requirements of the operations? Of the previous operation? Of the following operation?
10. Would changing the inspection requirements of the operation make the operation easier to perform?
11. Are the inspection points in the process in the most effective places?
12. Has agreement been reached by all parties as to what constitutes acceptable quality?

E. *Delays:*

Ask:
1. What is being delayed?
2. What type of delay is this?
3. What is the cause of this delay?
4. How could it be avoided?
5. Who is involved in this delay?
6. What is affected by this delay?

Find Out:
1. Are there idle men, machines, materials?
2. Is work piled up? Is it causing bottlenecks?
3. Are people waiting in line at any time for any reason?
4. Do skilled or highly paid employees have to go after tools, supplies, equipment, reports, etc. that could be obtained by helpers or messengers?
5. Should deadlines or schedules be set up to expedite paper work?
6. Why is the work-in-process (or paper work) not being worked on now?
7. Is there sufficient material-handling equipment of the sight kind at the right time?
8. Can the flow of work be regulated to eliminate peak periods?
9. Do delays prevent controls from being used soon enough to be most effective? Do inspection reports sit on desks while parts go through defective?
10. Are long, unnecessary conversations delaying the work?

F. *Storage*

Ask:
1. What is being done in this place of storage?
2. Why is it done?

3. In what other way could this result be accomplished?
4. Where is this storage? Why there?
5. In what other place could it be?
6. When is this storage done? Why then?
7. At what other time could it be done?
8. How is this storage handled? Why this way?

Find Out:
1. Is the amount of material in storage too much? Too little?
2. Is there storage of the material justified in terms of costs (including paper work) as against the possibility of loss or pilfering?
3. Should storage be centralized or decentralized?
4. Can the material be stored outdoors?
5. Could the space being used for storage be put to better use?
6. Are absolute parts and files consuming valuable storage space?
7. Are parts in storage protected against damage?
8. Are inventory control records too elaborate? Are they inadequate?
9. Is the storeroom set up so that parts can be easily located and quickly obtained?
10. Are all file copies essential? Need these copies be filed? For how long?

IX. *Presentation of Findings to Department Head and Manualization*

Since responsibility for operations of a department lies with the manager concerned, the findings seek to secure his conformity and decision on proposed procedures and his recommendations on how to improve the effective operation of his department.

The study should be presented in booklet form consisting of four parts:

1. Summary of Efforts being made to carry out Proposed Procedures, Functions, and Tasks on Operations of Department.
2. Summary of Recommendations
   - Statement of Policies, Rules, Procedures
   - Reorganization Recommendations

X. *Implementation and Monotoring of Effects/Results of New Procedures.*

The cost figures shall follow the standards to be developed for each office expense/cost item of each department by a cost accounting unit and HRM Department. Any variance should be analyzed as to the cause.

Corrective and preventive measures shall be incorporated in the manual of procedures as reinforcements to the developed standards.

STUDY/REVIEW QUESTIONS

1. What is the importance of a good human resource records program in attaining the corporate objectives?
2. How can we implement a good human resource records program?
3. What are the different personnel/human resource forms used in human resource management?

SUGGESTED ACTIVITIES AND ASSIGNMENT

1. Secure a whole set of all the personnel/human resource forms used in human resource management/personnel and criticize them.
2. Interview the record clerk of a human resources department and ask him to explain to you what records the department keeps and how they keep them.
3. List all the Filipino values that affect a good records program both adversely and beneficially.

REFERENCES FOR FURTHER READING

Angeles, Conrado et al. *Principles of Personnel Administration.* Quezon City: R.M. Garcia Publishing House, 1981.

Chruden, Herbert J. et al. *Personnel Management.* Chicago: South & Western Publishing Company, 1968.

Sison, Perfecto S. *Personnel and Human Resource Management.* Manila: Rex Book Store, 1981.

26

HUMAN RESOURCE ACCOUNTING AND MEASUREMENT

TODAY more and more firms are becoming interested in quantifying their human assets. There have been successful attempts by practitioners in various disciplines to define, evaluate, and measure human capital.

The Nature of Human Resource Accounting

Human Resource Accounting informs management what changes are occurring in the human resources of an organization. Thus, an attempt is made to identify, quantify, and report investments made in the human resources.[1] It monitors the manpower plan through quantifiable financial data. Its goal is to have both a balance sheet statement and an income and expense statement on human resources.

Human Resource Accounting can prevent approval of expenditures and programs which will cause serious human resource deterioration and refusal of programs with high potential for human resource appreciation. Furthermore, human resource accounting has possibilities for useful human resource investment management.

Human resource is viewed as human capital, that is, the quantity and quality of useful skills and knowledge acquired through various expenditures (investment). The various approaches to human capital measurement and evaluation are the following:

1. *Economic Value Approach.* This approach defines human capital value as the present value of that portion of the organization's

future earnings attributed to human resources. Expected wages are a basis for measuring the "portion of future earnings." Thus, the value of human capital is defined as the net present value of expected wage payments discounted at the economy rate of return on aimed assets for the latest year.

2. *Opportunity Cost Approach.* According to this approach human resources have worth in their best alternative use, where use is measured by the marginal productivity of the employee. Thus, we need information not only on the contribution of the employee in one position (probably the present one), but also on possible contributions in other positions.
3. *Value to the Undertaking Approach.* This approach is best demonstrated in a corporation that has several cost centers competing for the same employee, and the employee is allocated to the highest bidder, and the bid price measures the value of the employee to the corporation and to the cost center.
4. *Total Contribution Approach.* This approach measures the performance of the corporation and the contribution of human resources to this performance. In Rensis Likert's approach, three classes of variables and their inter-relationships are defined and measured. The three classes are the *causal* (independent variables which can be manipulated by management), the *intervening* (which reflect the capabilities of the organizations), and the *end results* (results achieved by the organization).
5. *Replacement Costs Approach.* Replacement costs are estimates of the recruiting, hiring, familiarization and training of individuals for potential vacancies, plus the costs of carrying a vacancy until replacement can fill it.
6. *Historical Cost Approach.* Expenses incurred in employing corporate personnel are viewed as investments in human capital. The balance is recognized as a loss if an employee leaves the corporation before the investment is fully amortized.

Since 1966, Eric Flamholtz, Lee Brummet, and William Pyle, along with the executives of the R.G. Barry Corporation, have conducted a research project and they have developed what is believed to be the first human resource accounting system.[2] This system intends to:

1. Provide managers with specific feedback information on their performance in managing the organizational assets entrusted to them.
2. Provide managers with additional information pertaining to

human resources to assist in their decision making.
3. Provide the organization with a more accurate accounting of its return on total assets employed.

Essentially this approach considers two major Human Resource Investment Areas: the direct out-of-pocket expenses for activities like recruitment and training; and the salary allocations of people during periods when the company is unable to benefit from a person's efforts such as familiarization, on-the-job training and the like. They made an annual financial report (see Table 1) depicting their efforts in quantification, allocation and amortization.[3]

Table 1
'THE TOTAL CONCEPT'
PRO-FORMA
(Conventional and Human Resource Accounting)[4]

Balance Sheet

Assets	*Conventional and Human Resource*	*Conventional Only*
Total Current Assets	P18,049,482	P18,049,482
Net Property, Plant & Equip.	3,709,132	
Excess of Purchase Price over Net Assets Acquired	1,417,299	1,417,299
Deferred Financing Costs	201,467	201,467
Net Investments in Human Resources	1,957,545	–
Other Assets	255,895	255,895
	P25,590,820	P23,633,275

Liabilities and Stockholders' Equity		
Total Current Liabilities	P 3,540,024	P 3,540,024
Long Term Debt, Excluding Current Installments	8,013,500	8,013,500
Deferred Compensation	128,386	128,386
Deferred Income Tax Based Upon Full Tax Deduction for HR costs	978,772	–
Stockholders' Equity:		
Capital Stock	2,000,658	2,000,658
Additional Capital in Excess of Par Value	5,552,228	5,552,228

Retained Earnings:		
Financial	**4,398,479**	**4,398,479**
Human Resources	**978,773**	**–**
	P23,590,820	**P23,633,275**

Statement of Income

Net Sales	**P43,078,531**	**P43,078,531**
Cost of Sales	**28,234,511**	**28,234,511**
Gross Profit	**P14,844,020**	**P14,844,020**
Selling, General and Administrative Expenses	**11,209,850**	**11,209,850**
Operating Income	**P 3,634,170**	**P 3,634,170**
Interest Expense	**604,147**	**604,147**
Income Before Income Taxes	**P 3,030,023**	**P 3,030,023**
Net Income in Human Resource Investment	**240,555**	**–**
Adjusted Income Before Income Taxes	**P 3,270,578**	**P 3,030,023**
Income Taxes	**1,555,777**	**1,555,777**
Net Income	**P 1,714,801**	**P 1,474,246**

On both the Assets and Liabilities portions of the HRA Balance Sheet, Human Resource are reported in money terms, resulting in a larger Assets and Liabilities versus the conventional approach. The HRA method reports a bigger bottom line than the conventional Income Statement at the Profit and Loss Statement below due to the Net increase in Human Resource Investment which amounts to P240,555. This figure represents the increase in investment made over the past year. (That is in the preceding year the company's net investment in Human Resources was P1,561,264, the next year this increased to P1,779,950 or an increment of P218,688). The human resource management efforts are now part of profits rather than expense. Furthermore,

Human Resource Accounting translates human resource development efforts in a language that is appreciated by top management.

The potential for human resource accounting is significant for both external and internal purposes. It can generate data highly useful to stockholders as well as to management. Human Resource Bookkeeping can be done to identify the information that must be kept or should be kept and to collect and have available for retrieval such information on a cost/efficiency basis. With human resource accounting and bookkeeping, management would be encouraged to give more serious consideration to human resource investment decisions and to the human resource impact of all of their decisions. Relevant information on human resource conditions and changes could improve substantially managers' decisions and organizational objectives. Human resource accounting's expansion requires development of data and guidelines for more effective management.

Areas that are partially cost-related in human resources are safety data, new hire costs, turnover data, cost of management data, budgeting and bookkeeping, and time-cost data. Areas that are of primary value as measurement information are attitude information, labor contract information, productivity data, critical positions, and consensus data.

Values related to human resources are made "measurable" by using the tools provided by human resource accounting. When this is done, the balance sheet and the profit and loss statement and their supporting records provide management with important sources of information about the loss exposures of the organization. A systematic study of each of the asset items on a balance sheet helps the management to locate loss exposures. Take for example employees' turnover. Conventional approaches to turnover provide management with percentages that lack information in terms of the value lost due to resignations or terminations. Magdaraog depicts in a chart (See Table 2) the traditional reporting of the turnover index in percentages.[5]

Table 2 reveals that Dept. C reported the largest percentage of turnover, followed by Dept. A, then Dept. B. However, if Human Resource Accounting is employed, analysis reveals that Dept. B has a higher turnover loss probably because the people who have left or were asked to leave were employees who were more expensive to recruit, train and develop versus the other Departments.

Table 2
TWO WAYS OF ANALYZING EMPLOYEE TURNOVER

Alternatives	*Dept. A*	*Dept. B*	*Dept. C*
Conventional Reporting Procedure-Percent Basis	10%	5%	25%
Human Resource Accounting Reporting Procedure-Money Loss Basis	P45,000.00	P78,000.00	P65,000.00

Uses of Human Resource Accounting Information

The following are some practical uses of human resource accounting information:

1. *Human resource investment management.* HRA has possibilities for useful development of human resource investment management. The conventional practice of "expensing" all human resource investments has deterred management from giving close scrutiny to expenditures in this area. With HRA capital budgeting procedures can be applied to human capital investments and post-audit techniques can be developed to increase the payoff of human resource investment pesos.
2. *Substantial improvement of short-term profit contribution measurement.* HRA information can improve substantially short-term profit contribution measurement. In general, management is encouraged to meet targets stated in terms of cost, revenues, or profits measured without regard to the changing condition of into the reckoning process can redirect management's thinking and action toward a broader and more realistic concept of the real contribution being made by segments of the organization.[6]
3. *Facilitation of accurate before-the-fact information.* HRA, in a sense, can give us this information. If we can measure and

assess the changing conditions of skills, attitudes and working relationships among people, we can predict the nature of their performances in the future. It is then possible to take action to improve or remedy these conditions and, by so doing, to prevent substandard performance that would otherwise have been inevitable.

4. *Change of management outlook on human resource.* Management has always thought that the things that "really count" are the things that "get counted." If HRA information includes measures of human resource condition and change in a form meaningful to management, that is, in peso terms, management will begin to consider this resource in a different light, giving much greater recognition to the "total" impact of their decisions.

Steps in Human Resource Accounting

Human Resource Accounting provides criteria for determining the optimum magnitude and mix of human capital expenditures. This involves measures of return on investments in recruiting, training, and experience-building activities and the related trade offs.

There are three steps involved in Human Resource Accounting. They are:[7]

1. Devising and establishing systems to evaluate all key areas where management attention is needed to develop strengths while minimizing weaknesses and to improve current and future human asset utilization.
2. Analyzing, appraising, and interpreting results; in other words, comparing plans and performance against opportunities. This involves an analysis of deviation from standard. It involves making adequate information available to all concerned, in advance if possible, so reasoned decisions can be made on the basis of facts.
3. Making known the systems, the media and the results to all those whose performance is measured so that this process of feedback will be used for continued individual and collective appraisal and readjustment of the work and its performance.

Tools for Measuring Human Resources

The traditional tools for measuring human resources were attitude surveys, turnover in terms of voluntary resignations, attendance, number or promotions made within the manager's operation and from his operation to other segments or functions of the enterprise, number, frequency, and severity of lost-time accidents and dispensary visits involving hourly employees, number and contributed value of ideas for improving operations which are submitted by hourly and salaried employees, training time and loss of productivity to break in new employees, the existence or lack of formal orientation and indoctrination programs and regular follow-up meeting, frequency of staff meeting, uses of management by objectives, the existence or absence of organizational charts, position descriptions, and performance standards, the number, nature and extent of expressed employee dissatisfactions at all levels, difficulty or ease of recruitment of exempt employees, that is, the ratio of job offers to acceptances, and what has been done to develop and improve the performance of key people.

Some of the newer tools and techniques for measuring human resources are: *quantitative data* such as ratio and levels of participation in programs, movement of talent, turnover, and absenteeism and their caused; *employee attitudes* based on periodic employee attitude surveys or other forms on organizational climate audit; *direct expenditures* for such programs as recruitment training and development; the *break-even point/payback period* for new hires; *productivity changes*, the impact of incentive compensation on productivity, and other factors affecting productivity; *recruitment results* such as optimal sources of recruits, recruitment practice and cost of recruiting versus developing talent available internally; and the *economics of layoff* and retention of good talent during periods of staff reduction.

Some of the activities of human resource management can be readily measured, but others are indirect or intangible, thus making it difficult to accurately gauge their value in terms of pesos and centavos.

STUDY/REVIEW QUESTIONS

1. What is Human Resource Accounting?
2. What are the advantages if companies in the Philippines adopt the Human Resource Accounting system in their organizations?

3. What are the uses of Human Resource Accounting?

4. How do we implement Human Resource Accounting in an organization?

5. Is there a need for Human Resource Accounting in the Philippines?

SUGGESTED ACTIVITIES AND ASSIGNMENT

1. Find out whether any Philippine firm has experimented in implementing a Human Resource Accounting system in their organization.

2. Identify Filipino values that have to do with Human Resource Accounting.

3. Write a letter to the Philippine Institute of Certified Public Accountants asking it to study the possibility of accepting Human Resource Accounting in Accountancy practice.

NOTES

[1]R.G. Barry Corp. 1969 Annual Report. Columbus, Ohio.

[2]"Human Resource Information Tools," R.G. Barry Corporation, December 1973, Columbus, Ohio.

[3]R.L. Woodruff Jr. "Measuring Staff Turnover," *Canadian Chartered Accountant;* February 1973.

[4]Victor L. Magdaraog, "Human Resources Accounting: Its Value and Contribution," *HR Magazine*, November 1978, p. 29.

[5]Ibid. pp. 30-31.

[6]From a speech by Arthur L. Litke, Chief Accountant, Federal Power Commission before the American Public Power Association Accounting and Finance Workshop, Anchorage, Alaska, September 1970.

[7].Robert L. Desatnick. *Innovative Human Resource Management.* U.S.A. American Management Association, Inc., 1972, pp. 86-87.

BIBLIOGRAPHY

A. Books

Andres, Tomas D. *Management by Filipino Values.* Quezon City: New Day Publishers, 1985.

____. *Human Resource Training and Development.* Quezon City: New Day Publishers, 1980.

____. *Organizational Development for Productivity in the Philippine Setting.* Quezon City: New Day Publishers, 1984. 4th ed.

Angeles, Conrado P. and Garcia, Ricardo M. *Principles of Personnel Administration.* Quezon City: R.M. Garcia Publishing House, 1981.

Belcher, David W. *Wage and Salary Administration,* 2nd ed., Englewood Cliffs, N.J.: Prentice-Hall, 1962.

Bennis, Warren. *Organizational Development: Its Nature, Origins and Prospects.* Reading, Mass.: Addison-Wesley Publishing Company, Inc., 1969.

Boydell, T. H. *A Guide to the Identification of Training Needs.* London, England: BACIE, 1971.

Byars, Floyd and Leslie Rue. *Personnel Management: Concepts and Applications.* Philadelphia: W. B. Saunders, 1979.

Cassell, Frank H. Corporate *Manpower Planning.* University of Minnesota, Minneapolis, Industrial Relations Center, February, 1968.

Coleman, Charles. *Personnel: An Open System Approach.* Cambridge, Mass.: Winthrop Pub. 1979.

Cooke, Morris Llewellyn and Philip Murray. *Organized Labor and Production; Next Steps in Industrial Democracy.* New York: Harper and Brothers, 1940.

Cornell, William B. *Business Organization and Practice.* New York: American Book Co., 1956.

Dale, Ernest. *Management Theory and Practice.*. 3rd Ed.. New York: Prentice-Hall, Inc.

Desatnick, Robert L. *Innovative Human Resource Management.* U.S.A.: American Management Association, Inc., 1972.

Donnely, James H., Gibson, James L., Inaneewick, John M. *Fundamentals of Management.* Austin, Texas: Business Publications, Inc., 1971.

Dooher, J. and Marquis, V. *The AMA Handbook of Wage and Salary Administration.* New York: American Management Association, 1950.

Dressler, Gary. *Personnel Management: Modern Concepts and Techniques.* Virginia: Preston Publishing Company, Inc., 1978.

Drucker, Peter, *Management.* New York: Harper and Row, 1974.

Flippo, Erwin B. *Principles of Personnel Management.* 3rd Ed., McGraw-Hill Book Co., New York, 1972.

Foulkes, Fred K. *Creating More Meaningful Work.* New York: American Management Association, 1969.

Gooding, Judson. *The Job Revolution.* New York: Walker, 1972.

Grove, Mock and Ehrenreich. *Human Resource Accounting Measurement.* Pergamon Press Ltd., 1979.

Gutenberg, Arthur W. and Richman, Eugene. *Dynamics of Management.* Seranton, Pennsylvania: International Textbook Co., 1968.

Haire, Mason. *Coming of Age in the Social Sciences.* Cambridge, Mass.: Massachusetts Institute of Technology, 1967.

Jenkins, David. *Job Power.* New York: Doubleday, 1973.

Jucius, Michael J. *Personnel Management.* Illinois: Homewood: Richard D. Erwin, Inc., 1975.

Klatt, Laurence A., Robert G. Murdick, Fred E. Schuster. *Human Resource Management: A Behavioral Systems Approach.* Illinois: Richard D. Irwin, Inc., 1978.

Koontz, Harold. *Principles of Management: An Analysis of Managerial Functions.* New York: McGraw-Hill, Inc., 1977.

Langsmer, Adolph. *Wage and Salary Administration.* Ohio: South Western Publishing Company, 1961.

Lanham, Elizabeth. *Administration of Wages and Salaries.* New York: Harper and Row Publishers.

Lynch, James J. *A Manpower Development System.* London: Pan Books Ltd., 1971.

Martinez, Esdras T. *Human Resources Management.* Manila: GIC Enterprises & Co., Inc., 1979.

____, Abasolo, Pacita A., Carlos, Crispiniano P. *Management Theory and Practice.* Manila: GIC Enterprises & Co., Inc., 1972.

Massie, Joseph. *Essentials of Management.* Englewood Cliffs, New Jersey: Prentice-Hall Inc., 1964.

McFarland, Dalton S. *Management Principles and Practices.* London: McMillan Company, 1977.

Megginson, Leon C. *Personnel: A Behavioral Approach to Management.* Illinois: Richard D. Irwin, Inc., 1977.

____. *Personnel and Human Resources Administration.* Illinois: Richard D. Irwin, Inc., 1977.

Nadler, Leonard. *Developing Human Resources.* Houston: Gulf Publishing Company, 1970.

Newman, William H. and Logan, James P. *Business Policies and Management.* 4th ed., Cincinatti, Ohio: Southwestern Publishing Co.

O'Donnel, Koontz. *Principles of Management.* New York: McGraw-Hill Incorporation, 1977.

Otis, J. L. & Leukart, Richard H. *Job Evaluation.* Rev. Ed., Prentice-Hall, 1954.

Patten, Thomas H., Jr. *Manpower Planning and the Development of Human Resources.* New York: Wiley-Interscience, A Division of John Wiley & Sons, Inc., 1971.

Patton, J. A. and C. L. Littlefield. *Job Evaluation.* 3rd Ed., Irwin, Homewood, Illinois, 1964.

Phelps, Earle B. *Public Health Engineering.* Vol. 1. New York: John Willey & Sons, p. 185.

Pigors, Paul and Myers, Charles A. *Personnel Administration: A Point of View and A Method.* New York: McGraw-Hill Book Company, Inc., 1961.

____. *Personnel Administration.* New York: McGraw-Hill Book Company, 1978.

Roethlisberger, F. J. and Dickson, W. J. *Management and the Worker.* Cambridge, Massachusetts: Harvard University Press, 1956.

Rosow, Jerome M., ed. *The Worker and the Job: Coping With Change.* Englewood Cliffs: N.J.: Prentice-Hall, 1974.

Scheer, Wilbert E. *Personnel Administration: Handbook.* U.S.A., 1969.

Seymour, W.D. *Industrial Skills.* London: Pitman, 1966.

Shartle, Carroll L. *Occupational Information.* Englewood Cliffs, N.J.: Prentice-Hall, Inc., 1952.

Sherman, Arthur. *Difficulties of Wages Administration.* Ohio: South-Western Publishing Company, 1961.

Shillinglaw, Gordon, & Ronen. *Accounting: A Management Approach.* 6th Ed. Irwin Dorsey Ltd. 1979.

Sison, Perfecto S. *Personnel and Human Resources Management.* Manila: Rex Printing Co., Inc., 1981.

Spriegel, William R. *Principles of Business Organization.* 3rd Ed., New York: John Wiley and Sons, Inc.

Stahl, Glen. *Public Personnel Administration.* New York: Harper Publishers, 1976.

Strauss, George & Sayles, Leonard R. *Personnel: The Human Problem of Management.* Englewood Cliffs, New Jersey: Prentice-Hall Inc., 1972.

Wellens, J. *The Training Revolution.* London: Evan Bros., 1963.

Yoder, Dale. *Personnel Principles and Policies.* 2nd Ed. New York: Prentice-Hall, Inc., 1959.

____. *Personnel Management and Industrial Relations.* 5th Ed., Asian Edition, Prentice-Hall, Inc., Maruzen Co. Ltd. Japan. 1962.

Zollitsch, Herbert A., and Adolph Langsner. *Wage and Salary Administration.* 2nd Ed., South-Western, Cincinnati, 1970.

B. Articles and Others

Agnir Wenceslao, Jr. "Salary Administration: Understanding the New System," *Far East Bank & Trust Company Primer on Salary Administration,* 1974.

____. "The Present Law on Preventive Suspension and Termination," *The Personnel Manager* (Official Organ of the Personnel Management Association of the Philippines), July 1977.

Barrett, James E. "The Case for Evaluation of Training," *Business Week* (1962).

Benge, Eugene J. "By-product of Job Evaluation," *Personnel Journal,* 29, No. 3 (July-August 1950): 94-99.

Burack, Elmer H. and Miller Edwin, "The Personnel Function in Transition," *California Management Review* (Spring 1976): 32-28.

Chalofsky, Neal E. and Cerio, Joseph A. "Professional Development Program for Federal Government Trainers," *Training and Development Journal* (December 1975): 18-20.

Clement, Ronald W, Walker, James W. and Pinto, Patrick R. "Changing Demands of the Training Professional," *Training and Development Journal.* (March 1979): 3-7.

Contreras, Nonong. "Accreditation (Professionalization)? of Personnel Function?, Personnel Manager? or PMAP?", *PMAP Convention Bulletin* (December 4, 1976).

Cooper, Lloyd G. "HRD-A Professional Manifesto" *Training and Development Journal* (September 1975): 26.

Davis, Louis E. "The Design of Jobs," *Industrial Relations.* 6, No. 1, (October 1966): 21-45.

____ & Werling, R. "Job Design Factors," *Occupational Psychology,* 34 (1957): 305.

____. "Toward a Theory of Job Design," *Journal of Industrial Engineering,* 8 (1957): 305.

____. Canter, R.R. and Hoffman, J.F. "Current Job Design Criteria," *Journal of Industrial Engineering,* 6 (1955).

____ and Canter, R.R. "Job Design Research," *Journal of Industrial Engineering,* 7 (1956): 275.

De Genaro, Guy J, and Rimler, George W. "Human Resource Development in Banks," *The Magazine of Bank Administration.* (March 1975): 47-53.

Fidelino, Rachel E. "Business With a Social Conscience—Living Allowances: A Challenge to Social Justice & National Unity," *Philippine Panorama.* 3 No. 17 (April 28, 1974): 3.

_____, "The Soaring Cost of Employee Compensation," *Business Week.* (September 7, 1974): 42.

_____, "How New Pension Law Will Affect You," U.S. *News & World Report* (Aug. 26, 1974): 37-38.

____. "Social Security Promising Too Much to Too Many?" *U. S. News & World Report* (July 15, 1974): 26.

Fitzpatrick, B.H., "An Objective Test of Job Evaluation Validity," *Personnel Journal,* 28, No. 4 (September 1949): 128-132.

Flowers, Vincent S. and Coda, Bernard A. "Human Resource Planning: Foundation for a Model," *Personnel* (Jan.-Feb. 1974): 20-42.

Fryer, D.H. "Training with Special Reference to its Evaluation," *Personnel Psychology.* 4 (1951): 19-37.

Giblin, Edward J. "The Evolution of Personnel," *Human Resource Management* (Fall 1978): 25-30.

Hedges, Janice. "Absence From Work: A Look at Some National Data," *Monthly Labor Review* (July 1973).

Heneman, Herbert, Carter Camaford, Judson Jasmin, "Standardized Absent Rate: A First Step Toward Comparability," *Personnel Journal* (July-August 1961): 114.

Horning, E.S., "Job Descriptions," *Management Record,* 7 No. 10 (October 1945): 277.

Kenny, John B. et al. "Core Competencies of the Trainer," *Canadian Training Methods* (December 1976).

Kilcourse, Tom. "IR Training: What Line Managers Need to Know," *Personnel Management* (August 1976).

Knight, J.F. "Fallacies in Job Evaluation," *Advanced Management* 15, No. 6 (June 1952): 351.

Louis Harris Associates. "Public Confidence in Institutions Mostly Lower," *Chicago Tribune* (September 30, 1974).

Martin, A.O. "The Assessment of Training," *Personnel Management* 39, no. 340 (1957).

Mayfield, Harold, "In Defense of Performance Appraisal," *Harvard Business Review.* Performance Appraisal Series, (1972): 27.

Mills, D. Quinn. "Human Resources in the 1980's," *Harvard Business Review* (July-August 1979): 154-162.

Mills, Ted. "Human Resources: Why the New Concern?," *Harvard Business Review* (March-April 1975): 120-134.

Nadler, Leonard and Lippett, George. "Emerging Roles of the Training Director," *Training and Development Journal* (June 1979): 26-30.

____. "Research: An HRD Activity Area," *Training and Development Journal* (May 1979): 60-64.

Oca, Roberto S. "Labor's Commitment to Human Resources Development," *PMAP 20th Anniversary Convention, Convention Bulletin* (1979).

Patz, Alan L. "Performance Appraisal: Useful But Still Resisted," *Harvard Business Review* (June 1975).

Pyle, William, "Accounting for Your People," *Innovation* (1971).

Rensis, Likert. "Guide On Human Resource Management". *Apex Journal* 10, no. 2:10-15.

Santos, Emmanuel Noli T., "What Is Voluntary Arbitration?" *Philippine Panorama* (October 5, 1975): 20-21.

Schrovoni, Michael R. "Employee Relations: Where Will It Be in 1985?" *The Personnel Administrator* (March 1978): 25-29.

Seev Neumann and Eli Segev, "Human Resources and Corporate Risk Management," *Personnel Journal* 57, no. 2 (February 1978).

Seitchik, Jack M. "A Humanistic Approach to Psychological Testing." *Personnel Management* (March 1979): 151-158.

Skjervheim, Terry F. "Training: Evolution of a Profession," *The Personnel Administrator* (October 1977): 16

Smardon, Raymond A., "Arbitration Is No Bargain," *Nation's Business* (October 1974): 80-83.

Stolz, Robert K. "New Perspective in Manpower Development," *Harvard Business Review.*

Velasco, Dante. "Needed: New Work Ethic To Spur Economic Development," *PMAP Convention Bulletin,* Manila (Dec. 4, 1976).

White, Tod. "Increasing Your Effectiveness as a Training and Development Professional," *Training and Development Journal* (May 1979).

Austin, David L. "Must the Past Be Prologue? Or, Why Can't We Do Things Differently?", 15th National Conference of the Personnel Management Association of the Philippines (PMAP), Baguio City, November 22-24, 1978.

Bacungan, Froilan M. "The Rights of Workers in the Philippines," U.P. Workers' Institute on Labor Law, Quezon City, 1980.

Burack, Elmer H., Miller, Edwil L. "The Personnel Function in Transition," 15th MAP National Conference, Baguio City, November 22-24, 1978.

Daltas, Arthur J. and Schwartz, Howard M., "Towards Human Resources Management," 15th PMAP National Conference, Baguio City, November 22-24, 1978.

Doromal, Quintin S. "Personnel Management in the Philippines: Retrospect and Prospect," PMAP 20th Anniversary Convention. Manila. 1977.

Hansen, Gary B. "Educating the HRD Practitioners of the 80s" Technical Paper No. 7934, 8th International Training and Development Conference, Manila, November 7-12, 1979.

Hoffman, Frank O. "Identity Crisis In the Personnel Function," 15th PMAP National Conference, Baguio City, November 22-24, 1978.

Hollingsworth, A. Thomas and Preston, Paul. "Corporate Planning: A Challenge for Personnel Executives," 15th PMAP National Conference, Baguio City, November 22-24, 1978.

Itchon, Gabriel. "Human Resources Management in National Development," PMAP 20th Anniversary Convention, 1977, Manila.

Jimenez, Elpidio C. "Human Resources Management: Concepts, Contents, Practices and Trends," 15th PMAP National Conference, Baguio City, November 22-24, 1978.

Lucero, Antonio, Jr. "Human Resources Management Planning: An Evaluation of Current Practices of Ten Selected Private Corporations," MBA Masteral Thesis, Ateneo de Manila University, Manila, 1977.

Manabat, Conchita L. "Motivation-Hygiene Theory, A Study on Job Attitudes of Philippine Middle Management Validation of Frederick Herzberg, "MBA Masteral Thesis, Ateneo de Manila University, Manila, 1972.

Miller, Edwin L. "The Emerging Personnel Function," 15th PMAP National Conference, Baguio City, November 22-24, 1978.

Muller, David G. "A Model for Human Resource Development" 15th PMAP National Conference, Baguio City, November 22-24, 1978.

Oca, Roberto S. "Trends and Prospects in Labor Relations," 16th PMAP National Conference of the Philippines, November 30, 1979, PICC, Manila.

_____. "Trends and Prospects in Collective Bargaining and Labour Arbitration in the Philippines," 16th PMAP National Conference, 1979.

Odiorne, George S. "Training Director-Personnel Manager, Who's In Charge Here?," 15th PMAP National Conference, Baguio City, November 22-24, 1978.

Ople, Blas. "Human Resource Management Practices 'Myths and Realities'" Keynote Speech at the 16th PMAP National Conference, Manila, November 28, 1979.

Pattenaude, Richard L. "Increasing the Importance of Personnel: A Strategy," 15th PMAP National Conference, Baguio City, November 22-24, 1978.

Soriano, Emmanuel. "The Future of Human Resource Development and the HRD Specialist," Keynote Paper No. 804, 8th International Training and Development Conference, Manila, November 7-12, 1979.

Sycip, David. "A Private Sector View of Human Resource Management," PMAP 20th Anniversary Convention, Manila, 1977.

Walter, Verne. "Self-Motivated Personal Career Planning: A Break- Through in Human Resource Management," 15th PMAP National Conference, Baguio City, November 22-24, 1978.